THE EAST GERMAN ARMY

The East German Army

A PATTERN OF
A COMMUNIST MILITARY ESTABLISHMENT

Thomas M. Forster

WITH AN INTRODUCTION BY
BRIGADIER W. F. K. THOMPSON, C.B.E.

Translated by
Antony Buzek

South Brunswick
New York: A. S. Barnes and Company

50,967

INTRODUCTION

by

BRIGADIER W. F. K. THOMPSON, C. B. E.

I greatly welcome this opportunity to introduce Herr T. M. Forster's meticulous study of the history, organization, training and equipment of the East German forces. In my opinion, its publication in English ist most timely, and its interest far wider than the purely military. By setting out the relationship between a communist government and its armed forces, and the methods used for their political indoctrination and control, we are forcibly reminded of how a gap still exists between the communist and democratic orders of society.

It is true that there are many signs of a change for the better in East/West relations in Europe but there is, as yet, no sign whatever of a Russo/German detente, and until this is accomplished the German question will remain the powder keg of Europe, and East Germany the most likely detonator.

To most Britons, East Germany is an aberration left over by the war, dangerous because of its ambiguous position but otherwise of little importance. It is as well, therefore, to be reminded that since its citizens were virtually interned, in 1961, by the building of the Berlin wall, and the strengthening of her western frontiers by minefields and barbed wire, against the escape of those who would seek political freedom in the West, East Germany has become the leading industrial country of Eastern Europe, and her army of six divisions the best equipped. Yet she remains a highly militarized island surrounded on all sides by barbed wire and under the domination of 20 Russian divisions.

The history of the build-up of the East German forces and the militarization of East Germany is an interesting one. The author relies on East German official sources for his facts and figures. I can vouch for the accuracy of his description of the origin of these forces, six years ahead of those of West Germany, for I was in a position to know at that time.

Russia's attitude towards the East Germans has always been ambiguous, she has an obsessional fear of all Germans. For both the Warsaw and the NATO pacts the question is: how far can the East Germans be relied on to fight West Germans? Russia has tried to make the East Germans reliable by intensive communist indoctrination, to make them willing to fight for 'the cause'. The priority, recently given, to re-equipping their forces suggests that Russia's confidence has grown in this respect. Nevertheless, Russia's governors must often reflect that it was for Russia and not for communism that Russians fought and died in the last war.

The peaceful evolution of all Europe towards a genuine detente must be persistently and soberly worked for, but to believe prematurely that such a situation has been achieved would be most mischievous to the cause of freedom, justice and peace. It is in this light that I hope many will study this book, whose German edition has already been well received in Austria and Switzerland, as well as in the Federal Republic.

CONTENTS

PART FIVE
THE NPA IN ACTION

CHAPTER

PART SIX
EVALUATION

CHAPTER

PREFACE

The habit of the communist regimes of surrounding all their activities with a veil of secrecy may make it difficult to draw a clear picture of the institutions in communist states. There are several reasons for this secretiveness which is mostly incomprehensible to western observers. Firstly, it is a tendency inherent in every dictatorship; it stands in sharp contrast to democratic theory and practice according to which the people – the real source of the constitutional rule – have the right and duty to be informed about everything. In addition, the natural inclination to secretiveness in every communist state has been strengthened by the influence of Russian communists who once regarded even the ownership of a photographic camera as being as dangerous to themselves as that of a submachine gun. Another important factor contributing to the communist hostility towards free information is the fact that the material situation in communist states is far behind the propagandist targets and the reality is thus something not to be talked about.

Yet there are certain possibilities for those who want to draw a proper picture of certain communist institutions, even when the institution concerned is – as in our case – the armed forces: an objective which, because of true security interests, is naturally treated, to a certain extent, as secret in democratic countries.

In fact, the communists are anything but reticent. In their incessant stream of agitation and propaganda they take stand towards everything and produce, in great quantities, propaganda literature with which they want to "reach the masses". But they are not content with only generally leading and directing the "masses" for which purpose propagandist assertions are, in the communist view, sufficient. In our highly technical age, with its special demands on everybody, the communists, too, must try by all means, including the means of information, to gain support from their subjects. They must tell their own people, in this case the officers and soldiers of the National People's Army (NPA), what precisely they want from them; especially because one of the main communist dogmas is that the "all embracing consciousness" is the most important force.

Thus anyone who undertakes to read carefully and compare the numerous pronouncements of the regime of the "German Democratic Republic" on its army, the propagandist works as well as the more factual instructions, can reach certain correct conclusions.

The most yielding sources in this respect are the periodical and non-periodical publications of the Deutscher Militärverlag (German Military Publishing House) in East Berlin which is in fact a department of the Ministry of National Defence and as such holds a sort of monopoly in the sphere of general and specialized military literature. Here, the difficulty was more in the abundance than in the scarcity of material.

Together with the numerous reports made by the refugees, particularly the former members of the armed forces, the material was completely "open". It is available to any scientific worker who wants to buy the cheap military publications of East Germany and plough through them – which is by no means an easy thing.

This work on the East German National People's Army is thus not a "secret study". A possibly disillusioned reader can take consolation in the view of the former director of the U. S. Central Intelligence Agency, Allen W. Dulles, who said that in peacetime 80 per cent of the information needed for the direction of American foreign policy is collected from open sources.[1] (The communists are, perhaps, able to collect 98 per cent of the information which they think they need on the non-communist world from publicly available sources.)

The western intelligence services are, of course, properly informed on the communist armies and also on the NPA. However, the authorities charged with the task of watching the "foreign armies" currently submit their secret reports and evaluations only to a limited and selected circle of politicians and officers. Yet it is also necessary to inform the larger public. This task, as far as the NPA is concerned, is undertaken by our publication which comes at a very opportune time when the build-up of the NPA has been essentially concluded.

More difficult than collecting the materials was their evaluation. The facts had to be laboriously sifted from the waste of propaganda in which they were wrapped by the communist authors. In this respect the author is indebted to many friends and acquaintances who are

---

1 Harry Howe Ransom, *Central Intelligence and National Security*, Harvard University Press, Cambridge, Massachusetts, 1958, p. 18–19.

experts and equally concerned with this army. Still, mistakes can crop up and the author would be therefore grateful if the readers of the book would let him know of any mistakes, in details or in general conception.

In the conception of this work one decision could not be avoided which has to be made by any author writing on communist affairs. It is the question whether the communist terminology should be taken over, to a certain degree, or whether, so to say, each communist term should be translated. The fact that the term "German Democratic Republic" entirely contradicts the reality of the communist dictatorship in this Soviet satellite does not require further explanation. More difficulties are created by terms which are not so current in the West. Would it not be better, from the standpoint of linguistic truthfulness, not to use at all such terms as the "National People's Army", the "German Frontier Police", the "People's Police"?

This work has essentially used the terms current in East Germany This enables the reader, when he wants to study personally the original sources, to orientate himself quickly. The communist designations and word compositions are, anyway, more and more detached from the original linguistic usage – especially the abbreviations.

Here and there, the reader will find repetitions and overlapping; this is because the book was not written only for the military experts. On the other hand, it could not be avoided that some themes could not be, at their first appearance, thoroughly dealt with. The "uniform" is, for example, described once in its ideological context – as the communists see it or pretend to see it; then in another passage it is shown in its details. An index will enable the reader to get quickly informed on some secondary themes in larger context.

Some readers may regard it as a disadvantage that, apart from a few exceptions, no comparisons are made with the situation in the West. To do this would mean increasing several times the present volume of the book.

The author only hopes that the book may arouse lively interest inside and outside the circle of military experts.

Cologne, 15 March 1967

Thomas M. Forster

PART ONE

HISTORICAL DEVELOPMENT

CHAPTER 1

THE DEVELOPMENT OF THE
MILITARY FORCES 1945 TO 1967

On 5 June 1945, one month after the unconditional surrender of Germany at the end of World War II, the Allied Great Powers – the United States, Great Britain, France and the Soviet Union – took over supreme power. The commanders-in-chief of their armies in the occupied country signed on that day the "Declaration on the Proceeding of Control in Germany". An *Allied Control Council,* which could make only unanimous decisions, was formed in Berlin.

Germany was divided into occupation zones. The *Potsdam Agreement* of 2 August 1945 submitted about 25 per cent of her state territory within the 1937 borders to Polish or Soviet administration; the provinces of Silesia, East Brandenburg, Pomerania and the largest part of East Prussia fell under Polish, the northern part of East Prussia under Soviet administration. The final demarcation of the eastern German border was reserved, under this agreement, for the peace conference. At the same time a thorough demilitarization, denazification and democratization of the German people was ordered.

Not even neutral historians doubt the fact that the victorious western powers felt themselves in the following years bound in their political decisions by the provisions of the Potsdam Agreement. This provided for the establishment of central administrative organs in the sphere of finance, transport, foreign trade and industry for the entire German state territory, and for the creation of administrations for the individual occupation zones on the basis of a "free, democratic, legal order".

By contrast, the Soviet Union from the very day of the signing of the Agreement abused its provisions, and also the directives of the Control Council, for her own aims. The Soviets had an interpretation of the term "free, democratic, legal order" quite different from that of the western powers. For them the "democratization" meant only a formal democratic façade behind which they could proceed with purposeful gradual sovietization of their occupation zone. The *Soviet*

Military Administration in Germany (SMAG), which was established on 9 June 1945 and which had its seat in the Berlin suburb of Karlshorst, was issuing, without regard to the jurisdiction of the Allied Control Council for the entire German state territory, arbitrary orders valid as law for the Soviet occupation zone. This was in clear violation of the provisions of the Potsdam Agreement.

These Soviet actions were not surprising in view of Stalin's attitude at the conferences with the statesmen of the United States and Great Britain in Teheran (November 1943) and Yalta (February 1945). The protocols of these conferences clearly show that the Soviet Union, contrary to the western powers, did not want to annihilate Hitler-Germany, but above all wanted to secure for herself the best power positions for the period after the war which they had fought together.

The Soviets conceived very early the idea of German rearmament under the conditions of a favourable (in their view) development. Amidst the war, on 6 November 1942, Stalin declared:

> We do not have such a task as the annihilation of all organized military strength in Germany because any half-literate man can understand that this is in relation to Germany as well as in relation to Russia not only impossible, but also, from the standpoint of victor, disadvantageous.[1]

The idea of subordinating German military potential to Soviet was realized when the Soviets, helped by German communist emigrés, founded on 12–13 July 1943 the *National Committee "Free Germany"* and on 11–12 September 1943 the *German Officers' League* among German prisoners of war. Though no military units came into being out of the National Committee, its members were individually used by the Red Army in its fight against the German Wehrmacht. The Soviets were also able to use the knowledge of German military experts and they obtained assistance later in the establishment of the German communist army in their occupation zone. That applied, for example, to the Wehrmacht generals Vincenz Müller, Arno von Lenski, Dr. Otto Korfes and Hans Wulz who were later active in setting up the armed forces of the Soviet Zone. Though the Soviets dissolved,

1 Translated from J. V. Stalin: *Über den Großen Vaterländischen Krieg der Sowjetunion* (On the Great Patriotic War of the Soviet Union), Publishing House of the SMAG, Berlin 1945, p. 59.

An honour-guard company of the NPA
at the Soviet War Memorial in East Berlin.

German prisoners of war in the Soviet Union in 1944. Many of them later went from the POW camps directly into the People's Police.

The former general of the Wehrmacht Vincenz Müller, in 1957 Chief of the NPA Main Staff, shaking hand with President Pieck. Right: The former Minister of Defence and now Chairmain of the Council of Ministers Willi Stoph. Second from the left: NPA-General Dickel, now Minister of Interior.

in autumn 1945, the National Committee and the German Officers' League, they nevertheless intensified the political re-education of the prisoners of war in the spirit of Marxism-Leninism, and this was all too often followed by military training.

Under the guise of police

Immediately after the war the Soviets started to set up systematically in their occupation zone German communist military units under the guise of police. Otto Opitz, a veteran communist who was until 1960 as head of the Office of the State President of the "German Democratic Republic" Acting Secretary of State, confirmed in October 1959 in a report of the Institute of Marxism-Leninism, specially written for the SED Political School, that "the hour of birth of the armed forces of the German working class" was as early as in October 1945:

> On 31 October 1945 the armament of the People's Police was approved by the SMAG. This became the birth-hour of the armed forces of the German working class, the birth-hour of the armed forces of the first Workers' and Peasants' Power in Germany ...
> The new police, which we founded in Dresden[2], had to be be built into a reliable instrument of the new anti-fascist order. Therefore the selection of the cadres[3] was the most important and responsible task. Today it is no longer necessary to prove that out of these élite cadres the armed organs have grown into a reliable instrument of the working class.

During May and June 1945 the non-military police forces in the three western occupation zones – in accordance with the decisions of the Yalta Conference – were strongly decentralized and in general established only on a municipal basis. Contrary to this, the decree of the SMAG, issued at the end of October 1945, gave the administrations of the then five existing *Länder* (states) of the Soviet Zone – Brandenburg, Saxony, Saxony-Anhalt, Thuringia and Mecklenburg-Pomerania – full powers to integrate municipal police forces and

2 Opitz was President of Police in Dresden in 1945–1949.
3 The term "cadres" generally means officers.

centralize them in each Land. Only two months later, in December 1945, the individual police forces of the Länder were subordinated to the Minister of Interior, a member of the communist party. Thus, half a year after the end of the war, there existed in each of the five Länder of the Soviet Zone a central organization for the police, the *Land Police Authority (LPA)*. This was a gross violation of the inter-Allied agreements.

With the beginning of 1946 the Soviets purposefully forged ahead with the build-up of the armed forces. Early in January "Neues Deutschland" (New Germany), central organ of the Socialist Unity Party of Germany (SED – Sozialistische Einheitspartei Deutschlands)[4], for the first time coined the term *People's Police*.

A new chapter in the development began with the centralized *German Administration of Interior (GAI)* which was established in East Berlin on the order of the SMAG under the guidance of the veteran communist Erich Reschke. The GAI was given authority to issue orders by-passing the ministers of interior in the individual Länder and thus it was made the supreme command organ for all units of the People's Police. The key positions within the GAI were given to proven communists, who in many cases were receiving their instructions directly from the SMAG in Berlin-Karlshorst.

This centrally commanded People's Police had at the end of November 1946 already 45 000 men.

On 28 November 1946 the SMAG gave the GAI another important military task. This was the instruction to the police authorities in the Länder to set up barracked *German Frontier Police (GFP)*. In December 1946, there were already 3 000 frontier policemen in the barracks; in the first half of 1947 they were trained and equally organized in all five Länder.

In September 1947 the GFP had 4 000 men armed with carbines 98k and pistols of the former German Wehrmacht.

The foundation of the German Frontier Police and its tasks were a clear violation of the Allied Control Council's instructions that the demarcation lines and frontiers were to be guarded, until the

---

4 SED was formed through the forced unification of the Social Democratic Party and the Communist Party ordered by the Soviets in their occupation zone.

conclusion of a German peace treaty, solely by the military personnel of the Allies. Though the Soviets had agreed to such directives of the Control Council, they had no intention of fulfilling them in their zone of occupation.

Hence it is not surprising that, despite the detailed measures for the demilitarization of Germany contained in the directives of the Control Council, the following centrally directed armed organizations were in existence in the Soviet Zone by April 1948: the People's Police with 60 000 men and the German Frontier Police with 10 000 men. In addition, the SMAG had already issued Order No. 60 under which the strength of the *Railway Police* (Transport Police) was increased to 7 400 men.

From 1948: Regular military forces

The decisive step was made by the Soviets in the summer of 1948 when, with the communist putsch in Prague, increased armaments in the USSR and the Berlin blockade, a sharper course in the foreign policy was started. The SMAG order of 3 June 1948 introduced the decisive phase in the build-up of the regular military forces. The German Administration of Interior was ordered to establish training institutions and units for the creation of military cadre formations.

The necessary personnel preparations had been, by that time, already set in motion. Their aim was to win over for the service in the new military forces of the Soviet Zone some 1000 officers of the Wehrmacht who were still held in the Soviet Union as prisoners of war.

Thus in the summer of 1948 there were in existence three branches of the armed forces:
– the (general) police,
– the German Frontier Police,
– the Barracked Alert Units.

All these forces were subordinated to the *Chief Department of the Frontier Police and Alert Units,* a newly formed department of the GAI. Corresponding departments were formed also in the Land Police Authorities in all five Länder.

The Alert Units were soon, though officially only from 1952, designated as the *Barracked People's Police (BPP).* They were the cadre formations of the future land, air and naval forces. Their first commander and chief inspector with the rank of major general became Hermann Rentzsch, a first lieutenant of the Wehrmacht, re-educated in 1943 in the Soviet camp for prisoners of war.

In August 1948 there were already 10 Alert Units with 250 men each, that is 2 500 men in all, with the former Wehrmacht officers and NCO's as the cadres.

The same tactics, under which the Soviets had begun the remilitarization immediately after the unconditional surrender of Germany on 8 May 1945 with the gradual centralization of the police, were now applied systematically to the creation of military cadres as the nucleus of a future army.

The then Minister of Interior of Brandenburg and former major of the Wehrmacht, Bernhard Bechler, mentioned this several times in his speech at the conference of the heads of personnel departments of the German Administration of Interior:

> ... a strong centralization of the police apparatus was necessary ... A municipal police system would have constituted danger to the democratic development. Neither district presidents nor mayors are, therefore, permitted to give instructions to the police.

In October 1948 the GAI decided to take the Departments of the Frontier Police and Alert Units in the individual Länder out of the jurisdiction of the Land Police Authorities, and subordinated them directly to its own Chief Department.

Parallel with this proceeded the formation of the *Transport Police (Trapo)* from the already existing Railway Police. This new force was, allegedly, only to take over the protection of railway installations and transport of goods and reparations to the Soviet Union, but it was built up as a police force with considerably expanded authority.

Towards the end of 1948, the barracked Alert Units of the BPP had 8 000 men. In all these units Soviet officers acted as *military advisers*, with General Petrakovski as their chief. Their use clearly shows the consistency with which the Soviet Union proceeded in the formation of effective military forces in its zone, since these soldiers could have hardly understood police tasks.

In the spring of 1949 the SMAG gave its first "purge order" (No. 204/2). This laid on that all persons who had close relatives in West Germany, who were for a considerable time detained in the West as

prisoners of war, who were refugees from the eastern German territories, who were politically unreliable and/or before 1945 members
of the German police, had to be dismissed from all armed forces.

The management of the disguised military forces, now standing
under the Chief Administration of Schooling, was taken over in September 1949 by Wilhelm Zaisser, a specialist in civil war who was
trained in the USSR and who made his reputation as "General
Gomez" in the Spanish Civil War. (For a time after 1945, Zaisser was
Minister of Interior in Saxony.) His deputy became Heinz Hoffmann,
also trained in the USSR, at the Frunze Academy. He, too, was an
officer of the *International Brigades* in Spain.

The training of the leading cadres was now increasingly intensified; the first 12-month courses for higher officers of the BPP began
in autumn 1949 at the Soviet military academy at Privolsk near
Saratov on the Volga.

From 1949: The foundation of the Services

A new development phase in the building of military forces in
East Germany began with the establishment of the "German Democratic Republic" on Soviet instruction in October 1949.

The Soviet Military Administration in Germany was dissolved and
replaced by the *Soviet Control Commission (SCC)* which from then
on exercised the supreme supervision of all military and police
forces.

The German Administration of Interior became the Ministry of
Interior (MI); within it was formed the *Chief Administration of the
German People's Police (CAGPP)* to which were subordinated the
general *German People's Police (GPP)* and the *German Frontier
Police (GFP)*.

The barracked Alert Units of the BPP remained to be subordinated
to the *Chief Administration of Schooling (CAS)* which began to
develop more and more into an independent chief command. A few
weeks later the units were divided into the forces of individual
services.

At that time the Federal Rupublic of Germany, established out of
the three western occupation zones, had no barracked police, not to
speak of the non-existent military units.

Taking into consideration the situation created in East Germany the *Allied High Commission* of the three western powers was issuing from then on directives under which each *Bundesland* (federal state) was authorized to organize its own police force while keeping within the regulations of the occupation statute. According to this, the cities could integrate their police forces with those of other municipalities "provided no such police force had more than 2 000 men and ... no territory integrated in this way was larger than that of an administrative district".

Even more significant for the situation in West Germany of that time was Act No. 16, issued by the High Commission in December 1949. It forbade, under the threat of a heavy penalty, all activities "directly or indirectly connected with teaching the theory and basic laws or technique of war or aimed at preparation of any military actions or at the resuscitation of militarism".

In East Germany, the Chief Administration of Schooling changed its name on 3 February 1950 and became *Chief Administration of Training (CAT)*. The supreme command, held until now by Wilhelm Zaisser, passed into the hands of General Inspector Heinz Hoffmann. Zaisser took over the *Ministry of State Security (MSS)* created by a law of 8 February 1950, and began to set up, from politically absolutely reliable men, the *Guard Regiment MSS*, a special military force of 5 000 men.

Besides the CAT, the Soviets also created, on 15 June 1950, out of a camouflaged department ZBV (for special duty) the *Chief Administration of the Naval Police (CANP)*. Its first units – the 1st Flotilla Zinnowitz (motor torpedo boats) and the 2nd Flotilla (mine sweepers) – had been commissioned a month before. Officially the tasks of the CANP were defined as "protection of the coast against smugglers and protection of own fishermen".

A newly founded department ZBV2 (for special duty) within the CAT became in December 1950 the nucleus of the command for the still missing Air Force.

The schooling of the officers of the BPP in the USSR was further intensified. In the last months of 1950 over 500 younger officers went to the Soviet Union to attend instruction courses for staff officers.

By the end of 1950 the armament of East Germany had reached the following state:

1. The barracked Alert Units (BPP) of the CAT and the units of the

CANP had:
- 39 alert units,
- 12 schools of the services,
- 12 officer schools,
- 5 special schools.

Total strenght: 70 000 men.
2. The German Frontier Police of the Chief Department of the Frontier Police had 18 000 men.
3. The Transport Police: 11 500 men.
4. The Guard Regiment MSS: 5 000 men.

To this was to be added the non-military part of the People's Police whose 80 000 men were employed in the criminal police, traffic police, general police and administrative police.

Only at this point did the West begin to consider whether the Federal Republic of Germany should be militarily armed again. After the communist attack on Korea on 25 June 1950, and in view of the increasing armaments in East Germany, the *Conference of Foreign Ministers* agreed in New York in September 1950 to the establishment of barracked police forces to at total strength of 30 000 men. On 16 March 1951 the President of the Federal Republic of Germany announced a bill for the foundation of a barracked and motorized *Federal Border Police* with 10 000 men; the Bundesländer agreed only reluctantly to the creation of their own alert units totalling 10 000 men in all.

Meanwhile the build-up of armed forces proceeded in East Germany systematically.

The barracked Alert Units were again reorganized and integrated into *People's Police Offices,* each of them corresponding to a strengthened regiment.[5] Thus came into being 24 equally organized cadre forces of mixed branches with a total target strength of 60 000 men. In all these units Soviet advisers were active, supervising the training which was now conducted more on Soviet lines. As chief of the Soviet

---

5 Military term; generally comprises one regiment of infantry, one section of artillery and armoured, engineer, reconnaissance, signal and transport units.

advisers' group, General Makarov now replaced General Petrakovski.

The Spring of 1951 saw the foundation of the first units of the "Air Police". The camouflaged department ZBV2 became, some 18 months later, in July 1952, the *Chief Administration of the Air Police (CAAP)*. Its command was taken over by the leading functionary of the *Free German Youth (FDJ* – Freie Deutsche Jugend), Heinz Kessler, who as a soldier on the German East Front deserted in 1941 to the Red Army and by 1952 was promoted to major general.

From 1952: "National armed forces" and Soviet weapons

Though in the previous years the existence of armed forces in East Germany was always hotly denied, in May 1952 the rulers admitted the build-up of "national forces". They tried to justify this by the alleged "war-mongering" in the West as well as "remilitarization of the Federal Republic of Germany", where at that time even the legal conditions for setting up the forces did not exist, not to speak of the existence of military units.

The attitude of East Germany was mainly based on the Soviet line towards Germany. The Soviet Union, trying to prevent the integration of the Federal Republic with the free West, sent a note to the western powers on 10 March 1952 pleading for a reunited and "democratized" (i. e. communist) Germany and promising her "her own national armed forces". With this note, far-reaching and wide-spread militaristic propaganda and militarization of the entire life of East Germany were set in motion. From then on, the leadership was proclaiming every year more persistently and impatiently the duty to serve in the armed forces.

Into 1952 and the following year also falls the foundation of communist *Combat Groups,* originally designated as Factory Combat Groups, and of the *Sport and Technology Association* serving as training body for the young people of both sexes.

Soviet initiative and guidance in the militarization of East Germany can be seen from the fact, among others, that since the beginning of 1952, on orders from the Soviet Control Commission, the weapons of the Wehrmacht used until then in training the BPP were gradually replaced by Soviet models.

The building of the East German armed forces was from then on, though still under the guise of the BPP, conducted openly, in line with contemporary military demands. The basis for the expansion of the future communist army was assured with the re-education and re-training of 15 000 officers and 30 000 NCO's.

The Chief Administration of Training, commanding authority of the land forces, was officially renamed
- Chief Administration of the Barracked People's Police (CABPP). Simultaneously the CABPP together with the
- Chief Administration of the Naval Police (CANP), commanding authority of the naval forces, and the
- Chief Administration of the Air Police (CAAP), commanding authority of the air forces
were subordinated to the Minister of Interior, Willi Stoph. Heinz Hoffmann, until then inspector general, was promoted to lieutenant general and appointed Chief of the Barracked People's Police.

Police ranks were replaced with military ranks and instead of the old blue uniforms, new khaki ones were introduced resembling in style and colour Soviet uniforms.

On 5 July 1952 the Council of Ministers of the GDR, on instruction from the Central Committee of the SED, decided upon the foundation of four Army Groups. The Army Group North, consisting of three divisions (Eggesin, Prora on the Island of Rügen and Prenzlau) and corresponding army troops, could be set up, due to favourable conditions, as early as late summer 1952.

Earlier, in May 1952, the units of the German Frontier Police were taken out of the authority of the Ministry of Interior and were subordinated to the Ministry of State Security.

Parallel with the build-up of the land, air and naval forces, within the framework of the German People's Police, the barracked *Technical Stand-by Commands* were being established. These had in their ranks by the end of December 1952 in the 14 districts of the Soviet Zone – the Länder were meanwhile dissolved – and in the Soviet Sector of Berlin a total of 13 000 men.

The build-up of the Recruiting and Replacement Organization, too, was essentially finished by the end of 1952, and first releases of men, after three years of service, could now be undertaken, creating thus the first reserves of men for the armed forces.

On 19 February 1953 the Council of Ministers, "with a view to strengthening further the power of the state", founded within the Ministry of Interior a *State Secretary's Office of Interior*. This office was supposed to fulfil the traditional duties of the Ministry of Interior while the rest of the ministry now took over the tasks of a Ministry of Defence.

At this time began also the setting up of the so-called *Territorial Administrations*, new cover name for military commands:

– Territorial Administration 4000 (Pasewalk),
– Territorial Administration 3000 (Dresden),
– Territorial Administration 5000 (Schwerin),
– Territorial Administration 6000 (Leipzig).

Only the Territorial Administration 4000 (corresponding to the Army Group North) had more than three divisions at its disposal. The Territorial Administrations 3000, 5000 and 6000 each consisted of three infantry formations in regimental strength, one armoured regiment, one artillery regiment and later one anti-aircraft regiment, as well as of corresponding operational and service troops.

After the popular rising of 17 June 1953, during which the BPP did not fulfil its tasks as a SED-Party force, a second big purge was started and 12 000 men of all ranks were dismissed as "unreliable elements". Supervision by Soviet "advisers" was temporarily increased.

The next organizational step was made in September 1953. The Chief Administrations of the Barracked People's Police, Naval Police and Air Police were integrated into one central command within the framework of the Ministry of Interior under the name of the *Ministry of Interior/Barracked People's Police (MI/BPP)*. The Territorial Administrations 3000 and 5000 were dissolved and within the Territorial Administration 6000 was set up the Army Group South (Leipzig), consisting of three divisions (Dresden, Halle and Erfurt) and one additional division as counter-attack reserve of the MI/BPP in Potsdam.

At the end of 1953 the MI/BPP had at its disposal more than seven divisions.

In June 1954 the Supreme Command of the BPP (MI/BPP) was further separated from the ministry by having its headquarters transferred from East Berlin to Strausberg. Here, at the same time, anti-aircraft units were set up. They formed the nucleus of the 1st Anti-Aircraft Division established in August 1957.

When Willi Stoph, the Minister of Interior, handed over, on 30 June 1955, his office to the then head of the Chief Administration of the German People's Police, Inspector General Karl Maron, the entire apparatus of the BPP was definitively taken out of the Ministry of Interior and subordinated to Willi Stoph in his capacity as Deputy Chairman of the Council of Ministers. Stoph, who appeared for the first time in the uniform of colonel general in the summer of 1955 at a military parade, took over as the highest ranking officer the military supreme command of the BPP. Lieutenant General Heinz Hoffmann, until then Chief of the BPP, went to the Soviet Union to attend a course.

In 1955 the training and equipment of units were generally improved. The training places of the troops were extended. In October of the same year the first large-scale autumn manoeuvres took place in which several divisions participated.

1956: Act on the Foundation of the NPA

The People's Chamber, the sham parliament of the East Germany, passed on 18 January 1956 the *Act on the Foundation of the National People's Army and the Ministry of National Defence.* This Act, which was supposed to give the NPA the seal of legality, formally acknowledged a state of affairs long existing, known throughout the world and officially admitted by the East German authorities as early as 1952. It was presented by propaganda as a "spontaneous" reaction to the discussion conducted in the Federal Republic of Germany on the necessity of a German contribution to the western defence organization. In fact, however, the first great phase in the build-up of the Soviet Zone's armed forces was, by the beginning of 1956, already concluded. Their total strength was 120 000 men. (The Federal Republic of Germany, at that time, only started recruiting the first 1 000 volunteers for the establishment of the *Bundeswehr* – federal defence forces.)

The present Supreme Command of the BPP was given the name of the *Ministry of National Defence.* At its head now stood formally the Deputy Chairman of the Council of Ministers, Colonel General Willi

Stoph, aided by *Chief of Staff of the Ministry of National Defence*, Lieutenant General Vincenz Müller (former lieutenant general of the Wehrmacht and member of the National Committee "Free Germany") and by Deputy Chief of Staff, Major General Bernhard Bechler (former major of the Wehrmacht and member of the National Committee "Free Germany").

The traditional German uniform was re-introduced (only the steel-helmet of the Soviet Army was retained). This was meant to stress outwardly the alleged national character of the NPA in accordance with the efforts of the Soviet Zone to gain official recognition and sovereignty. At home, the SED leadership apparently hoped that the publicly manifested continuation of German military traditions would induce the population to approve of the unpopular NPA.

In the Order of the Day on 7 October 1956, issued on the occasion of the "7th anniversary of the GDR", Stoph declared that the National People's Army was now established. The units were further modernized and soon reached such a state of preparedness that the Soviets were able gradually to recall their advisers.

The military formations of the Alert Units, Frontier Police and Transport Police were also strengthened while their subordination to the Ministry of State Security or the Ministry of Interior was, from time to time, changed.

In autumn 1957 the German Frontier Police was reorganized on military lines and divided into brigades, regiments and battalions. Its subordination to the Ministry of Interior was terminated on 15 September 1961 and it was taken over by the NPA as locally stationed frontier troops under the designation of the *National People's Army/Frontier Command*. Its units have been using since April 1962 military designations.

The Alert Units, too, were in the years 1958–1961 better trained, equipped and organized. In 1962 they were decentralized so that they could be speedily used locally as military security troops. The units of the Transport Police remained, within the framework of the Administration of German People's Police, under the jurisdiction of the Ministry of Interior.

Since East Germany had, as the only member of the Warsaw Pact, to put all its military units at the disposal of the United Command, the Frontier Troops, too, now came under this supreme command.

In the last quarter of 1958 the 6th Motorized Infantry Division Prenzlau was dissolved and later the armed forces of the NPA were divided into the *Military Districts* (in time of war: Armies) III, Leipzig, and V, Neubrandenburg (each with one armoured and two motorized infantry divisions and with units directly subordinated to military districts), and, from 15 September 1961, a *Frontier Command* in Pätz.

In July 1960 Colonel General Heinz Hoffmann became Minister of National Defence.

On 10 February 1960 the People's Chamber established the *National Defence Council* and appointed as its chairman Walter Ulbricht, Chairman of the State Council and leader of the SED. This emergency organ, working in greatest secrecy, bears responsibility for all measures connected with the security of East Germany, and all other state organs are subordinated to it. The National Defence Council can issue decrees in case of state emergency and since October 1963 has issued several important government decrees.

On 13 August 1961, when the building of the infamous "Berlin Wall" was started, together with the NPA were used also the formations of the Alert Units, Frontier Police and Combat Groups in cutting off West Berlin. The two frontier brigades, used for this purpose, were established in June 1961 out of the selected cadres of other Frontier Police units.

The Act on the Defence of the German Democratic Republic, passed on 20 September 1961, put down the basic principles of further militarization of the GDR and confirmed the emergency powers of the National Defence Council. According to paragraph 4, section 1, the Council can declare "in case of danger or attack on the GDR, or when the fulfilment of international alliance duties it requires" a "state of defence". Since for example the building of the Berlin Wall on 13 August 1961 was "justified" with the alleged attack planned by the West, and since also the popular uprising on 17 June 1953 was allegedly started by western provocateurs, the formula "in case of danger or attack" offers possibilities of action against inner disorders. The Act further confirmed the basic civic duty to military service in the NPA or in other armed organs and civil defence.

1962: The NPA under universal conscription

When, despite all enforcement and terror, the number of "volunteers" was insufficient, the *Act on Universal Conscription* was formally introduced on 24 January 1962. At the same time an *Order of Listing* and an *Order of Mustering* were issued, accompanied by *General Regulations, Order of Reservists, Pay Regulation Order, Order of Maintenance* and an *Order of Advancement* concerning the members of the NPA released from the active military service. Together with the General Regulations was introduced the *Oath of Allegiance* binding the NPA soldiers to unconditional obedience to the government and to unconditional support of the "Soviet Army and armies of our socialist allies".

On 23 August 1962 the NPA took over from the Soviets the garrison headquarters in the Soviet Sector of Berlin and Major General Helmut Poppe was appointed "Commander of the GDR capital".

Another sign of progressing militarization was the *Order of Military Tribunals* of 4 April 1963 regulating the establishment and jurisdiction of military tribunals. Simultaneously it was ordered that all cases of military offences had to be, as from 1 July 1963, handed over by civil courts to military tribunals.

In autumn 1963 the entire officers' schooling in the NPA was reorganized and as much as possible centralized with the establishment of central schools for the officers of land forces, frontier troops, naval and air forces respectively.

Building a modern army with nuclear weapons

Continuous supply of the latest modern Soviet weapons and equipment improved the material combat strength of all three services of the NPA. This fact was further underlined by the re-formation of conventional and nuclear forces and units.

In sharp contrast to the hypocritical declarations of the zonal functionaries on the dangers of spreading nuclear weapons, the armament of the NPA services includes rocket carriers for nuclear warheads. Their existence became known in 1963, but the nuclear field weapons were publicly displayed for the first time only on 7 October 1964 at the NPA parade on the occasion of the 15th anniversary of the GDR. The NPA/People's Navy had shown missile motor gun boats at a simultaneously staged parade in Rostock.

Also the NPA/Air Force is equipped for nuclear warfare with modern, highly efficient aircraft. And moreover, there have been hints from East Germany that further specialized units of the NPA are going to be equipped with nuclear weapons.

Army General Heinz Hoffmann, Minister of Defence, stated in April 1965 that the NPA belongs, together with the armies of the Soviet Union, Poland and Czechoslovakia, to the First Strategic Echelon of the Warsaw Pact. This only emphasizes the high value of the NPA acknowledged by its communist allies, and it shows how near it is to the level of the Soviet Army.

In the first quarter of 1966 the peace-time strength of all armed forces of East Germany, including the police and paramilitary units of the Combat Groups was as follows:

– Land Forces (including Frontier Troops)	155 000
– Air Force and Air Defence	35 000
– People's Navy	20 000
– Police Alert Units (including Guard Regiment of MSS)	20 000
– Transport Police	8 000
Barracked military units – total	238 000
– Combat Groups	400 000
– (general) People's Police	80 000
– Customs Administration	10 000
Non-barracked paramilitary units and organizations – total	490 000
Total strength of all armed forces	728 000

Summary

The evolution of military forces and para-military units and organizations in East Germany faithfully mirrors Soviet policy towards Germany.

Until 1952 the build-up of the Barracked People's Police as an unmistakably military institution was conducted in great secrecy and under disguise. Its military value was rather limited. Nevertheless, it was an important factor in Soviet foreign policy which was planning for, and aiming at, a settlement of the German problem which would create favourable conditions for a communist putsch in the Federal Republic of Germany.

These Soviet hopes were, however, dwarfed by the continuing integration of the Federal Republic into the western community. The Soviets increased, therefore, the militarization of their zone. The existence of "national military forces" was officially admitted and their necessity justified by the alleged West German "revanchism". Yet, for the time being, the cover name of the Barracked People's Police was retained.

Only when the beginning of the build-up of the Bundeswehr within the defence alliance of NATO – as the result of the Soviet threat – could not be any longer prevented, the existence of the East German military forces was confirmed by law in January 1956 and simultaneously the BPP was renamed the *National People's Army.* In line with communist distortion practice, the East German functionaries were declaring that this was a new-type army, necessitated only by the alleged "remilitarization" in the Federal Republic. The falseness of such communist accusations and their practices of covering up or distorting truth is illustrated by, among others, the fact that while the GDR was a full member of the Warsaw Pact from its foundation on 14 May 1955, this was officially admitted only on 28 January 1956. Then it was stated, on the occasion of renaming the BPP as the NPA, that the GDR was a "fully recognized military member of the Pact".

The importance of East Germany for the Soviet Union was increased considerably by the conclusion of the *Treaty on Mutual Assistance and Cooperation* on 12 June 1964.

In building the armed forces in their occupation zone the Soviets never felt themselves prevented by the decisions on German demilitarization made by the Allies at the end of World War II. By "demilitarization" they apparently understood only the persecution of all persons who opposed communist penetration. "Militarists", who are willing to collaborate with communists, are not regarded "obnoxious" as long as they are needed or as long as they loyally serve the communist regime. This is well illustrated by the use of former Wehrmacht officers in the BPP and NPA.

The NPA tries to assume the air of a national German Army.

Commander-in-Chief Ulbricht inspecting a unit of the People's Navy.

Erich Honecker, head of the Commission for National Security of the SED Politburo (left), and Army General Heinz Hoffmann, Minister of National Defence.

The propaganda machinery of the NPA puts great stress on German-Russian comradeship in arms. Right: An NPA-soldier and a Russian "talk" during a break in joint military exercise.

Below: Russian Cavalry and Prussian Home Guard on the Kreutzberg in Berlin 1813; such pictures are frequently used to create a new tradition.

Within the framework of the Soviet Union's German policy it could therefore have corresponding specific tasks. In this role, the NPA represents a particular danger to the Federal Republic, since there has not been any trustworthy hint that the communists have definitively given up their intention of a possible violent solution of the German problem.

PART TWO

ORGANIZATION AND EQUIPMENT

CHAPTER 2

ORGANIZATION AND STRUCTURE OF THE ARMED FORCES

The Ministry of National Defence (MND)

The highest military command and administrative organ of the NPA is the *Ministry of National Defence (MND)* headed by the *Minister of National Defence*, a veteran communist, Army General Heinz Hoffmann. He holds supreme command within the NPA.

According to the law, the MND "organizes and leads the NPA (land, air and naval forces) in accordance with the laws, decrees and decisions of the People's Chamber[1] and the Council of Ministers"[2]. The tasks of the MND are "decided by the Council of Ministers"[3].

Superior state organs for the MND are the *State Council of the GDR*, whose *Chairman* (and therefore also head of state) is Walter Ulbricht, and the *National Defence Council* of the GDR, whose *Chairman* is again Ulbricht. He is sometimes also called *Supreme Commander*. The *Secretary* of the National Defence Council is a veteran communist, Erich Honecker.

Even more relevant for the MND are, however, the directives, instructions and orders of the *Central Committee (CC)* of the SED whose *First Secretary* is again Ulbricht. Members of the CC are also Honecker and Minister Hoffmann, as well as several other holders of important command posts in the NPA.

The *Politburo*, the real leading organ within the CC, decides the basic questions for the NPA.

1 People's Chamber – sham parliament of East Germany.

2 Council of Ministers – designation of the government introduced in 1954 on the Soviet model. (The powers of the Council of Ministers were several times changed and substantially reduced.)

3 *The Act on the Foundation of the National People's Army and the Ministry of National Defence*. Here quoted from "Neues Deutschland", 19 January 1956.

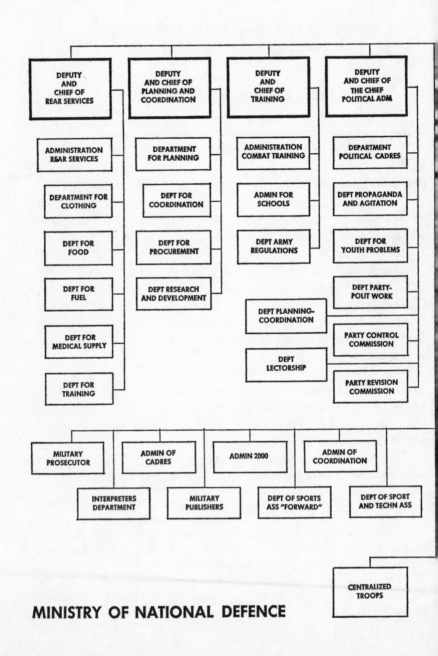

DEPUTY AND CHIEF OF REAR SERVICES	DEPUTY AND CHIEF OF PLANNING AND COORDINATION	DEPUTY AND CHIEF OF TRAINING	DEPUTY AND CHIEF OF THE CHIEF POLITICAL ADM
ADMINISTRATION REAR SERVICES	DEPARTMENT FOR PLANNING	ADMINISTRATION COMBAT TRAINING	DEPARTMENT POLITICAL CADRES
DEPARTMENT FOR CLOTHING	DEPT FOR COORDINATION	ADMIN FOR SCHOOLS	DEPT PROPAGANDA AND AGITATION
DEPT FOR FOOD	DEPT FOR PROCUREMENT	DEPT ARMY REGULATIONS	DEPT FOR YOUTH PROBLEMS
DEPT FOR FUEL	DEPT RESEARCH AND DEVELOPMENT		DEPT PARTY-POLIT WORK
DEPT FOR MEDICAL SUPPLY		DEPT PLANNING-COORDINATION	PARTY CONTROL COMMISSION
DEPT FOR TRAINING		DEPT LECTORSHIP	PARTY REVISION COMMISSION

MILITARY PROSECUTOR	ADMIN OF CADRES	ADMIN 2000	ADMIN OF COORDINATION
INTERPRETERS DEPARTMENT	MILITARY PUBLISHERS	DEPT OF SPORTS ASS "FORWARD"	DEPT OF SPORT AND TECHN ASS

CENTRALIZED TROOPS

MINISTRY OF NATIONAL DEFENCE

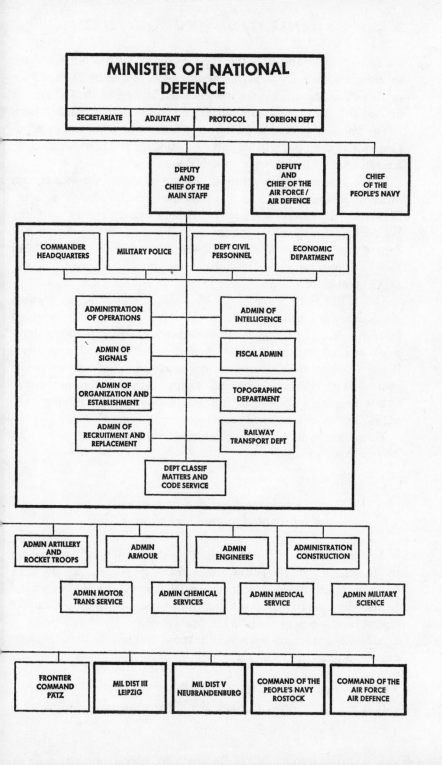

Security tasks and also the special control in the NPA are the sphere of the *Security Department* of the CC headed by Major General Walter Borning. Thus the influence and control of the CC are not limited only to party affairs but extend to the purely military field.

The Minister of National Defence is assisted by a number of deputies; each of them is a reliable party functionary and is responsible for a certain spere of work within the NPA.

In the process of strengthening the top of the ministry, a certain order of precedence was introduced among the minister's deputies. Previously the head of the Political Administration (today the Chief Political Administration) took the first place; later the post of the first deputy minister went to Kurt Wagner who was promoted in March 1966 to colonel general. After him come the members of the CC, Colonel General Kessler and Admiral Verner.

The MND is organized into *Main Staff, Chief Administration, Administrations* and *Departments* of varying importance, size and independence. The complicated organizational structure of the ministry – which a Western observer can understand only with difficulty – is explained by the fact that it was modelled strictly on its Soviet equivalent and that the NPA was originally developed from the Barracked People's Police. Also different conceptions of military and political tasks of the armed forces played their role.

The administrations and departments of the MND can be divided into five main groups.

Administrations and departments subordinated to the Chief of Main Staff

Among the tasks of the Main Staff are those which are essential for the functioning of the entire armed forces in peace and war, their deployment etc. Since there is no special supreme command for land forces, the operational tasks for them must be elaborated on the highest level – that of the Chief of Main Staff.

Altogether there are six administrations and five departments subordinated to the Chief of Main Staff.

ADMINISTRATION OF OPERATIONS
It is responsible for planning the deployment of the NPA units

within the framework of the armed forces of the Warsaw Pact according to the directives of the *Supreme Commander of the United Forces.*

ADMINISTRATION OF INTELLIGENCE

It evaluates all information on foreign military forces and corresponds in its sphere of activities, perhaps, to the G_2-Intelligence of the NATO armed forces.

ADMINISTRATION OF COMMUNICATIONS (SIGNALS)

It is responsible for the entire communication system within the NPA and for its coordination with that of other members of the Warsaw Pact to facilitate the use of the NPA forces in joint operations. It is also responsible for supplying the troops with communications apparatus and its maintenance.

ADMINISTRATION OF ORGANIZATION AND ESTABLISHMENT

It keeps the records on the strength of the armed forces and their equipment (strength returns, disposition plans etc.). It also elaborates mobilization plans.

FISCAL ADMINISTRATION

It presents the yearly military budget, controls the use of the appropriations by individual departments and is responsible in general for all military expenditure.

ADMINISTRATION OF RECRUITMENT AND REPLACEMENT

Its sphere is the recruitment of both conscripts and volunteers. It cooperates with the military sub-district commands. Among its task is also the listing and care of all reservists.

TOPOGRAPHIC DEPARTMENT

It is responsible for a new topographic survey conducted by local surveying offices, for elaborating the existing military maps and charts and evaluating and filing new ones. It provides the troops with maps and charts.

RAILWAY TRANSPORTATION DEPARTMENT

It is responsible for the entire transport of supplies and transport by rail.

DEPARTMENT OF CLASSIFIED MATTERS AND CODE SERVICE

It elaborates regulations for handling classified matters and supervises their fulfilment. It also lays down the methods for the preparation of codes for the use in ministries and in tactical and operational service by the armed forces.

COMMANDER HEADQUARTERS

This office is in charge of the entire bureaucratic management of the personnel within the MND.

MILITARY POLICE

Its sphere of tasks corresponds to that of the western military police. Its range of competence is limited to the MND and the Garrison Command, Strausberg. Here the Military Police controls the behaviour of officers, NCO's and soldiers and supervises the fulfilment of regulations issued by the post headquarters.

DEPARTMENT OF CIVIL PERSONNEL

It deals with the employment, promotion and dismissal of civil personnel within the NPA.

ECONOMIC DEPARTMENT

It regulates all economic questions of supply in the entire sphere of the MND.

Administrations and departments subordinated to the Deputies of Minister for Training, Planning and Coordination of Rear Services

The Chief of Training, responsible for the entire training of land forces is in charge of two administrations and one department:

ADMINISTRATION OF COMBAT TRAINING

It is responsible for combat training projects in all motorized infantry formations. It currently evaluates the experiences of the troops and elaborates them into relevant general directives which are later reflected in regulations.

ADMINISTRATION OF SCHOOLS

It prepares syllabuses for military schools and the Military Academy and controls the training of officers.

DEPARTMENT OF ARMY REGULATIONS

It lays down and issues service regulations for the troops.

The Chief of Planning and Coordination is responsible for the supply of equipment and material to all services. He is assisted in this by:

DEPARTMENTS OF PLANNING AND COORDINATION

These two departments coordinate the plans of needed materials for all services and divide them according to the industry branches. The total plan is then agreed with the State Planning Commission and afterwards passed on to the Department of Procurement.

DEPARTMENT OF PROCUREMENT

It translates the plan into individual orders and concludes supply contracts with industries.

DEPARTMENT OF RESEARCH AND DEVELOPMENT

It allocates to the industries orders for the development of new equipment, weapons and tools.

The Chief of Rear Services is competent for the supply of general goods to the armed forces. In this he is assisted by the

ADMINISTRATION OF REAR SERVICES

with the departments for the supply of clothing, food, fuel, medicaments, and one department for training.

Chief Political Administration (CPA)

Its task is to guide and control the entire political work within the NPA. Since the execution of military oders and also the military offences committed by the soldiers can constitute a "political problem", the CPA is concerned with practically everything. It plays a very important role in the NPA and is therefore dealt with separately in Chapter 5.

Administrations and departments subordinated directly to the Minister

According to their tasks they are divided into four different groups:

Administrations responsible for logistic planning, procurement and distribution of supplies for *individual branches,* principally however for the training of the branches:

ADMINISTRATION OF ARTILLERY AND ROCKET TROOPS

Its task is to equip the artillery and rocket troops with weapons and to teach them the theory of modern weapons and train them for combat.

ADMINISTRATION OF ARMOUR

It is responsible for the equipment, supply and maintenance of tanks and armoured vehicles for all troops and for technical and combat training of armoured troops.

ADMINISTRATION OF MOTOR TRANSPORT SERVICE

It is competent for the equipment, supply and maintenance of non-armoured tracked and wheeled vehicles for all troops and for the necessary training.

ADMINISTRATION OF ENGINEERS

It has to supply the troops with engineer equipment, war material and explosives and also bears responsibility for specialist training of all engineer formations.

ADMINISTRATION OF CHEMICAL SERVICES
Its task is to supply the troops with ABC defensive weapons and to train specialists in their use.

ADMINISTRATION OF CONSTRUCTION
In its competence falls all construction and building work of military character (comparable with the Infrastructure of the NATO armed forces); it closely cooperates with various specialized ministries.

ADMINISTRATION OF MEDICAL SERVICE
It supervises the entire medical service in the army and is responsible for equipping and supplying necessary tools and goods. It is in charge of training specialists for all medical units.

Specialized administrations of particular importance for the entire armed forces:

MILITARY PROSECUTOR'S OFFICE
This is the highest prosecution authority of the NPA, responsible for issuing relevant decrees in the sphere of the military criminal law. It also issues directives to the military prosecutors of subordinated organs.

ADMINISTRATION OF CADRES
In its sphere fall the personnel affairs concerning the officers of all services; it keeps their personal files, records of their commissions, promotions, transfers, awards and decorations.

Espionage and counter-espionage:

ADMINISTRATION OF COORDINATION
It is the superior authority of the military espionage service directed against the Federal Republic of Germany, West Europe and the NATO in general. It is responsible for the collection of military and military-political reports and information on the weapons and their production in the West. (Its activities are dealt with in greater detail

in Chapter 16, The psychological offensive against the Bundeswehr.)

ADMINISTRATION 2000
It serves as the liaison office to the Ministry of State Security (MSS) and is responsible for security affairs within the entire armed forces. It employs officers of the MSS who are not, however, outwardly recognizable as such. They are listed on all levels, down to the regiment staff, in the corresponding military posts.

Other departments directly subordinated to the Minister:

FOREIGN DEPARTMENT
It guides the affairs connected with the work of military attachés, their training and appointment, and serves also as the liaison office for contacts with, and care of, foreign military attachés accredited in East Berlin.

INTERPRETERS DEPARTMENT
It supervises the staff of interpreters employed by the ministry.

ADMINISTRATION OF MILITARY SCIENCE
It elaborates questions of military history and conducts basic research into military problems.

GERMAN MILITARY PUBLISHING HOUSE
Its task is to publish and distribute military literature in the broadest sense of the word within the NPA, other armed forces and among the public.

DEPARTMENT
OF THE ARMY SPORT ASSOCIATION "FORWARD"
It guides sporting activities within the armed forces concentrating not only on the masses of soldiers but also on prominent soldier-sportsmen in all sports disciplines; it also organizes international sports meetings.

DEPARTMENT OF THE SPORT
AND TECHNOLOGY ASSOCIATION
It serves as the liaison organ for this pre-military organization,

issues directives for the pre-military training and puts army personnel at its disposal.

Chiefs of the
Air Force/Air Defence and of the People's Navy
directly subordinated to the Minister

AIR FORCE / AIR DEFENCE

The *Chief of the Air Force/Air Defence* is also the *Chief of the Command of the Air Force/Air Defence* which was taken out of the sphere of the ministry. (Its seat is in Strausberg-Eggersdorf.) Being also the Deputy Minister of National Defence, he can assure good cooperation with the ministry.

PEOPLE'S NAVY

The *Chief of the People's Navy* is also the *Chief of the Command of the People's Navy* which, too, was taken out of the sphere of the ministry. Its headquarters are in Rostock.

Command organs subordinated to the MND

The *Frontier Command*, which has its seat in Pätz near Königs-wusterhausen and is headed by the Chief of Frontier Troops, Major General Erich Peter, is competent for the entire Frontier Troops; these were until September 1961 subordinated to the Ministry of Interior as the *German Frontier Police* and then incorporated in the NPA.

The *Air Force/Air Defence Command*. It has its headquarters in Strausberg-Eggersdorf and its chief is Colonel General Heinz Kessler.

Military District III. Its command is in Leipzig, its chief ist Major General Hans Ernst.

The *People's Navy Command*. Its seat is in Rostock and its chief is Vice Admiral Willi Ehm.

Military District V has its command in Neubrandenburg and Major General Horst Stechbarth is its chief.

LAND FORCES

MINISTRY OF NATIONAL DEFENCE

MIL DIST III LEIPZIG

- 4th MOT INF DIV ERFURT
- 11th MOT INF DIV HALLE
- 7th ARM DIV DRESDEN

- ART REGT LEIPZIG
- NCO TRAINING REGT EILENBURG
- AA REGT LEIPZIG
- SIGNAL BN LEIPZIG
- ENGR BN GERA
- ART RECON BN LEIPZIG
- CHEM CO GERA
- TRANS BN COTTBUS

MIL DIST V NEUBRANDENBURG

- 1st MOT INF DIV POTSDAM
- 8th MOT INF DIV SCHWERIN
- 9th ARM DIV EGGESIN

- ART REGT TORGELOW
- NCO TRAINING REGT TORGELOW
- AA REGT PRENZLAU
- ENGR BN PASEWALK
- ART RECON BN TORGELOW
- CHEM COM PASEWALK
- TRANS BN PASEWALK
- SIGNAL BN NEUBRANDENBURG

(MND direct)

- SIGNAL REGT NIEDERLEHME
- ENGR REGT DESSAU
- ENGR REGT STORKOW
- GUARD REGT KOEPENICK
- MOT TRANS BN STRAUSBERG
- ART BRIG TORGELOW
- RAD INTEL BN DESSAU

- MIL ACADEMY "FRIEDRICH ENGELS" DRESDEN
- OFFICER SCHOOL NAUMBURG
- OFFICER SCHOOL "ERNST THÄLMANN" LOEBAU

Land forces

The land forces – apart from the Frontier Troops – are guided (without any intermediary organ of a command staff) directly by the MND through Military Districts III and V. At the beginning of 1966 they had, including the Frontier Troops, a total strength of 155 000 men. They included:
- 2 armoured divisions,
- 4 motorized infantry divisions,
- troops of the direct command of the land forces headquarters and corresponding schools,
- army troops and army schools,
- Frontier Troops (their total strength at the beginning of 1966 was 50 000 men. They are organized in 10 frontier brigades and 2 independent frontier regiments.)

The organization of land forces in East Germany basically corresponds in its armoured divisions and motorized infantry divisions to the Soviet model. The still existing differences in material equipment are being steadily removed. The supporting troops have not yet, in their equipment and number, reached the strength usual in the Soviet land forces. Nuclear delivery systems (NATO's designation: FROG and SCUD) are, however, already in service to the same extent as in the Soviet units.

The land forces of the NPA are in their training and equipment equal to the requirements of a modern, nuclear war.

The NPA/Frontier Troops are divided into *Frontier Brigades* and independent *Frontier Regiments*. In 1966 there were 10 frontier brigades: 6 brigades on the demarcation line with the Federal Republic of Germany, 3 brigades for interdiction of West Berlin, 1 brigade on the Baltic coast *(Frontier Brigade Coast)*. One independent frontier regiment is stationed on the Oder-Neisse line and one on the frontier with Czechoslovakia.

Among the frontier brigades, as far as their deployment is concerned, the Frontier Brigade Coast is subordinated to the People's Navy and the three brigades used for the interdiction of West Berlin are subordinated to the East Berlin City Commandant, Major General Helmut Poppe.

The frontier brigades deployed on the demarcation line are, in general, organized and equipped in the same way.

MOTORIZED INFANTRY DIVISION

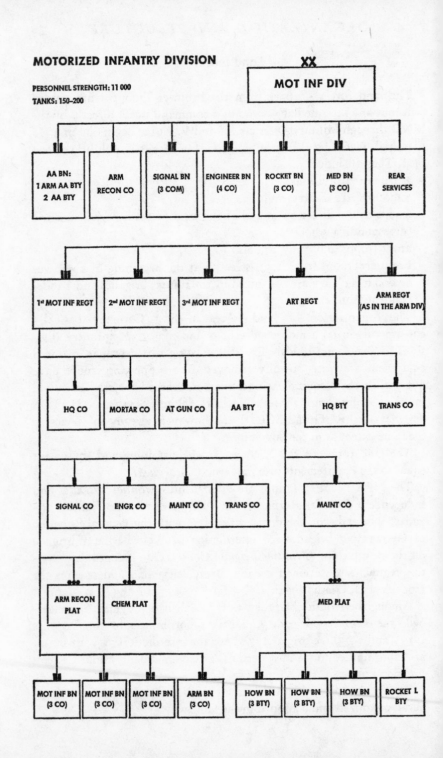

PERSONNEL STRENGTH: 11 000

TANKS: 150–200

XX

MOT INF DIV

| AA BN: 1 ARM AA BTY 2 AA BTY | ARM RECON CO | SIGNAL BN (3 COM) | ENGINEER BN (4 CO) | ROCKET BN (3 CO) | MED BN (3 CO) | REAR SERVICES |

| 1st MOT INF REGT | 2nd MOT INF REGT | 3rd MOT INF REGT | ART REGT | ARM REGT (AS IN THE ARM DIV) |

HQ CO | MORTAR CO | AT GUN CO | AA BTY | HQ BTY | TRANS CO

SIGNAL CO | ENGR CO | MAINT CO | TRANS CO | MAINT CO

ARM RECON PLAT | CHEM PLAT | MED PLAT

MOT INF BN (3 CO) | MOT INF BN (3 CO) | MOT INF BN (3 CO) | ARM BN (3 CO) | HOW BN (3 BTY) | HOW BN (3 BTY) | HOW BN (3 BTY) | ROCKET L BTY

ARMOURED DIVISION

PERSONNEL STRENGTH: 9000
TANKS: 300 T-54, 20 PT-76

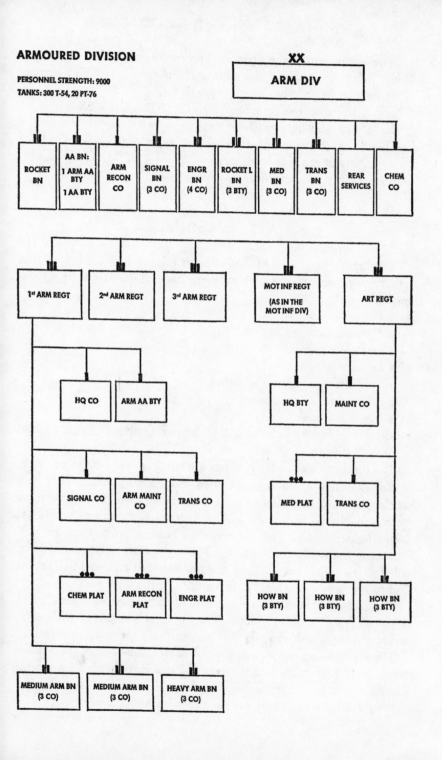

The equipment of the Frontier Troops consists essentially only of light infantry weapons and of some armoured personnel carriers. One frontier brigade has at its disposal:
- about 10 armoured personnel carriers BTR-40 or BTR-152,
- about 250–300 light machine guns,
- about 250–300 light anti-tank guns of type LPAG 40 mm (RPG-2 = anti-tank grenade launcher),
- about 200 trucks and other equipment.

Air Force/Air Defence

The highest command of the NPA for this service ist the *Air Force/ Air Defence Command* in Strausberg-Eggersdorf. It has at its disposal:
- 2 fighter divisions,
- 1 fighter training division,
- 1 transport group,
- 1 helicopter group,
- 5 anti-aircraft rocket regiments,
- 2 radio engineer regiments,
- 1 signal regiment,
- aircraft technical battalions and supply facilities of the ground organization.

The total strength of the personnel in autumn 1965 was 35 000 men. The divisions are entirely equipped with Soviet aircraft. They had, at the beginning of 1966 600 machines; among them there were more than 320, that is about 180 MiG-17 and MiG-19 and 150 MiG-21, in the fighter groups. The Air Force has been intensively modernized in recent years. Not only has the MiG-15 totally disappeared from all fighting units, but also the present standard fighter MiG-17 has had to give way to the highly efficient MiG-21.

The anti-aircraft division was originally equipped only with barrel weapons (57 mm and 100 mm); after 1961 it was armed with anti-aircraft rockets and now has five anti-aircraft rocket regiments.

The air warning service and ground control service have two radio engineering regiments, and the ground organization of the airborne divisions has numerous airborne technical battalions.. In addition there are service units and various other installations.

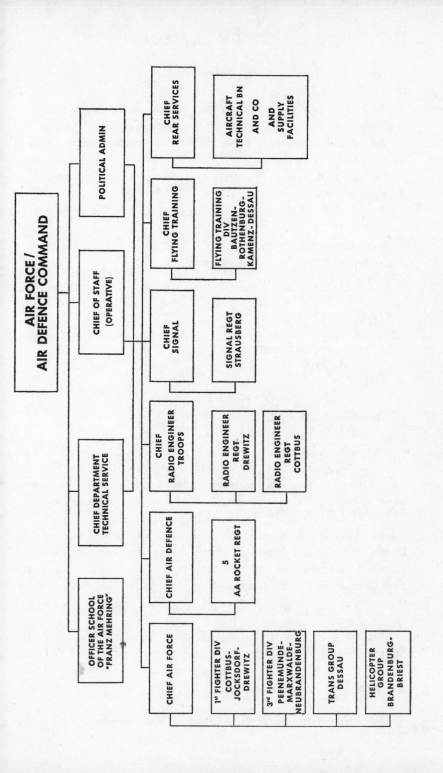

AIR FORCE / AIR DEFENCE COMMAND

OFFICER SCHOOL OF THE AIR FORCE "FRANZ MEHRING"

CHIEF DEPARTMENT TECHNICAL SERVICE

CHIEF OF STAFF (OPERATIVE)

POLITICAL ADMIN

CHIEF REAR SERVICES

AIRCRAFT TECHNICAL BN AND CO AND SUPPLY FACILITIES

CHIEF FLYING TRAINING

FLYING TRAINING DIV BAUTZEN-ROTHENBURG-KAMENZ-DESSAU

CHIEF SIGNAL

SIGNAL REGT STRAUSBERG

CHIEF RADIO ENGINEER TROOPS

RADIO ENGINEER REGT. DREWITZ

RADIO ENGINEER REGT COTTBUS

CHIEF AIR DEFENCE

5 AA ROCKET REGT

CHIEF AIR FORCE

1ˢᵗ FIGHTER DIV COTTBUS-JOCKSDORF-DREWITZ

3ʳᵈ FIGHTER DIV PEENEMUNDE-MARXWALDE-NEUBRANDENBURG

TRANS GROUP DESSAU

HELICOPTER GROUP BRANDENBURG-BRIEST

The naval forces

The highest command of the naval forces, which are designated as the *National People's Army/People's Navy (NPA/PN)* after the "People's Navy Division" (which played an important role in the civil war 1918–1919), is the *People's Navy Command* with headquarters in Rostock and headed by the Chief of the People's Navy, Vice Admiral Willi Ehm.

The People's Navy has 20 000 men and more than 300 ships, among them:
- 4 coastal defence ships,
- 22 motor mine layers and mine sweepers,
- 50 mine sweepers,
- 22 submarine chasers,
- 50 motor torpedo boats,
- 16 missile patrol boats,
- 60 coastal defence boats,
- 45 patrol boats,
- 16 landing craft.

The units of the People's Navy are divided in 3 flotillas:
- 1st flotilla in Peenemünde
- 4th flotilla in Warnemünde
- 6th flotilla in Sassnitz

In addition there are two coastal rocket battalions, the Frontier Brigade Coast; they, too, are subordinated to the NPA/PN Command as are also the signal unit on the island of Rügen and supply units.

The NPA/PN had, when it started, only ships of Soviet origin. This changed later and today all mine layers and mine sweepers are of East Germany's own design and production. Also the landing craft, mine sweepers, patrol boats and auxiliary vessels have been built in the East German shipyards. On the other hand, all coastal defence ships, the older motor torpedo boats and submarine chasers are of Soviet type and production.

Thus the NPA/PN is still dependent on the material aid from the Soviet Union. It is not, as yet, equipped with submarines; it has several Soviet helicopters for liaison and reconnaissance service and recently was also given some helicopters for detecting and chasing the submarines.

The testing centre of the NPA/PN is in Wolgast where there is also

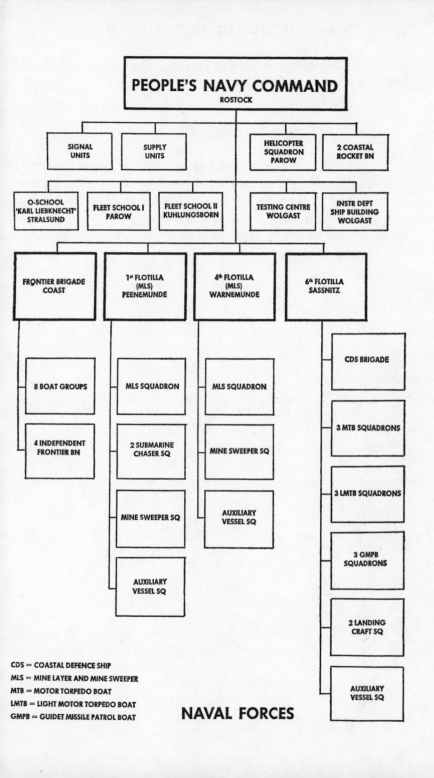

PEOPLE'S NAVY COMMAND
ROSTOCK

- SIGNAL UNITS
- SUPPLY UNITS
- HELICOPTER SQUADRON PAROW
- 2 COASTAL ROCKET BN

- O-SCHOOL 'KARL LIEBKNECHT' STRALSUND
- FLEET SCHOOL I PAROW
- FLEET SCHOOL II KUHLUNGSBORN
- TESTING CENTRE WOLGAST
- INSTR DEPT SHIP BUILDING WOLGAST

FRONTIER BRIGADE COAST
- 8 BOAT GROUPS
- 4 INDEPENDENT FRONTIER BN

1ˢᵗ FLOTILLA (MLS) PEENEMUNDE
- MLS SQUADRON
- 2 SUBMARINE CHASER SQ
- MINE SWEEPER SQ
- AUXILIARY VESSEL SQ

4ᵗʰ FLOTILLA (MLS) WARNEMUNDE
- MLS SQUADRON
- MINE SWEEPER SQ
- AUXILIARY VESSEL SQ

6ᵗʰ FLOTILLA SASSNITZ
- CDS BRIGADE
- 3 MTB SQUADRONS
- 3 LMTB SQUADRONS
- 3 GMPB SQUADRONS
- 2 LANDING CRAFT SQ
- AUXILIARY VESSEL SQ

CDS = COASTAL DEFENCE SHIP
MLS = MINE LAYER AND MINE SWEEPER
MTB = MOTOR TORPEDO BOAT
LMTB = LIGHT MOTOR TORPEDO BOAT
GMPB = GUIDET MISSILE PATROL BOAT

NAVAL FORCES

an instruction department in ship building. The crews for the newly built ships are also trained here.

Summary

The organization and structure of the individual services of the People's National Army show its dependence on the Soviet armed forces. There is no room for independent operations of the East German army; this has clearly assigned tasks within the framework of the wider Soviet strategy, as is manifested in its deployment, training and equipment.

CHAPTER 3

THE NPA AND THE WARSAW PACT

The Warsaw Pact is a "Treaty of friendship, cooperation and mutual assistance between the People's Republic of Albania, People's Republic of Bulgaria, Hungarian People's Republic, German Democratic Republic, People's Republic of Poland, Rumanian People's Republic, the USSR and the Czechoslovak Republic"; it was concluded, after long preparations, at the fourth conference of the East bloc states in Warsaw between 11 and 14 May 1955. In its military part the treaty states (among other things):

> Article 4. In the event of an armed attack in Europe on one or several states that are signatories of the treaty by any state or group of states, each party to this treaty shall, in the exercise of the right to individual or collective self-defence in accordance with Article 51 of the U.N. Charter, render the state or states so attacked immediate assistance, individually and in agreement with other states that are parties to this treaty, by all the means it may consider necessary, including the use of armed force . . .[1]

Of course, the states of the Warsaw Pact decide on their own, in the event of an international conflict, who is the attacker and who is the attacked. In 1950 the Soviet Union declared South Korea, which was attacked by communist North Korea to be the attacker – contrary to the findings of the U.N.

According to Article 5 of the treaty the signatories agreed

> to set up a united command for their armed forces, which shall be placed under this command by aggreement among the parties, and which shall function on the basis of jointly defined principles.

A special announcement, issued after the conclusion of the conference, declared that the Supreme Commander of the United Armed Forces should always be a Soviet officer holding at the same time the

---

[1] Full text of the treaty can be found in *Keesing's Contemporary Archives*, Vol. X. 1955–6, p. 14250–1. Published in Bristol, Britain.

function of First Deputy Minister of Defence of the USSR. The first Supreme Commander was (until 25 July 1960) Marshal I. S. Koniev; he was succeeded by Marshal A. A. Grechko[2]. Ministers of Defence of all other participating states are Deputies of the Supreme Commander.

The Supreme Commander is supported by a Staff of the United Supreme Command consisting of officers from all armies of the Pact. The post of the Chief of Staff is always held by a Soviet officer. The first Chief of Staff was (until 29 October 1962) Army General A. I. Antonov, then this post was held by Army General B. J. Batov who was succeeded in November 1965 by Army General M. J. Kazakov.

Subordinated to the United Supreme Command in peace time is the Group of the Soviet Armed Forces in Germany with its staff in Wünsdorf. Its chief is Army General P. K. Koshevoy.

This is not the place to analyze whether, and if so to what extent, the founders of the Warsaw Pact pursued, from the very day of the establishment of the institution, the aims which can be discerned today. It can be argued that the Pact was originally meant only to strengthen the bargaining position of the communists (for example to prevent the integration of the Federal Republic into NATO) or to strengthen the military forces of the Soviet bloc.

At the time of signing, on 14 May 1955, the Pact was apparently intended to regulate the relations of the Soviet Union to some of the satellites rather than to be used as the means of political and military integration of East Germany. Thus the Soviets were, for example, obliged to withdraw, after the Austrian State Treaty became valid in May 1955, their troops from Hungary and Rumania since their task there was only to maintain communications and supply lines to the Soviet occupation troops in Austria. The Warsaw Pact enabled the Soviet Union to keep troops and commands in all satellite states, even in Czechoslovakia where at that time it had none, and in Poland where it had until then only small units.

The following passage deals with the process of integrating the East German forces into the military potential of the Soviet bloc, the present state of affairs and possible future developments.

---

2 When Grechko became Minister of Defence, in April 1967, Marshal I. Yakubovski was nominated Supreme Commander.

The integration of the NPA

The passage of the resolution dealing with the establishment of the United Supreme Command says:

> The participation of the German Democratic Republic in the United Command would be examined later.

This statement, made apparently with an eye on the public, was necessary because at that time East Germany already had armed forces in the shape of the Barracked People's Police (BPP) which had all the outward signs of a regular army but were still disguised as police. It is significant that the GDR was also represented at the Warsaw Conference by the commanders of the BPP, Minister of Interior, Willi Stoph and his deputy, Lieutenant General Heinz Hoffmann, while other states did not send their ministers of interior or "police generals".

Only on 28 January 1956 did the *Political Consultative Committee*, the highest organ of the Warsaw Pact, decide in Prague to integrate the National People's Army and all its units in the United Armed Forces. Shortly before, on 18 January 1956, the People's Chamber of East Germany had passed the Act on the Foundation of the NPA under which the Barracked People's Police was renamed.

In the first years of its so-called sovereignty the GDR was militarily isolated from the other states of the bloc. It did not participate in the bilateral military agreements which the satellite states concluded among themselves and with the Soviet Union. Even after the conclusion of the Warsaw Pact the GDR remains the only partner which – apart from agreements with the Soviet Union – is militarily allied with other communist states in East Europe only on the multi-lateral level of the Pact. Another specific status has also been maintained until now, namely that the NPA forces are fully subordinated to the United Supreme Command while the other members have only a certain part of their armed forces at its disposal.

Until 1957 the GDR's membership in the Warsaw Pact had hardly any effect on the NPA. It is possible that the organization was given new impetus by the revolutionary events in Poland and Hungary in the autumn of 1956. Since 1957 the Soviets have used the Warsaw Pact not only as a political forum but also as an institution to – control the armed forces of the satellites,

- indoctrinate the troops,
- improve and build up the armed forces,
- integrate the military potential of the satellites into their military planning.

A certain role herein is played by the *United Secretariat* which conducts the work of the Political Consultative Committee between its sessions. It is headed by the Chief of Staff of the United Supreme Command and has subcommittees on, for example, for research, armaments and logistics.

In the ten years of the NPA's membership of the Warsaw Pact three development phases can be discerned:

Firstly: 1956–1958.
In this period the organizational build-up of the NPA was completed; the armed forces were modelled in their structure on the Soviet Army. The weapons, training and command were organized along the standard Soviet lines; the forms of political leadership within the armed forces of the Pact were equalized.

Joint training and exercises were at that time apparently very rare, limited mostly to the staffs, command troops or cadre units of two or more members of the Pact. The absence of a joint command basis made cooperation extremely difficult at the beginning; but the basis was established towards the end of this period.

Secondly: 1959–1961.
Within this period falls the political decision to make the NPA a full member of the alliance. Military consequences of this were the increased Soviet efforts to raise the manpower and material potential of the NPA. Until then the NPA was the only army with voluntary recruitment. In this period the cadres for the future regular army based on compulsory service were systematically selected and trained. The prestige of the NPA was, however, considerably affected by the great number of deserters who were more or less forced by the party and trade union functionaries in the factories to "volunteer" for the NPA.

Joint training activities began to increase. Numerous officers and specialists returned to the NPA from training courses in the Soviet Union and strengthened the efforts for uniformity.

The cooperation within the Warsaw Pact was first tested in connection with the Berlin crisis in 1961. The NPA was then for the first

THE NPA-DIVISIONS WITHIN THE SOVIET ORDER OF POWER

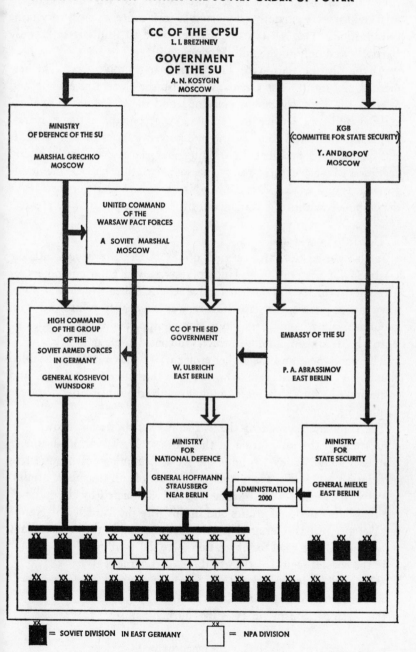

= SOVIET DIVISION IN EAST GERMANY   = NPA DIVISION

time fully involved in the large exercises held towards the end of the crisis which were partially conducted as staff exercises with very large ramifications. The NPA was, however, able to fulfil its tasks only partially and only to the middle command level.

At the turn of 1961–1962 important changes took place. The hermetical closure of East Germany against the Federal Republic and West Berlin from the summer of 1961 and the introduction of compulsory military service in January 1962, based on the universal conscription, helped to allay the manpower worries of the NPA. It did create some problems in training, but the rise in the level and readiness to service of the reserve personnel, obedient to the inevitable force, was noticeable. Thus the basis for the third phase of the NPA's development within the framework of the Warsaw Pact was created.

Thirdly: 1962–1966.

In this period the three services of the NPA were issued with the latest Soviet weapons. The land forces received good equipment of armoured vehicles and nuclear field weapons. The air force was given all-weather interceptors, air defence was effectively reinforced with ground-to-air rockets. The navy was equipped with guided-missile patrol boats and amphibious vehicles in considerable quantity.

This equipment and the higher efficiency of the cadres now enabled the NPA to participate also in the large-scale exercises and manoeuvres[3] which were increasingly organized by the United Supreme Command.

The command system of the Warsaw Pact, however, shows – in contrast with the integration in the staffs of NATO which has now reached its highest level – only the weak beginnings of an effective integration of staffs from the personnel of all member armies. Usually, the exercises and manoeuvres are conducted by the staffs of the individual national armies and in this way the Ministry of National Defence of East Germany is also participating in them. Important milestones on this road to integration were the exercises

– in the coastal region of the Middle Baltic in 1962,
– "Quartet" in September 1963 in Saxony,
– the Berlin harrassing manoeuvres in April 1965,
– the "October Storm" in 1965 in Thuringia and

3 See Chapter 15, The NPA in the manoeuvres.

—the "Vltava" manoeuvres in 1966 in southern Bohemia.

They serve to improve the self-assurance of the NPA, its integration into the operative planning and military targeting of the Soviet Union and its cooperation and amalgamation with the armies of the other Warsaw Pact states, above all with those of the Soviet Union, Poland and Czechoslovakia.

The NPA as member of the First Strategic Echelon

From at least 1965 the NPA has been a member of the so-called *First Strategic Echelon* of the Warsaw Pact system. That means that its forces belong to the formations which would be, in the event of war, immediately drawn into the operations in Central Europe.

The land forces of the NPA would then fight either in army formation with the assigned Soviet troops or they would be assigned to large Soviet formations and deployed within the Soviet-led front (army group). The land forces of the NPA, covered by the Frontier Troops, are deployed against the Federal Republic of Germany and one cannot exclude the possibility of an independent employment of these forces against the Federal Republic if the Soviets, tempted by a favourable political situation, came to the conclusion that they could achieve their aims by a localized military action. On the other hand, the Soviets were able to hold the reins on the NPA tightly because of its logistic dependence on the Soviet Army.

The naval forces of the NPA (the People's Navy) guard, even in peace time, the Baltic Sea in close cooperation with the *Polish Navy* and the *Baltic Red Banner Fleet* of Russia. In war, the People's Navy's task is to cover, together with the other Baltic fleets of the Warsaw Pact states, the sea flank of the attacking communist land forces and to help advance their offensive by amphibious actions and logistic support.

The Air Force of the NPA has, above all, to secure the air defence and is fully integrated with the Soviet air defence system. For this purpose not only the numerous missile units and anti-aircraft artillery are used but also the bulk of the flying forces.

Hand in hand with this integration of planning and commanding tasks through the United Supreme Command goes political penetration and indoctrination with the ideological principles of communism. The foremost aim of political work in the NPA is to imbue the soldiers with a vivid feeling of a true and unbreakable comradeship in arms with the armies of the Soviet Union and other communist states. With this in mind, Defence Minister Hoffmann stated in September 1965:

> Our political-ideological work is focused on the education of our soldiers to comradeship-in-arms, love of the socialist fatherland and pride in being the weapon bearers of the free German workers and peasants. In this work, the education to comradeship in arms with the Soviet Union is given special attention because it is the touchstone of socialist internationalism in the military field.[4]

This indoctrination is also aimed at destroying the feeling of kinship and togetherness of the two parts of Germany divided by the demarcation line, and thus to achieve unconditional reliability of the NPA soldiers in the event of a potential conflict. Until now this work has shown only minimal results but the efforts will be, necessarily, increased in future.

4 *Ten years of the National People's Army – ten years of defence of peace and socialist construction in the GDR. Report by the Minister of National Defence, Army General Heinz Hoffmann, at the conference of the Institute for German Military History on 15 to 17 September 1965 in Brandenburg/ Havel.* "Volksarmee" (People's Army), Documentation, November 1965, P. 5.

CHAPTER 4

THE ARMED FORCES
OF THE MINISTRY OF INTERIOR
AND PARAMILITARY FORMATIONS

Besides the armed forces subordinated to the Ministry of National Defence there are in East Germany other military and paramilitary forces playing an important part in internal politics of the "German Democratic Republic". They mostly come under the Ministry of Interior (MI) and mainly comprise:
- the *Alert Police (AP)*,
- the *German People's Police (GPP)* including the *Transport Police (Trapo)*.

Placed unter the MI are also the *Combat Groups of the Working Class (CG)*, similar to militia, and the civil organization of the *Air Raid Protection (ARP)* as far as their training, equipment and partly also their employment are concerned.

It is important to note that within the framework of the MI and within its structure of command organs and formations the Alert Units of the People's Police are in personnel, training and equipment questions subordinated to the independent *Department of Alert Units* in the MI but in their employment they are placed at the disposal of the *Regional Commands of the German People's Police (RCGPP)*. Thus the RCGPP is also the commanding authority of the military and paramilitary forces of the MI within the corresponding region. (Its subordinated organs are the *District Offices of the GPP.*) In the *RCGPP* there is an *Operation Direction* with an *Operation Staff* to which are also subordinated the *Staffs of the Combat Groups* with the corresponding *Combat Group Battalions of the Regional Reserve*, while the *General Combat Group Battalions*, *General Hundreds* and *Independent Platoons* are placed under the operational directions of the district offices of the People's Police.

From this subordination system can also be traced the sphere of

tasks of the armed forces of the MI:
- suppression of inner disorders in peace and war,
- coverage of the rear areas in the event of threatening war or during fighting,
- support of own and allied forces in the event of war by covering the rear against sabotage and by defence against airborne troops.

The Alert Police (AP)

The AP has about 16 000 men and consists of *21 People's Police Alert Units* in battalion strength, all equally trained and equipped. Normally, there is one Alert Unit in each of the fourteen regions of East Germany but the key regions of Leipzig, Halle and Magdeburg with their strong working class population and Potsdam have two units; the *Presidium of the People's Police* in East Berlin has in Basdorf three Alert Units. This shows that the regime does not regard the workers as sufficiently politically reliable and expects – partly on the basis of the experience of the popular rising on 17 June 1953 – disorders in these industrial centres.

The 21 PP-Alert Units consist in general of:
- 3 motorized companies,
- 1 armoured personnel carrier company,
- 1 artillery battery,
- 1 staff company with
   signal platoon,
   engineer platoon,
   chemical platoon,
   reconnaissance platoon,
   transport platoon,
   supply section,
   control section,
   medical section.

The units are equipped with light and medium infantry weapons. The few medium infantry weapons (each unit has three 45/57 mm anti-tank guns, three 76 mm anti-tank/field guns, three 82 mm mortars) are to be regarded obsolete. The uniform is grey-green, like that of the general People's Police.

The party attaches great importance to the political reliability of the AP because its units are supposed to be used against the population as reliable tools in the event of social disorders.

The German People's Police (GPP)

Minister of Interior and simultaneously also Chief of the GPP is Colonel General Dickel, his deputy for the armed organs of the MI, who is also Chief of Staff, is Lieutenant General Willi Seifert.

Subordinated to the MI and its staff are:
- the Chief Administration of the GPP (CAGPP) and
- other organs of the MI: Fire Service, Penal Service and Air Raid Protection for which new regulations (order of official) were issued on 9 December 1964.

The Chief Administration of the German People's Police has departments for various spheres of tasks of all branches such as Common Police, Traffic Police, Transport Police, Criminal Police. From the military standpoint most important ist the *Transport Police Department* to which are subordinated so-called *Operational Companies* within the *People's Police Sectors of the Transport Police* always covering the same area as *Regional Railway Directorates*. Their task is to protect all railway installations and transports.

Each company has 150 men equipped with pistols, carbines, sub-machine guns as well as light and heavy machine guns. Their uniform is dark-blue.

The Chief Administration of the People's Police has the following subordinated commands:
- the 14 Regional Commands of the German People's Police,
- the Area Command of the GPP Wismut Karl-Marx-Stadt in Sieg-mar-Schönau (to protect the enterprise of Wismut-AG),
- the Presidium of the GPP Berlin (East) with eight *Police Inspectorates* and one *River Police Inspectorate* (operating on the sector border and at sector crossing points).

The Air Raid Protection (ARP)

The Administration of the Air Raid Protection within the MI has the following departments among others:
– communication, warning and alarm service,
– medical and veterinary service,
– salvage and maintenance service,
– technical service,
– transport service,
– supply service,
– fire service,
– chemical service,
– self-defence,
– Organization of Voluntary Air Raid Protection Helpers.

Placed under the Administration of the Air Raid Protection are the *Departments of the ARP* in the Regional Commands and District Offices of the German People's Police. They are in charge of the entire civil air defence.

The responsibility for organizational preparation and conduct of the air raid protection of the civil population in regions, districts, cities, towns and communities rests with the *local organs of state administration*. The *chairmen of local councils,* that is the government commissioners in the regions and districts, are in charge of the air raid protection within their area. They are assisted by *ARP Staffs* consisting of full or part-time functionaries.

The most important instrument of local organs in this respect is the *Organization of Voluntary ARP Helpers.* It accepts members of both sexes from their fourteenth year of age and is subordinated to police commands and in the highest instance to the Ministry of Interior. It closely cooperates with the *German Red Cross Society,* the *Sport and Technology Association,* the *Society for Promotion and Dissemination of Scientific Knowledge* and the *Voluntary Fire Brigades.*

The various air raid protection services are placed under the charge of the heads of corresponding departments in the local administration. Thus the salvage and maintenance service is subordinated to the construction department in the town council, the supply service is under the commerce and supply department, the communication service falls under the German Post etc.

The Air Raid Protection in the East Germany is part of the coordinated defence system. It is noteworthy that in the explanation of the Act on the Air Raid Protection the protection of the "entire population" came only after the "defence of the territory and socialist achievements".[1] In the training of ARP functionaries great stress is laid also on military training and above all on political indoctrination. Thus out of the 800–850 hours in the half-year course for full-time functionaries 214 hours are provided for military traning and 162 for political education.

The armed forces of the Ministry of State Security (MSS)

The MSS had at the time of the establishment of armed formations in East Germany, in line with the Soviet practice and its place in the state apparatus, an important role to fulfil. In February 1957 the Alert Police, the Frontier Police and the Transport Police were taken out of the sphere of the MSS and placed under the authority of the Ministry of Interior. Since then the Ministry of State Security has had at its disposal only one *Guard Regiment MSS*.

This regiment had, at the end of 1965, 4000 men and its task is to protect government buildings and high officials.

It is divided into four operational battalions, one heavy battalion and one training battalion. The regiment has the same training and equipment as the units of the Alert Police. In addition, its battalions are equipped with modern anti-tank guns, anti-aircraft weapons and mortars.

The members of the Guard Regiment MSS are selected among the most reliable recruits or volunteers and have to do a minimum service of three years.

Among the other organs of the State Security Service one must also mention the *Chief Administration of Intelligence*, the most important East German espionage centre aimed above all against the Bundeswehr. (See also Chapter 16, The psychological offensive of the NPA against the Bundeswehr.)

---

1 State Secretary Grünstein explained the Bill on the Air Raid Protection in "Neues Deutschland" of 10 January 1958.

The Combat Groups (CG)

The Combat Groups, which had in the middle of 1966 about 400 000 men, are the embodiment of the Marxist idea of the "armed working class" and they are, therefore, officially designated the *Combat Groups of the Working Class*. Their tradition is derived from communist rebellions, especially in the first years of the Weimar Republic 1918–1923, and from the *Association of the Red Front Fighters* (1924–1933). In the practice the CG are to be employed in the event of civil disorders or war as special SED troops and as such they are the most important part of the paramilitary formations in East Germany.

They can be compared with the factory units of the *Workers' Militia* which played a very important role in the successful communist putsch in Czechoslovakia in February 1948.

The CG were developed mainly after the popular rising in June 1953 and were originally intended only as *Factory Combat Groups* with the task of protecting the enterprises in the event of social disorders or disasters.

But as early as in 1955 the CG were divided into mobile units and units based on their working place. The general units are closely tied to their local basis, nationalized enterprises, state and local administration offices and other working places, and their organization and employment does not extend over the district level. The motorized units, which also have the designation of *Battalions of the Regional Reserve*, can be employed outside their local and district area. The fact that the CG can be employed not only for the protection of enterprises but also for military operations is clearly shown in the "vow" which the members have to make.[2]

The CG were placed by the decree of the *Politburo of Central Committee (CC)* of the SED of 31 May 1955 under the authority of the CC whose First Secretary is Walter Ulbricht. Directly responsible

---

2 "I am ready, as fighter of the working class, to fulfil the directives of the Party, to protect the German Democratic Republic, its social achievements at any time with weapon in hand, and to risk my life for them. This I vow." – Quoted from "Der Kämpfer" (The Fighter), organ of the Combat Groups of the Working Class, published by the Central Committee of the SED, East Berlin, June 1959.

for the CG, and also for all other armed forces, is the *Commission of National Security* attached to the Politburo of the CC; the Commission is headed by veteran communist Erich Honecker.

Politically-administratively the CG are directed by the *Security Department of the CC* whose chief is Major General Walter Borning. It exercises decisive influence on the CG, especially in connection with the selection of "cadres", through the regional and district organs of the SED.

As for military training, equipment and employment of the CG the responsibility lies with the Ministry of Interior which has a *Department of Combat Groups* headed by Major General Mellmann.

The *First Party Secretaries* are on the regional and district levels chairmen of the so-called *Operational Directions* to which also belong the commanders or commissioners of all military units stationed in the area. The first party secretaries are, in addition, also superiors of the CG.

The commanders of the CG are selected by the party organizations in the factories. They must be confirmed by the regional or district SED committees to which they also have to report regularly on the progress of military training. Commanders are allowed to issue orders on the employment of the CG only on approval by the competent party organs.

Originally only the SED members were allowed to join the CG. Since the party could not supply enough new men it was decided in 1954 to accept also non-party members who were then, after having proved themselves reliable, induced to join the SED. Members join the CG "voluntarily" but the party exercizes, as everywhere else where it deems it right, great pressure and workers who refuse to join the CG lose their jobs.

The members of the CG are between twenty five and sixty; the men over fifty five form the reserve which is to be employed only within the enterprises. Men under twenty five, insofar as they do not serve in the NPA or other formations of the armed forces, are expected to join the Sport and Technology Association.

The personnel basis of the CG ist the enterprise where the individual *fighters* (as the members of the CG are called) are under the control of the party.

The basic unit is a *hundred*, divided into three platoons, each of them consisting of three groups. The *commander of the hundred* has two deputies: one *political deputy* and one *general deputy*. He is further supported by one *supply officer* and one *chief medical orderly*. One *inspector of the People's Police* assists the commander in the training of men.

The hundred further has three platoon leaders, three deputy platoon leaders, nine group leaders, eighty one fighters and one medical orderly per platoon.

Three or four hundreds form a *CG battalion*. In the *CG Battalions of the Regional Reserve*, the so-called Heavy or Motorized Battalions, all hundreds are fully motorized and they, too, are called Heavy Hundreds.

The CG have light and medium infantry weapons, vehicles and technical equipment for reconnaissance, simple communication lines and light engineer work. Simple personal means are supposed to give the men protection against the ABC weapons.

The fighters, clad in "stone grey" uniforms, are equipped with carbines; the commanders of hundreds and platoon leaders have pistols. The CG also have submachine guns, assault rifles, hand grenades, smoke grenades and light machine guns.

The heavy or motorized CG battalions use for transport the trucks of their "home" factories or of the local nationalized haulage firms. They have machine guns, light and medium mortars, anti-tank launchers, anti-tank guns. In some cases the CG have also been issued with anti-aircraft machine guns, reconnaissance tanks and armoured personnel carriers of old types.

The basic training of the CG is done in 132 training hours divided into 33 training weeks. It has to be attended, like all other duties of the CG, outside the normal working hours, that is in the evenings and during the weekends.

The CG were employed on a large scale, for the first time, during the closure of East Berlin in August 1961 (the 8000 CG men formed about 20 per cent of all employed armed formations). Only specially reliable CG were selected for this task and they distinguished themselves – compared with the other participating units – by extraordinary fanaticism.

For the second time the CG were employed in larger numbers a month later, in September 1961, to assist in the strengthened sur-

A special branch of
the People's Police:
Factory Guards.

Left below: Members of a special unit of the Air Raid Protection of the People's
Police. Right below: NCO of the Alert Police.

The NPA City Commander General Poppe (right) taking over in 1962 the Frontier Brigades 1 and 2 which had been until then subordinated to the Ministry of Interior.

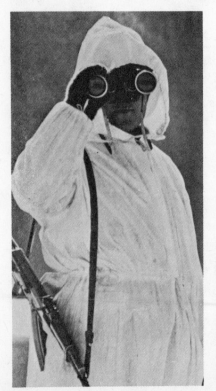

Left: Policeman wearing a winter camouflage cloak.

Below: A policeman (centre) and soldiers of the Frontier Troops trying to hide the body of a refugee shot dead on the barbed wire.

A unit of the Combat Groups deployed at the Brandenburg Gate in Berlin in August 1961 when the Wall was built.

Combat Groups in street fighting exercise under the guidance of the officers of the People's Police.

Combat Groups in river-crossing exercise.

Combat Groups and Frontier Troops on the demarcation line in the autumn of 1961.

Female members of
the Sport and Tech-
nology Association,
armed with air guns,
at a party assem-
bly in 1956.

Since then the Sport
and Technology As-
sociation has be-
come a paramilitary
organization with
many special branch-
es; parachutists at a
parade.

veillance of the demarcation line with the Federal Republic; in many cases the fighters were presented to the Frontier Troops as models for emulation.

There are some 130 motorized CG battalions and they represent an important factor in the total military strength.

They are particularly suitable for suppression of any signs of internal opposition to the regime among the population and above all among the industrial workers.

Together with the security troops, police and army units they are also capable of crushing larger rebellions and uprisings.

In wartime, the CG can take over, within the framework of regular military formations, the tasks of mopping up and securing the rear areas. Their equipment and organization, however, enable them also to fulfil independent combat tasks such as fighting small enemy groups in the rear.

Training and education are aimed at enabling the CG to force, in the event of war, the workers in the occupied areas of West Germany and West Europe to continue their work in the industry and supply services.

In times of tension and in war, the CG are a very useful instrument able to fight according to military regulations or with the methods of guerilla warfare. This considerably increases the combat value of the CG.

The Sport and Technology Association (STA)

After the Soviet Union pronounced herself on 10 March 1952 in a note addressed to the Western powers in favour of granting "Germany her own national armed forces" and started to rearm openly East Germany, the SED introduced the pre-military training. Particularly the East German youth organization, the *Free German Youth (FDJ)*, was pressed to train its members in the use of arms. The FDJ statute, confirmed in May 1955, obliged every member "to be ready to defend peace and the fatherland".

The task of giving pre-military training to the young people of both sexes between fourteen and twenty five was given to the Sport and Technology Association wich was established in August 1952 by a government decree. It was closely modelled on the Soviet DOSAAF

(Voluntary Society for Support of Army, Air Force and Navy) which has several million members.

The Association originally came under the Ministry of Interior which was at that time responsible for the establishment of military units. After its foundation in January 1956 the Ministry of National Defence took over the responsibility for guiding this organization and for approving its budget.

The Association had in the autumn of 1963 nominally about 450 000 members; 70 per cent of them were active. It has a *Central Executive* and 14 *Regional Unions* corresponding to the administrative regions of East Germany.

The Central Executive is responsible for carrying out the decisions of the *Congress*, the highest organ of the STA, which has to be convened according to the statute once in four years. The executive forms, from its own members, the *Secretariat* headed by the First Secretary who is the leader of the organization. At present the First Secretary is veteran communist Kurt Lohberger, major general of the reserve. The seat of the executive is in Neuenhagen near Berlin.

The regional unions are divided into *District Unions* and these are further subdivided into *Basic Organizations* of the STA. The basic organizations are formed mainly in the nationalized enterprises (VEB), agricultural cooperatives and schools; to a lesser extent also in residential districts.

The training is officially designated "pre-military training" and is carried out in the basic organizations in the following six "sports disciplines":

– shooting and field sports,
– aviation sports (gliding, training in sports aircraft, parachuting),
– auto and motorcycle sports,
– sea sports (navigation, signals, diving etc.)
– communications sports (radio, telephone),
– animal sports (horses, dogs, carrier pigeons).

Recently the "animal sports and other sports disciplines as well as hunters' societies were taken out of the sphere of the STA. This has enabled us to concentrate even more purposefully on our main task, socialist military education".[3]

3 Artur Dorf, Deputy Chairman of the STA Central Executive, *All are called to cooperate with us.* "Sport und Technik", Organ of the Central Executive of the STA, East Berlin, April 1964.

The training of the STA members is conducted and controlled by the reservists and active officers and NCOs of the NPA.

Every member of the Association is obliged to go through the so-called *general training* comprising field sports, training in the use of arms, map reading, military drill, protection against nuclear weapons, first-aid service. After eighty hours of general training the members of the STA can pursue the sports disciplines of their own choice; even here, however, training for military purposes is to be given priority. Shooting practice (carbines, submachine guns, light machine guns) is obligatory throughout the membership in the STA. Training in parachuting is also very intensive.

The STA is not an organization in which members could pursue sport for enjoyment; it is an organization for pre-military training and its task is to prepare and train the men of military age so that the basic training in the army during the regular active service can be shortened and conditions for efficient specialist training created. Thus the STA is a valuable auxiliary organization of the NPA.

In addition to the STA, the Free German Youth (FDJ) conducts pre-military training. Prominent in this are the *Order Groups of the FDJ*. They were established in 1959 and two years later, in connection with the war hysteria in August of 1961, they were considerably expanded. They are used not only as political youth police; in some cases they founded armed operational groups, the so-called hundreds in which the young men who are not members of the STA are trained. Also girls are trained in these Order Groups, mainly as radio and teleprinter operators etc. The Order Groups of the FDJ have about 40 000 members.

Aims of militarization

The numerous paramilitary organizations in East Germany reflect the total militarization of the population in a communist state.

The immanent communist tendency to centralization resulting from the power monopoly of the party is also apparent in the military apparatus. The centralization is achieved through the decisive influence of the party at all levels of leadership. This system also suppresses all aspirations of the huge military apparatus to independence which could threaten the ruling party group and finally lead to power grab by the highest military leaders. The ruling party group has also divided the subordinated military apparatus into various organizations and thus, in the event of one organization becoming politically unreliable, the armed formations of other organizations, such as the troops of the Ministry of Interior, can be used to restore and strengthen the threatened rule of the party. In this context has to be understood also the role of the Combat Groups; they are clearly becoming a party militia which can be quickly mobilized against internal disorders and strikes among workers.

Since the Peoples' Police, the Combat Groups and the Air Raid Protection have tasks which pervade the life of every citizen, the SED can through them not only exercize additional control but also extend its influence.

This is especially true in the case of the Combat Groups (CG). The soldier released from active service and transferred into the reserve has to continue his service in the CG. His activity in the CG has influence on his job and earnings. His promotion depends on the good record of his training with the CG because the party committee in the enterprise decides in practice everything.

To a smaller extent this is valid also for the Sport and Technology Association (STA) in the schools and universities. The STA has not only the task of preparing the youth for military service and thus of shortening the basic service in the NPA; it also has the function of exercising an early control over the willingness to military service of each citizen. (The SED members occupy in all organizations leading positions regardless of their qualification or seniority and thus the party can at any time remove unreliable non-party members and replace them by proven communists.) Thus the paramilitary organizations exercise an indirect control aimed at strengthening the regime of the communist party; in this respect they fulfil the political tasks as efficiently as civil organizations of the party.

CHAPTER 5

THE POLITICAL ORGANIZATION OF THE NPA

In East Germany, the SED has realized its ambition – to exercise total power. The SED is the State Party and the state an instrument of the party. The leadership of the SED, the Central Committee (CC), decides on all bills, decrees and decisions before they reach the *People's Chamber*, the *State Council* or the *Council of Ministers*. This monopoly of power turns the armed forces, too, into the tools of the party regime. This is clearly stated in the *Programme of the SED*[1], approved in January 1963:

> The most important source of army's strength is the fact that it is led by the party of the working class. The party makes sure that all members of the armed forces become class-conscious socialist fighters, ready to use their strength and lives for the protection of the people and socialist property as close comrades-in-arms with the Soviet Army and other armies of the socialist camp.

In this system it is most important to make sure of the loyalty of the military apparatus to the party and its state. It is therefore only natural that Walter Ulbricht, First Secretary of the CC of the SED, has been standing at the head of the Defence Council, whose task it is to ensure unity between the party and the armed forces, since its establishment in February 1960. It is also only natural that the CC guides the entire political apparatus of the forces. No officer can, unpunished, give an order which does not, directly or indirectly, come from the CC or is not approved by it. Nobody can become a general without the CC's approval; no officer is promoted without the approval of the corresponding party organ.

In the list of 121 members of the CC, published at the end of

---

1 *Programme of the SED, part 2, IV. The tasks of the Socialist Unity Party of Germany in the development of the German Workers' and Peasants' State.* Here quoted from the weekly "Volksarmee" (People's Army), Appendix 15/1962, p. 20.

the Sixth Party Congress in January 1963, there are only three members of the NPA: the Minister of National Defence, *Army General Heinz Hoffmann*, and his two deputies, *Colonel General Heinz Kessler* (Chief of the Air Force/Air Defence) and *Admiral Waldemar Verner* (Head of the Chief Political Administration of the NPA). As collaborators of the CC must be also included both leading representatives of the NPA in the Security Department of the CC, *Major General Walter Borning*, head of the department, and *Vice Admiral Bruno Wansierski*. They are not the spokesmen of the armed forces in the CC; they were delegated into the armed forces by the CC as its functionaries.

As the *Plenun of the CC* is convened, as a rule, only twice a year, the real leading political body is the *Politburo of the CC*. Among its 14 members there is – not taking into account the former Army General Willi Stoph – not one officer-functionary. The day-today affairs of the CC are conducted by seven secretaries of the CC together with 2500 officials of the Secretariat. Ulbricht, as First Secretary of the CC, member of the Politburo and Chairman of the State Council, has concentrated in his hands power over all the secretaries and officials of the CC. The Politburo has a *Commission for National Security* charged with the supervision of the armed forces; its chairman is Erich Honecker. Its routine work is conducted by the *Security Department* of the CC. Borning as its head is responsible directly to Ulbricht for the transmission of Central Committee's directives to, and their execution by, the Ministries of Defence, Justice, Interior and State Security.

This close liaison between the Politburo, the Central Committee and the Ministry of National Defence does not in itself satisfy the SED; it has created for itself a wide-spread apparatus within the NPA in the form of *Politorgans* (Political Organs). But even this was not sufficient for the party and it had built up within the NPA another network of *Party Organizations* and *FDJ Organizations*. In this way the party is always able to influence the officers on three organizational levels.

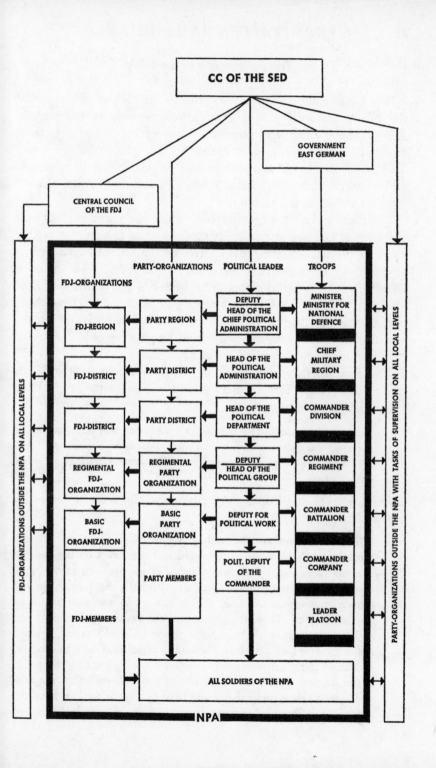

The Politorgans in the NPA

The *Chief Political Administration,* as the highest politorgan of the NPA, has built a vast organization penetrating horizontally and vertically the forces from the Ministry of National Defence down to companies and batteries, including the NPA/Frontier Troops. It also has a thorough system of channelling its orders to all levels and ranks. Its head is Admiral Waldemar Verner, Deputy Minister of National Defence.

The Chief Political Administration, which has within the Ministry of National Defence the authority corresponding to that of a *department of the CC,* is under the control of the CC SED. Its task is to guide the entire political work within the NPA which includes: coordination of political planning in the NPA, political schooling of soldiers and officers and party schooling of SED and FDJ members, strengthening of fighting morale, control of the execution of orders, cooperation in all personnel affairs and keeping personal files of all cadres on their political reliability and progress.

The *Directives for the work of political organs of the NPA,* confirmed by the CC SED on 17 June 1958, oblige the head of the Chief Political Administration

> to report immediately to the CC any wavering and irregularities in the issue of orders, violations of party decisions and laws of the Workers' and Peasants' Power by commanders as well as all other serious cases.

These directives stipulate in the introduction the tasks of the politorgans thus:

> The politorgans are the leading organs of the SED for political work in the NPA which is organized and conducted on the basis of Marxism-Leninism, the Statute of the SED, the decisions of the party congresses and conferences and of the CC SED, the decisions of the Government of the GDR as well as the orders and instructions of the Ministry of National Defence and the Political Administration.
> The party organs are responsible to the CC and to their superior politorgans for their activities. The leaders of political departments are, as leading party functionaries, subordinated to the next highest politorgan. In their function as deputies for political work they are subordinated to their commanders and have to account to them for their work. Disciplinarily they are subordinated to the next highest com-

The standard weapon of the NPA rifleman is the submachine gun Kalashnikov (left). The light machine gun Degtiarov (right) will be replaced by the light machine gun Kalashnikov.

Light mortar 82 mm.

152 mm howitzer M-1943.

Antitank launcher RPG-2.

85 mm auxiliary-powered anti-tank gun.

Antitank guided rocket ("Snapper")

14.5 mm anti-aircraft heavy machine gun (ZPU-4).

Above: 57 mm anti-aircraft gun M-1950.

Self-propelled anti-aircraft gun SU-57-2.

240 mm rocket launcher (12-round) BM-24.

Surface-to-air missile SA-2 "Guideline".

Left: Free rocket over ground (FROG 4).

Surface-to-surface guided missile, SS-1 "SCUD".

Medium tank T-34, to-day only a training vehicle.

Left: Medium tank T-54.

Below: Medium tank T-54 with snorkel can travel under water.

Armoured personnel carrier BTR-50 (P).

w: Reconnaissance amphibious tank PT-76.

Armoured personnel carrier BTR-40 (A).

Armoured personnel carrier BTR-152.

Below: Amphibious vehicle P2S.

Amphibious truck K-61

Amphibious truck BAV.

Earth driller.

Ditching plough.

Opposite page, top: T-54 with mine clearing equipment PT-54;
centre: Ditching machine.

Below: Bridge-laying tank on T-54 chassis.

Soldiers putting on ABC protective clothing.

mander. The Minister of National Defence or the commanders have the right to give to the Political Administration or to the political departments directives for tackling and solving certain tasks and to demand information from them.

To fulfil these tasks the Chief Political Administration is organized into departments and subdepartments, the most important being among them the *Department for Propaganda and Agitation;* it also has the widest range of tasks.

To the Chief Political Administration also belong the *Party Control Commission* and the *Party Revision Commission,* each with 11–13 members. They are appointed by the head of the Chief Political Administration but they have to be confirmed by the Central Party Commission and the Central Party Revision Commission.

Though the head of the Party Control Commission is subordinated to the head of the Chief Political Administration, he also has a direct contact with the Central Party Control Commission of the CC SED; he also closely cooperates with the representative of the State Security.

The Party Control Commission has authority to:
- consider all party disciplinary actions against party members in their function of commanders or on similar duties, as well as against all members of politorgans,
- supervise the subordinated party control commissions,
- control the fulfilment of the Party Statute,
- control the realization of party decisions,
- maintain the party's general line.

A liaison office of the *Ministry of State Security*, the *Administration* 2000 in the Ministry of National Defence, supervises the entire NPA, including the Political Administration and its organs.

The Political Administration in its activities is not confined to the NPA; it has numerous links to other state and party offices.

Of particular interest is the *Independent Department* of the Ministry of National Defence receiving instructions from the Chief Political Administration. The department is situated in Berlin-Schöneweide. Its task is to conduct agitation and infiltration in the Federal Republic of Germany among the members of the Bundeswehr, the youth of age classes who were not liable to military service until now, and former soldiers and officers, especially those in the veteran organizations. It publishes numerous propagandist and sensational pamphlets and maintains special radio broadcasts addressed to the members of the Bundeswehr. The activities of the Independent Department are described in greater detail in Chapter 16, The psychological offensive of the NPA against the Bundeswehr.

In its work in the NPA the Chief Political Administration is assisted by its own apparatus built from the top down to the company level. Subordinated to it are:
- *political administrations* in the military districts, Frontier Command, People's Navy Command and Air Force/Air Defence Command;
- *political departments* in the divisions and units of similar rank in the commands of the Frontier Troops, People's Navy and Air Force/Air Defence;
- *political groups* in the regiments and units of similar rank with the deputies of regimental commanders for political work (political deputies) as their heads;
- *deputies of battalion commanders for political work* (political deputies) in the battalions and units of similar rank;
- *deputies of company commanders (battery commanders) for political work* (political deputies) in independent companies of the NPA, in all companies of the NPA/Frontier Troops and in corresponding units of the People's Navy and Air Force/Air Defence.
The political organs are not elected; they are appointed on the basis of proposals by the head of the Chief Political Administration and heads of political administrations of military districts of the Peoples' Navy and Air Force/Air Defence.

The heads of political administrations of military districts and corresponding areas of responsibility are, at the same time, *political deputies* of the chiefs of military districts or of other areas of responsibility. In addition, they are ex officio first party secretaries of the leading organs of the SED party rayons in the NPA. The deputies of the heads of political administrations are always second secretaries of the SED party districts in corresponding areas of responsibility.

Each political administration has one party control commission and one party revision commission charged with the control and revision in the subordinated political departments. The commissions, consisting of 3–7 members, are elected at the conferences of delegates.

The heads of political departments in the divisions, schools and units of the same rank in other services are, at the same time, *political deputies* of divisional commanders. They are first secretaries of the SED district leadership. Their deputies are always second secretaries.

The political departments have subsections in which work 15 officers always as:
- head of the political department,
- debuty head of the political department,
- chief instructor for political work,
- chief instructor for agitation and propaganda,
- chief instructor for political schooling,
- chief instructor for political schooling of troops,
- chairman of the party control commission,
- chairman of the party revision commission,
- assistant for youth problems (FDJ),
- instructors for work with youth (2 officers),
- instructor for political cadres,
- instructor for party information,
- instructor for cultural mass work,
- instructor for personal records (party and FDJ files).

The political department has, above all, to supervise the conduct of political work in the troops in line with the directives of the political administrations of military districts and to issue party documents. The 7–11 members of the party control and revision commissions are elected at the SED party district conferences of delegates. Their tasks are similar to those of their superior commissions.

Regiments and units of the same rank have political deputies of regiment commanders as heads of political groups. They are supported by:
- chief officer for agitation and propaganda,
- chief officer for cultural mass work,
- head of the club and library,
- SED secretary (elected and chiefly acting only within the party

organization without being in any way subordinated to the commander),
– FDJ secretary.

The political deputy of the regiment commander has to school not only the non-commissioned officers, rank-and-file and members of the SED and FDJ, but also the officers of the regiment.

The *political deputies of the battalion commanders,* supported by three officers, are charged with political work in battalions and units of similar rank. The functions are divided in the following way:
– political deputy of the battalion commander (direct superior to all soldiers),
– officer for propaganda,
– SED secretary (elected and chiefly acting only within the party organization without being in any way subordinated to the commander),
– FDJ secretary.

The political deputy of the company commander (battery commander) in all independent companies (batteries) and similar units of the NPA and in all companies of the Frontier Troops has to advise politically the company commander, to supervise the fulfilment of orders and directives and to control the mood of the troops. In all companies where there ist no appointed political deputy, the company commander is personally responsible for the tasks.

The special position of political organs whose functionaries (political workers, political officers) are "built" into the military leadership but are not subordinated to it, enables them to supervise each commander through their own channels. They considerably strengthen the situation under which the commanders are the executors of the party's will.

Latent tensions had arisen, from the very beginning, between the military commanders and political officers of the NPA. They ceased only when the SED regime gave up the original form of the "political-only-officers". Clashes often occurred because the political officers – fulfilling their tasks – interfered in the education and training of troops without having the necessary military experience or knowledge. Thus, they became unpopular with officers as well as soldiers.

The NPA School for Political Officers in Treptow was therefore dissolved. All cadets now receive during theirs 3-year term of training instruction in "socio-political sciences" corresponding with a syllabus of one course in the SED district school. In this way, all officers are, in accordance with the demands of the SED, simultaneously educated both as military specialists and party functionaries.

At the end of 1962 the offices of the heads of political sections in divisions and political administrations of military districts and services were filled with functionaries who had received academic, political and military education.

The SED organizations in the NPA

Apart from the military political organs appointed from above and the civil local party organs which control the fulfilment of party instructions by the units stationed in their sphere of authority, the army and its officers are controlled by pseudo-democratically functioning organizations of the SED (and FDJ) within the NPA. There are about 97 per cent of party members among officers, 80 per cent among career non-commissioned officers, 35 per cent among "conscripted" NCOs and 10 per cent among soldiers.

Naturally, only the SED has the right to form party organizations in the NPA. The satellite parties[2] are denied this right.

The party organizations in the NPA have, above all, the task of indoctrinating *all* soldiers of the army, not only the members and candidates of the party, in the spirit of Marxism-Leninism. They are also obliged to spur all party members and candidates to conscientious fulfilment of their military duties. They have to influence the Marxist-Leninist indoctrination and military education of officers and to exercize the necessary control. They have the right to submit

2 In East Germany there are, besides the SED, officially licenced: the *Christian Democratic Union*, the *Liberal Democratic Party of Germany*, the *National Democratic Party of Germany* and the *Democratic Peasants' Party of Germany*. All of these parties explicitly recognize the "leading role of the SED".

to the commanders proposals for improvements in the training and education and for the selection of potential officers among the youth.

The Central Committee of the SED is the supreme organ for these party organizations as is stated in the *Party Statute* of 19 January 1963:

> The party organizations in the German People's Police, National People's Army and Transport System are working according to special instructions confirmed by the Central Committee.
>
> Their political departments and party organs are obliged to maintain close contacts with local party organs.[3]

The "Instruction for the party organizations of the SED and politorgans in the NPA" was approved and released by the CC SED in the autumn of 1963.

Subordinated directly to the Central Committee is in this hierarchy of party organizations within the army the Chief Political Administration in the Ministry of National Defence; it forms, at the same time a *SED Regional Directorate* and as such directs the entire party work in the NPA. The head of the Chief Political Administration is also first secretary of this highest party grouping in the NPA.

The regional party organizations are subdivided into *Party Districts, Regimental Party Organizations, Basic Party Organizations* and *Party Groups.*

The commanders of the units have to be, whenever possible, members of the leading party organs.

If a commander or his political deputy loses the "trust" of the party organization, its leading organ can demand from the higher organ their removal. In practice this could happen only when the officers concerned were to be removed in any case, and the party organ in the unit had acted on a hint from above.

3 *The Statute of the Socialist Unity Party of Germany, Section IX: The party organizations in the German People's Police, National People's Army and Transport System.* Here quoted from "Volksarmee", Appendix 13/1962, p. 31.

The basic party organizations are the most important organs of the SED in the NPA because they, as the proper organizations of party members, have to fulfil the task to "put in force the leading role of the party within the armed forces". According to their sphere of tasks, which is laid down in the party statute, the basic organizations have to convene each month a plenary meeting of their members to discuss political problems and proposals for the training of the troops, and to exercise "criticism and selfcriticism" of inadequate performance of duties and violations of party discipline.

The basic organization must fulfil the decisions and directives of the higher party organization, to spur its members to participate in socialist emulation, to increase the "socialist consciousness" of its members and to give directives to the FDJ organization for its work among the youth.

The control of party members is secured by the task "fearlessly to expose the defects in the work and behaviour of every member and to report them to the higher political organs", if necessary even to the Central Committee itself.

A soldier of the NPA can become a member of the party only within the basic organization in his unit. He has to file a written application and, if accepted, he has to undergo a one-year term of candidature during which he has to fulfil a number of party tasks. It is practically impossible for members to leave the party. The party cards of soldiers are issued by the political sections.

Party members are expected, and required, to be model soldiers in their behaviour and performance of duties. If they violate discipline, they are punished not only by their military superiors but also have to submit to a party disciplinary procedure. Because of this the soldiers are reluctant to become party members.

Paragraph 7 of the Party Statute dealing with disciplinary matters is very vague and allows very broad interpretation; thus party disciplinary procedure against soldiers can be started on rather flimsy grounds. The paragraph says:

> Who violates the unity and purity of the party, does not fulfil its decisions, shows no concern for inner party democracy, violates party discipline or misuses his membership and his functions, shows himself in his private and public life not worthy of being a party member – is to be called by the basic organization or a higher organ to responsibility.

Among the party punishments which can be meted out are: censure, strong censure, transfer of a member into candidature for a year, and, finally, expulsion from the party. For minor offences the statute provides for criticism of the erring member, expression of displeasure and warning; these punishments are called "means of party education".

Party procedure against officers with the rank of battalion commander and higher ranks are generally conducted by the appropriate party control commission.

In practice any offence committed on military service can be used as ground for party procedure.

Like all communists, the party members in the NPA have to pay party contributions which are calculated on the basis of monthly salary. Thus a major general, with eleven years of military service, married, with three children and a monthly salary of 4085 DM East (with all allowances) has to pay 122.55 DM-East monthly (= 3 per cent). Or a major with 15 years of service, married, with one child pays monthly 59.55 DM-East from an income of 1985 DM-Ost.

The FDJ organizations in the NPA

The third channel, through which the SED politically influences the NPA is the apparatus of the FDJ organizations which is, in the armed forces, organized in the same way as the party. From battalion level upwards there are officers in the political organs who are primarily concerned with youth problems. The FDJ is a *mass organization* to which belong about 80 per cent of soldiers up to their 26th year.[4] As a state youth organization it serves entirely the interests of the party, on which it totally depends. This is often mentioned in the Party Statute of 1963:

> The Free German Youth (FDJ), the socialist youth organization in the GDR, is an active assistant and reserve of the party. It assists the party to educate the youth in the spirit of socialism for active participation in the vast construction of socialism and for the protection of socialist fatherland . . .[5]

4 This age limit was removed by the VII Parliament (Congress) of the FDJ in June 1963.

And further the statute says:

> The FDJ recognizes in its decisions the leading role of the working class party.[6]

At the same time, the FDJ sees as its task to rouse "in the hearts of the youth a passionate hatred and abhorrence of militarism and revanchism in West Germany".

With all these tasks and the designation of the FDJ as "party youth" it is not surprising to find in the Statute of the FDJ the following regulations concerning its work in the armed forces:

1. The FDJ organizations in the armed forces of the German Democratic Republic base their work on the Statute of the Free German Youth and on the instructions confirmed by the CC FDJ; they have to assist in the realization of tasks issued by the leadership of the party and state for the protection of the construction of socialism in the GDR.

2. The FDJ organizations in the armed forces educate their members, and all young soldiers not organized in the FDJ, on the basis of the oath of allegiance in the spirit of socialist internationalism and comradeship in arms with the Soviet Army and the armies of the socialist camp, as true patriots ready to use their knowledge and capabilities as well as to sacrifice their lives for the protection of the construction of socialism.

3. The FDJ organizations in the armed forces maintain close contacts with local organizations of the FDJ and support the basic organizations especially in the socialist military education of the youth. They consider it as an important task to prepare all young members of the armed forces to be ready, after the conclusion of their military service, to work in key points at socialist construction.[7]

This shows that the FDJ is only an adjunct of the party in the armed forces. Acting on the instruction of the SED organization, it uses all oportunites to rouse young soldiers to fulfil their tasks. In this "youth organization" there is no room for youth freedoms

5–6 *The Statute of the SED, Section VIII, The Party and the Free German Youth*, p. 65–66.

7 *The Statute of the Free German Youth, Part IX, The FDJ organizations in the armed forces of the GDR.* Translated from "Volksarmee", Appendix 1966/1, p. 32.

and a life compatible with the ideas of the young. Whenever there are "all-important tasks" to be fulfilled, the FDJ organization takes the initiative. It is the driving force of "socialist emulation" for the "best soldier" in the NPA; it forms circles in which even the leisure of the soldiers is politically organized.

Summary

The political organization is an inherent part of the communist armed forces. Political organs, party organizations and FDJ organizations are decisive components of the security structure of the SED, holding soldiers constantly in a tight grip. This structure not only suppresses the professional soldiers' pride but also gives possibilities of control undreamed of in non-communist armies.

Communists often attempt to compare these institutions with the educational and training facilites of other armies. It is only natural for them to discredit, for example, the leadership of the Bundeswehr as an "instrument of the Adenauer Party". They deliberately conceal the fact that every type of state institution in a democratic state must be in essence approved by people's representatives elected in free elections. They also suppress another fact, namely that the educational tasks of a non-communist army are conducted by military institutions under the responsibility of the supreme command, but not by any political party.

In the communist power system, political organization receives its directives from the party leadership which, at the same, exercises its influence and control on all levels of the apparatus. All these efforts are not aimed at preparing the soldier to fulfil his service as a civic responsibility for a community guided by generally accepted moral norms, but at educating the soldiers as fanatical, ideologically drilled communists ready to fight with weapons for the goals fixed by the political leadership.

CHAPTER 6

WEAPONS AND EQUIPMENT

The weapons of the NPA are almost exclusively of Soviet origin. The NPA has a diversified arsenal, though not always the latest weapon models. New models are usually given to the other communist armies two or three years after their introduction in the Soviet Army. Some weapons have not as yet been handed over to the NPA.

While the weapons of the infantry, equipment of the armoured units and general supply of specialized vehicles correspond to the requirements of a modern army, the equipment of anti-aircraft units is not yet satisfactory. The troops are still equipped with heavy anti-aircraft guns which are not up to modern standards. On the other hand, the modern anti-aircraft rocket (ground-to-air) is being steadily introduced.

In the military parade on the occasion of the "15th birthday of the GDR" the army has shown, for the first time, potential nuclear carriers.

Of particular interest ist the good equipment of the army with amphibious vehicles, also of Soviet origin. East Germany produces its own vehicles of all sizes.

The Air Force already has the highly efficient jet fighter; other types of modern construction are continuously introduced.

The People's Navy employs mostly units of Soviet production.

Good armament and outfit enable the NPA to fulfil all tasks connected with its membership of the Warsaw Pact.

I. Land Forces

INFANTRY WEAPONS

Pistol Makarov (PM) – This Soviet pistol appears to be very much like the German Walther pistol, calibre 9 mm, short cartridge. The magazine capacity is 8 rounds; effective range 55 yd (50 m).

Submachine gun Kalashnikov (AK) – The AK, which is like the German "assault rifle" 44, can be described also as submachine pistol (MPi-K), though it fires short cartridge. There are two types: the standard (fixed stock) type has replaced the existing rifles and carbines; the folding stock variety (MPi-KmS) is especially suitable for street fighting and for tank crews. Its effective range in short bursts of uninterrupted fire is up to 330 yd (300 m), in interrupted firing up to 440 yd (400 m). Its effect is lethal up to 1650 yd (1500 m). The muzzle velocity is 2145 f/s (710 m/s); practical rate of fire in short uninterrupted firing is 90–100 rpm, in interrupted fire 40. The weight of the weapon, without magazine and outfit, is slightly more than 8 lb (3.8 kg). The box magazine has a capacity of 30 rounds. The AK is simple and robust.

Light machine gun Kalashnikov (LMG-K) – The LMG-K was introduced in the NPA in 1964; it has been developed from the submachine gun Kalashnikov (see above). The LMG-K differs from this in having a thicker and longer barrel with bipod and various magazines (also MP magazines can be used). It is intended to be used by one soldier and weighs, together with the bipod and the magazine over 10 lb (5 kg). The drum magazine's capacity is 75, that of the box magazine 40 short cartridges (Mod. 1943, 7.62 mm). The rate of fire in uninterrupted firing is between 150 and 600, in interrupted firing 50 rpm.

Light machine gun RP-46 (Degtiarov) – The company machine gun RP-46 is the most important weapon of the motorized infantry company. It is used against group targets and important individual targets up to 1100 yd (1000 m) and against air targets up to 550 yd (500 m). This weapon fires the old Russian infantry rimmed cartridge (7.62 mm x 54 R) and was fitted, after the war, with a metallic belt with capacity of 250 rounds. The barrel is interchangeable. The gun's practical rate of fire is 230–350 rpm.

Hand grenade F-1 – This is a defensive hand grenade with time fuse and fragmentation radius of 220 yd (200 m); it is thrown only from cover. It requires time fuse F-1 with time delay of 3.2 to 4 sec.

Hand grenade RGD-5 – It is used as offensive or defensive grenade. When it is thrown, the safety lever pivots upward and over the grenade body and releases the spring loaded firing pin which actuates the delay element and detonates the grenade in 3.2–4 sec.

Because of its light weight (0.75 lb or 315 g) it can be thrown to a distance of 55 yd (50 m); its fragments are effective up to 22 yd (20 m). The RGD-5 is used especially by the NPA/Frontier Troops.

Hand grenade 42 (RG-42) – This is an offensive weapon with a fragmentation effect and time delay. It detonates within 3.2–4 seconds.

Hand grenade RPG-43 – This tank hand grenade weighs 42.5 oz (1.2 kg) and can be thrown at a distance of only 22 yd (20 m). It penetrates armour of 2.95 in (75 mm) thickness and its fragments are effective within the radius of up to 22 yd (20 m).

82 mm mortar – The mortar platoons of the motorized infantry divisions use the 82 mm M-1937, the M-1941 and the M-1943. These conventional mortars can also fire 81 mm ammunition. Their horizontal range is around 3300 yd (3 km). The projectile weighs 7.25 lb (3.3 kg). The difference between the three models is in the base plates and the mounts.

120 mm mortar M-1943 – This is the weapon of regimental mortar companies and generally corresponds to the mortars of same calibre used in the West. For pack transport, it breaks down into three loads, or it can be towed behind an truck or armoured personnel carrier; also a caisson is available when animal draft is necessary. The base plate is round. The mortar's range is about 6600 yd (6 km).

LPAG 40 mm RPG-2 – This light anti-tank launcher is similar to the wartime German "Panzerfaust", but it can be reloaded and fired as many times as needed with rocket ammunition. The supercalibre shell weighs about 3.3 lb (1.6 kg) and its effective range is 165 yd (150 m). This is the standard weapon of each rifle squad.

ARTILLERY WEAPONS

57 mm anti-tank gun M-1943 – This gun originated from the 7.62 cm field gun widely used during World War II; it is mounted on a self-propelled carriage and is provided with a large protective shield, but has no muzzle brake. With a hardcore shell it can penetrate armor of up to 3.9 in (95 mm) thickness at 1100 yd (1000 m) distance; at 2200 yd (2000 m) the armour penetration is down to 2.9 in (72 mm). It is now being replaced with the 57 mm anti-tank gun M-55 (HA) which is standard equipment of anti-tank platoons of motorized infantry battalions under the designation of "57 mm SFK".

85 mm anti-tank gun (HA) M–1945 – This gun, designated in the NPA as the self-propelled gun SFK 85, is a multi-purpose weapon employed by the anti-tank companies of motorized infantry regiments. It is driven by a 750 ccm two-stroke motorcycle engine. The 14 ft 10 in long tube (4.5 m) has a muzzle brake. Maximum range is 10 miles (16 km). With armour ammunition it penetrates armour thickness up to 37 in (100 mm). The gun was introduced in the Soviet Army after 1945 and is still in effective use.

122 mm FH M–1938 – This obsolete light field howitzer is still a standard weapon of divisional artillery regiments. It is a pre-war model, robust and efficient but rather heavy. It is towed by truck; its maximum range is some 13 000 yd (12 km); the weight of explosive shell is 48 lb (22 kg), almost double that of the 85 mm shell. Like most other types of light and medium artillery guns this model, too, was replaced in the Soviet Army in 1955 by a lighter model (122 mm FK M–1955) with longer range.

152 mm FH M–1943 – Mounted on the same carriage as 122 mm FH, this model can be distinguished by a stronger muzzle brake. It is part of the equipment of artillery regiments in military districts and corresponds, perhaps, to the American 155 mm FH. It is towed by truck M–50. Its maximum range is 13 000 yd (12 km). The weight of explosive shell is 88 lb (40 kg). The Soviets have replaced it by a more efficient gun howitzer M–1955 (203 mm).

152 mm KH M–1937 – This gun was the principal Soviet weapon for counter-battery and other long-range destructive and interdiction fire in World War II, but it is no longer in use in the Soviet Army. Artillery regiments of military districts of the NPA, however, still employ it. It, too, is mounted on the standard carriage of the 122 mm FH; it weighs 7.82 short tons (7.1 t); its maximum range is 18 880 yd (17.2 km). The explosive shell weighs 96 lb (44 kg); the armour penetration explosive shell weighs 107.6 lb (49 kg). Only four shots can be fired in one minute.

160 mm mortar M–1943 – This mortar provides an important source of cheap firepower for Soviet artillery. It is, unlike the guns of smaller calibre, breech-loaded. It is towed by its muzzle behind truck. Its maximum range is 5460 yd (5 km); the projectile weighs 88 lb (40 kg).

Multiple rocket launcher BM–24 – This weapon is a further development of the Soviet "Katyusha" used in World War II. It is excellent against flat targets and for direct fire support of attacking troops. The launcher, mounted on a truck and also fired from it, has 12 rockets (calibre 240 mm). They are arranged in two rows, six rockets in each, on superimposed open launching frames. The total weight of the BM-24 (launcher and truck) is 9.9 short tons (9 t); the rocket itself weighs 248 lb (112 kg); its maximum range is 7700 yd (7 km).

Anti-tank guided rocket – This weapon (NATO assigned name "Snapper") was shown by the NPA for the first time in 1964, but it had appeared a year earlier in other satellite armies. It is part of the equipment of motorized infantry divisions. This rocket, mounted on a "small terrain vehicle" (0,5 t truck GAS-69; cruising range 460 miles or 650 km, speed 56 mph or 90 km), is about 4 ft (120 cm) long; it has stabilizing fins and a thick, cone-shaped warhead. The rockets are always hanging on four launching rails and can be guided by the driver from the truck cabin or from outside by wire. Their range is between 440 and 2200 yd (400 and 2000 m), and their penetration force is high.

Free rocket over ground – Among other "modern technique" shown by the NPA in the parade on the "15th birthday of the GDR" (7 October 1964) was also this rocket, displayed in Moscow as early as in the May Day parade of 1960. This weapon (NATO designation FROG 4), mounted on a light, self-propelled modified chassis of the tank PT-76, has with its multi-purpose warhead a range of 12.5 to 37 miles (20 to 60 km). The carriage, marked by very good cross-country mobility, has – at an average speed of 29 mph (45 km) – a cruising range of 156 miles (250 km). The rocket is especially suitable for direct support of land forces in tactical and operational range. It is fired electrically from a slanting rail and is driven by two jets using solid fuel. It is 33.6 ft (10.2 m) long and weighs some 4800 lb (2200 kg). The cone-shaped warhead weighs 660 lb (300 kg). The total weight of the weapon, with carriage, is 16.5 short tons (15 t).

Ground-to-ground guided missile – This, the heaviest artillery guided missile (NATO designation "Scud-A"), fired vertically from a modified tank chassis, was shown in East Berlin for the first time on 7 October 1964. It belongs to the Soviet missile family displayed first in Moscow in the November parade in 1957, and it is comparable to the American "Corporal". With atomic warhead, this 33-35 ft (10-10.7 m) long, electrically fired one-stage missile, driven by liquid fuel and guided by radio, has a range of about 100 miles (160 km); with conventional warhead up to 170 miles (275 km). The weight of the missile is 5.5 short tons (5 t), together with the carriage about 38.5 short tons (35 t). The cruising range of the carriage is 110 miles (175 km), the speed 20 mph (35 km). With this guided artillery missile the NPA has, for the first time, a weapon of superior warfare.

ANTI-AIRCRAFT WEAPONS

14.5 mm anti-aircraft heavy machine gun (ZPU) – The 12.7 mm calibre, which was earlier used as machine gun and anti-aircraft machine gun, is being replaced by the standard weapon ZPU. As twin ZPU-2 it is used in ships and sometimes mounted also on the armoured personnel carries BTR-152. In its quad version, ZPU-4, it is employed in the light anti-aircraft platoons of regimental units. In this form the weapon is mounted on a two-wheel carriage towed by truck. Its weight in firing position is about 1.1 short ton (1 t). Effective vertical range is slightly below 1100 yd (1000 m) horizontal range 2200 yd (2 km).

23 mm twin anti-aircraft gun ZU-23 – This modern weapon is being issued, from 1965 on, for air defence in the combat zone. It can reach targets vertically up to 1650 yd (1500 m) and horizontally up to 2750 yd (2.5 km). Theoretical rate of firing is, according to Soviet data, 800-1000 rpm per barrel; practical rate is, however, around 400.

57 mm anti-aircraft gun M-1950 - The medium anti-aircraft gun M-1950 is issued to anti-aircraft regimental batteries and also to divisional anti-aircraft sections. This very powerful weapon has a vertical range of 2200 yd (2000 m) and a horizontal range of 7.3 miles (12 km). The projectile (explosive shell) weighs 6.2 lb (2.8 kg). The rate of fire is 60 rpm. The gun can be effectively used also against tanks – its penetration of armour is slightly below 4 in (100 mm) at 1100 yd (1000 m). The long tube (14 ft 6 in or 4.4 m with muzzle brake) is also used for the self-propelled anti-aircraft gun SU 57-2 (57 mm anti-aircraft SFL) as twin.

100 mm anti-aircraft gun M-1949 – It was introduced to the anti-aircraft regiments of military districts as a replacement for the no longer satisfactory 85 mm anti-aircraft gun. This weapon weighs in firing position 12.1 short tons (11 t); it was made mobile by being mounted on a simple four-wheeled carriage towed by truck (ZKW M-1954). Its vertical range is effective up to 13 300 yd (12 km), maximal up to 16 500 yd (15 km); horizontally it can hit targets up to 13.5 miles (21 km). The rate of fire is about 15 rpm; the projectile weighs 35 lb (16 kg).

Anti-aircraft missile – Since 1962, the NPA has had a ground-to-air guided missile of type "SA-2 Guideline" (NATO designation) which had been used by the Soviet Army for the previous 9 years and shortly after 1962 was replaced by a new model. The SA-2 type is a two-stage missile capable of reaching the altitude of 60 000 ft (18 km); its slant range is 15 miles (28 km). Maximum fully effective altitude is 40 000 ft (12 km) – in slant range 33 miles (60 km).

TANKS

Reconnaissance tank PT-76 – This tank is among the standard equipment of reconnaissance companies; its chassis is also used for armoured personnel carriers BTR-50 (P) and tank mortars BB 1/PT. It is 7 ft (2.16 m) high; it has a weak armour but good weapons. The Soviets have armed their reconnaissance tanks with a conventional gun (76 mm). As secondary armament the PT-76 has a 7.62 mm machine gun; it carries a crew of three and weighs 15.4 short tons (14 t). Its diesel engine has 240 hp; speed on land is 28 mph (45 km), in water (driven by a hydrojet system) – 10 mph (16 km). Its cruising range is about 160 miles (250 km).

Medium tank T-54 – This modern, medium combat tank has been issued in large number to the medium tank units of the NPA. Prominent on it is its cruising range of some 250 miles (400 km) on good roads, its very good form and the heavy 100 mm gun, the ballistic efficiency of which cannot, however, be fully exploited because of insufficient sighting devices (there is no range finder). Another of its disadvantages is that it cannot store adequate quantity of ammunition. Two 7.62 mm machine guns serve as secondary armament. The 520 hp diesel engine gives the vehicle, which weighs 39.6 short tons (36 t), a speed of 30 mph (50 km). It is 7 ft 10 in (2.35 m) high.

Medium tank T-55 – This new development of T-54, which was to be introduced in the NPA in 1966, can travel under water; all

openings can be closed water-tight, a snorkel 4 yd (about 4 m) long
pulled out and antenna correspondingly extended.

BTR-40 – This robust, but simply built vehicle is employed by
tank reconnaissance companies as armoured personnel carrier or reconnaissance tank. Its height is 6 ft 2 in (1.9 m); it accomodates a
crew of two and eight soldiers (one group). The 80 hp engine has a
maximum speed of 50 mph (80 km); its cruising range is 170 miles
(280 km). Its mobility in terrain is, however, limited. Normally it
is armed with one 7.62 mm machine gun, but it can also be equipped
with a twin 14.5 mm anti-aircraft gun (ZPU-2).

BTR-40 (A) – In the May Day parade in 1960 the NPA displayed for the first time this light reconnaissance tank, a variation of
the BTR-40. It is a four-wheel drive car accomodating in addition
to the driver three or four men. It has only one machine gun and is
without revolving turret; therefore its outline is rather low. The amphibious BTR-40 (A) is mainly used by the reconnaissance units of
motorized infantry divisions and tank engineer troops, but it is sometimes employed also as armoured vehicle for staffs and also as armoured radio vehicle. To improve on the rather low distance between the
ground and the body of the tank, two adjustable auxiliary axles with
smaller wheels are added; when they are lowered the body of the tank
is raised.

Rocket-equipped tank destroyer 40 (A) – The chassis of the above
type was adapted to accomodate firing and guiding systems for three
anti-tank guided rockets ("snappers"). The whole system is vertically adjustable. When the weapon system is in lowered position the
vehicle is covered by top flaps.

Armoured personnel carrier BTR-152 – This three-axle carrier
with drive on all wheels is open at the top and rather high (without
armament 7 ft or 2.1 m). It can transport 15 men; its six-cylin-
der 110 hp petrol engine permits a road speed of about 47 mph
(75 km). In cross-country travel it is, because of its primitive construction, rather uncomfortable. The cruising range is about 400 miles
(650 km). In combat it gives the crew protection from grenade
splinters and projectiles of infantry weapons. It is supposed to reduce
pressure and radiation effects of nuclear weapons, but it is not
suitable for nuclear warfare, since it is not fully enclosed. Its normal
armament consists of one 12.7 mm or 7.62 mm machine gun; some
vehicles also mount the twin 14.5 mm anti-aircraft machine gun.

Armoured personnel carrier BTR-50 (P) – While the BTR-152 is built on the chassis of the standard tank, this type is mounted on the chassis of the reconnaissance tank PT-76. Its height is 6 ft 1 in (1.86 m). It is the first tracked armoured personnel carrier employed by the Soviet Army and has been, since 1962, issued also to the NPA, especially to its reconnaissance tank units. The latest version can be fully closed at the top, but it has no mounted weapons under the armour. The BTR-50 (P) can take twelve passengers and the crew of three. Its diesel engine has 240 hp and gives the vehicle a speed of 25 mph (40 km) on land, 6 mph (10 km) in water. The cruising range is around 160 miles (250 km).

Tank recovery vehicle T-34 BG – The NPA employs for tank recovery purposes the turretless T-34. It is insufficiently equipped, has no shovel and no crow-bar, but it is robust and can deal with the T-34 or T-54.

AMPHIBIOUS VEHICLES

Amphibious vehicle P2S – This all-wheel drive vehicle is standard equipment of reconnaissance troops and is also employed for command and liaison. The petrol engine has 65 hp and permits a maximum speed of 59 mph (95 km) on the road; in water it is driven by a three-bladed propeller and has a speed of 6 mph (9 km). The cruising range is 200 miles (320 km). The vehicle is almost 17 ft long (5 m). The P2S is built in East Germany from the blueprints of the Soviet GAZ-46.

Amphibious truck BAV – This Soviet copy of the American DUKW from the World War II has become – as BAV – the standard vehicle of all engineer units of the NPA. It can transport 20–25 men or a light gun with its crew. The petrol engine has 110 hp and enables this 31 ft (9.45 m) long vehicle weighing 7.7 short tons (7 t) to reach almost 40 mph (60 km) on road and slightly above 6 mph (10 km) in water. Its cruising range is 300 miles (480 km).

Tracked amphibian K-61 – The K-61 is a large, fully tracked vehicle capable of carrying a payload of 3.3 short tons (3 t) on land and 5.5 short tons (5 t) in water. With the K-61 the amphibious engineer units can transport howitzers, trucks, anti-tank guns or 40 men. The 135 hp diesel engine gives it a speed of 24 mph (36 km) on land or 6 mph (10 km) in water (driven by two propellers). This very robust vehicle was, according to Soviet reports, employed even in rivers during the ice-drift periods.

ENGINEER VEHICLES

The NPA, following its model the Soviet Army, pays great attention to the use of earth moving machines. Mounted on the chassis of the fully tracked tractor K-10 is the large *ditching machine* with a comparatively high digging speed (960-1200 cubic metres per hour) in straight ditch-line. A *ditching plough* is employed for digging smaller ditches. The NPA engineers also have at their disposal an *earth driller* which can be mounted on a tractor. It is used for quick drilling of holes of about 0.5 yd (0.5 m) in diameter. The *diesel rammer DCB-6*, of Czechoslovak production, is used as piledriving machine for many purposes.

Bridge laying machine – This machine was displayed for the first time by the NPA, and with great pride, in the May Day parade in 1963. Mounted on a T-54 medium tank chassis, it has been used by the Soviet Army for a long time. The one-part bridge laid by the machine is 13.2 yd (12 m) long and 3.83 yd (3.5 m) wide; it is capable of carrying any armoured vehicle developed in the Soviet Union.

Mine laying machine MLG-60 – The NPA employs a Soviet mine layer which is towed by an armoured personnel carrier and can quickly lay mines which slide down on a slanted platform and are evenly distributed. At the end of the platform there is a plough and behind it rough brushes to camouflage the laid mines.

T-54 with mine clearing equipment PT-54 – The armoured engineers of the NPA use the Soviet machine PT-54 consisting of a number of loose cast-iron rollers hanging from bars mounted forward of the T-54 tank. When lowered, their pressure on the ground is so strong that it detonates, in front of the tank, all anti-tank mines not equipped with time fuses. The system of rollers is easily mounted on any mass produced tank.

Tank dozer BTU – Standard tanks can be adapted for earth-moving work by a hydraulically movable strong steel-blade. A bar fixed in the middle of the blade helps in levelling the unevenness of ground.

II. Air Force/Air Defence

The Air Force/Air Defence employs the following aircraft of Soviet origin:

MiG-15 – This was the first arrow-winged jet airplane developed by the Soviet designers Mikoyan and Gurevich and introduced in the Soviet Army in 1949. The MiG-15, which had shown its mettle in the Korean war, is now outdated as a single-seat fighter and is used in the NPA and other satellite armies as a fighter-bomber. Its maximum speed is about 660 mph (1050 km) and its range 770 miles (1200 km). It is armed with two 23 mm and one 37 mm guns.

MiG-17 – This one-jet fighter is an improved development of the MiG-15 and is built in many versions; among them the MiG-17D and MiG-17E are regarded as the best armed all-weather fighter. The MiG-17 is a standard fighter of the NPA's Air Force. It has a maximum speed of around 770 mph (1200 km) and a normal range of 770 miles. (The MiG-17PF can be fitted with reserve fuel containers under the wings and its range is thus considerably extended.) Maximum altitude is 10 miles (16.6 km). Its armament consists of two 23 mm and one 37 mm gun.

MiG-19 – In contrast to the MiG-15 and MiG-17 this is a two-jet improved development which, because of its high climb-rate, can qualify also as an interceptor-fighter. The MiG-19, too, is produced in several versions; among them are the all-weather types B and C. Its specifications: maximum speed 906 mph (1450 km), range 1125 miles (1800 km), maximum altitude 11 250 yd (18 600 m). The MiG-19 is armed with two 23 mm guns and air-to-air missiles.

MiG-21 – This single-jet, single-seat highly efficient fighter with deltoid wings was displayed in the Soviet Union for the first time in 1956 and is now being introduced also in the NPA. Its maximum speed is 1250 mp (2000 km) – that is 2 Mach; it normally has a range of 1250 miles and can climb to an altitude of about 21 000 yd (19 000 m). It is built in two versions. One is armed with two 37 mm guns and rockets, the other only with rockets.

IL-28 – The IL-28 was designed by the Soviet designer Ilyushin and has been built, since 1950, in large numbers. This light (tactical) bomber has two jets and carries a crew of three (pilot, bombardier and aft-gunner). Maximum speed is 562 mph (900 km); normal range is 2350 miles (3900 km); maximum altitude is about 14 000 yd (12 900 m). It is armed with two 23 mm and two 20 mm guns and bombs.

AN-2 – This strutted bi-plane is a short-distance, multipurpose aircraft employed as a light cargo and ambulance carrier. It was developed in 1947–50 by the Soviet designer Antonov and is capable of transporting, together with a crew of two, cargo weighing 1.5 t or six stretchers with two accompanying persons. Its air-cooled radial engine develops a maximum speed of about 155 mph (250 km) with a service ceiling of 3.12 miles (5 km).

IL-14 – This machine is employed as a medium cargo and personnel carrier and is also used by parachute troops. It very much resembles the slightly faster American Convair 440 (Metropolitan). With its two double-radial engines it is capable of a maximum speed of 250 mph (400 km) and has a normal range of 1000 miles (1600 km). Its service ceiling is at 4.2 miles (6.7 km).

IL-18 – This modern transport aircraft with four turbo-propellers is used on both the domestic and international services of the Soviet Aeroflot. It has accomodation for 75–98 passengers. The NPA had, in the first half of 1966, three machines of this type. The maximum speed of IL-18 is 406 mph (650 km); its range – 3370 miles (5400 km); its service ceiling – 5.6 miles (9 km).

Yak-11 – This aircraft is driven by an air-cooled radial engine and is employed as a standard trainer for advanced trainees in the Soviet Army and for the same purpose and also for civil services in other communist states. This well-proved, two-seat model has a maximum speed of 287 mph (460 km); its range is 780 miles (1270 km) and service ceiling 4.4 miles (7.1 km).

Yak-18 – This is a single-engine aircraft used by the Soviet and satellite armed forces to train beginners. It has a max. speed of 147 mph (235 km), a range of 625 miles (1000 km) a service ceiling of 2.5 miles (4 km).

L-60 – This is a single-engine, short- take-off airplane used for surveillance, liaison and ambulance purposes. It is produced by Czechoslovakia; it can accomodate two pilots and two or three passengers or two stretchers and one accompanying person. The L-60 has an air-cooled cylinder in-line engine and is capable of attaining a maximum speed of 125 mph (200 km) with a normal range of 440 miles (710 km) and a service ceiling of 2.5 miles (4 km).

Mi-1 – This four-seat, multi-purpose helicopter was developed in 1949 by the Soviet designer Mil and is used for liaison and ambulance purposes; for the transport of wounded soldiers special basket-type containers can be fitted on the fuselage. The Mi-1 is driven by one radial engine, has a maximum speed of 112 mph (180 km) and a normal range of 220 miles (350 km). Its service ceiling is slightly below 3 miles (4.5 km).

Mi-4 – This helicopter is employed for transport – it has accomodation for a crew of two and fourteen fully equipped soldiers, or for corresponding freight (11 600 lb or 5220 kg). The aircooled radial engine is mounted in the fuselage nose and the aft is thus very easily accessible. The maximum speed of the Mi-4 is 110 mph (175 km); its normal range is 250 miles (400 km) and the maximum altitude – 3.3 miles (5.3 km). The helicopter is armed with one machine gun.

III. People's Navy

The NPA/PN employs the following types of ships of Soviet or East German production:

COASTAL DEFENCE SHIPS

These are the Soviet frigates of Riga type built in 1950–53. Displacement 1200 t, lenght 278.8 ft (91 m); machinery: geared turbines; speed 28 kt; complement 180 men. Weapons: three 100 mm, four 37 mm anti-aircraft guns paired vertically; 2 tubes; 4 depth bombs projectors; 50 mines; anti-submarine rocket projector. The four existing coastal defence ships are named: "Friedrich Engels", "Karl Marx", "Ernst Thälmann" and "Karl Liebknecht".

MINE LAYERS AND MINE SWEEPERS

Habicht-I Class – Built in East German shipyards in 1952 – 54, these ships are similar to the mine detecting boat 40 of the former German "Kriegsmarine". Displacement – 610 t; length 193 ft (59 m); diesels; speed 17 kt; complement 85 men. Weapons: one 85 mm, eight 25 mm anti-aircraft guns; 36 mines and depth bombs.

Habicht-II Class – Developed in East Germany, it is similar to the mine detecting boat 43 of the "Kriegsmarine". It was built in 1954–56; displacement 700 t; length 213 ft (65 m); two diesels;

speed 17 kt; complement 85 men. Armament as in the Habicht-I Class.

Krake Class – Another development of East German ship-yards. Outwardly very similar to modern salvage tugs. Built in 1956–58; displacement 740 t; length 229 ft (70 m); diesels; speed 17 kt; complement 90 men. Armament: one 85 mm, ten 25 mm anti-aircraft guns, 32 mines and 32 depth bombs.

The 22 existing mine layers and mine sweepers bear among others the names of district capitals (Magdeburg, Schwerin, Halle, Gera, Erfurt, Frankfurt, Brandenburg, Potsdam, Cottbus etc.)

MINE SWEEPING BOATS

Schwalbe-I Class – Built in East Germany in 1953–54; displacement 75 t; length 85 ft (27 m); diesels; speed about 12 kt; complement 14 men. Weapons: four anti-aircraft machine guns.

Schwalbe-II Class – Built in East Germany in 1954–58; displacement about 100 t; length 105 ft (32 m); diesels; speed about 13 kt; complement 14 men. Armament: two 25 mm anti-aircraft guns.

The People's Navy has some 50 mine sweeping boats.

PATROL VESSELS

SO-1 Class – Soviet type, built in 1957. Displacement 215 t; length 122 ft (40 m); diesels; speed about 40 kt; complement 30–40 men. Armament: four 25 mm anti-aircraft guns, 4 × 5 anti-sub-marine rockets, 24 depth bombs (2 depth bomb projectors).

The PN has 16 vessels of this type.

Hai Class – Built in East Germany in 1962. Displacement about 300 t; driven apparently by gas turbines; speed about 25 kt.

The PN has 6 vessels of this type.

MOTOR TORPEDO BOATS

P-6 Class – Soviet type, built in 1952–53. Displacement about 70 t; length 85 ft (27 m); diesels; speed about 42 kt; complement 15 men. Armament: four 25 mm anti-aircraft guns, two tubes, 12 depth bombs.

MiG-17, the standard fighter of the NPA-Air Force.

MiG-19.

Sketches of the jet fighters employed in the NPA-Air Force.

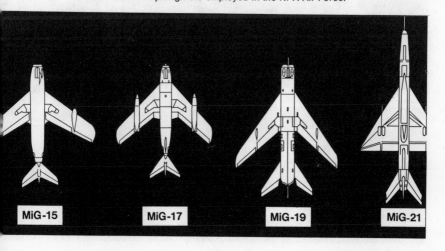

MiG-15   MiG-17   MiG-19   MiG-21

Tactical bomber Il-28.

Sketches of the aircraft employed in the NPA-Air Force.

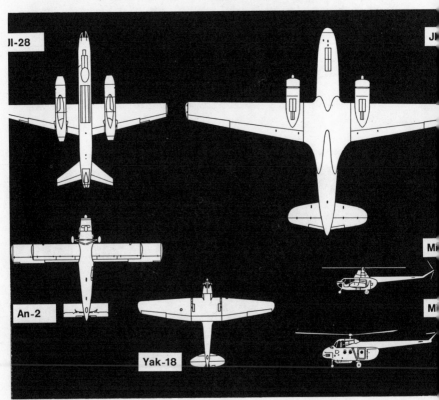

Medium cargo and personnel carrier Il-14.

Multipurpose aircraft An-2.

Transport helicopter Mi-4.

Paratroopers in exercise:
in the foreground a parachuted armoured vehicle.

There are 34 motor torpedo boats employed by the PN, commissioned in 1958.

Seeteufel Class – Built in East Germany. Displacement 150 t; speed about 35 kt. Weapons: two 57 mm anti-aircraft guns, two tubes.

The PN has about four vessels of this type.

Forelle/Iltis Class – Built in East Germany in 1962. Displacement about 55 t; speed 40 kt. Armed with two 25 mm and four 14.5 mm anti-aircraft guns, two tubes.

The PN has more than 12 boats of this type.

GUIDED MISSILE PATROL BOATS

Osa Class – Later Soviet type, designated in the PN as "rocket motor boat". Displacement 160 t; speed 35 kt. Weapons: four 25 mm anti-aircraft guns and four launchers for short range rockets.

The PN has more than 16 boats of this type.

COASTAL DEFENCE BOATS

Built in East Germany in 1953–54. Displacement about 78 t; length 85 ft (28 m); diesels; speed about 24 kt; complement about 20 men. Armed with one anti-aircraft machine gun and depth bombs.

The PN has more than 60 of these boats.

HARBOUR DEFENCE BOATS

Tümmler Class – Built in 1953–56. Displacement 50 t; length 70 ft (23 m); diesels; speed about 10 kt; complement 7 men. Armament: four 14.5 mm anti-aricraft guns.

Delphin Class – Built in East Germany in 1953–54. Displacement 50 t; length 88 ft (29 m); diesels; speed about 27 kt; complement about 14 men. Weapons: one 12.7 mm anti-aircraft machine gun.

The PN has more than 45 defence boats of both types.

LANDING CRAFT

Robbe Class – Newly built in East Germany. Displacement about 600 t (fully loaded about 800 t); speed 12 kt. Armament: two 57 mm and four 25 mm anti-aircraft guns.

The PN has more than 6 craft of this type.

Labo Class – Newly built in East Germany. Displacement about 500 t; speed about 10 kt. Armed with four 25 mm anti-aircraft guns. The PN has more than 10 craft of this type.

CHAPTER 7

LOGISTICS OF THE NPA

Among the military terms commonly used in the National People's Army neither the term *logistics* nor any comparable expression is to be found. The entire sphere of the East German military supply system, however, corresponds to the basic meaning of this word as understood in the West. It includes: development, production, procurement, administration and preservation or maintenance, transport and distribution, salvage and safeguarding of supplies and equipment of all sorts as well as medical supplies and care.

Compared with the situation in the western armed forces the supply system of East Germany is essentially more closely connected with the economy of the state. This is the result of the totalitarian state organization, central planning and direction of the economy by the state.

Armaments industry

The highest organs of the armaments industry are the State Planning Commission, closely cooperating with the Research Council and the State Secretariat of Research and Technology, and the Council of National Economy. They both base their work on the decisions of the Central Committee of the SED and the government.

The Department of Special Requirements at the State Planning Commission is competent for the supply of the NPA and is headed by a major general of the NPA.

Enterprises which produce the equipment for the NPA are guided, on behalf of the Ministry of National Defence, by *VVB Unimag*, an association of nationalized enterprises.

Heavy weapons, which are as yet not produced in the East Germany, are imported from the Soviet Union and other countries of the Soviet bloc. Apart from small arms, the armament industry of East Germany hardly produces any war materials. It concentrates on the production of components, instruments and tools of all kind such as communication apparatus, optical instruments, motor vehicles, coastal defence ships, leather and other articles for the outfit of soldiers.

In its organization and structure the supply system of the NPA is entirely based on the Soviet model.

Organization and tasks

General responsibility for the supply of the armed forces lies with the Minister of National Defence who has delegated his duties for individual spheres of supply within the Ministry and subordinated commands in the following way:
- the Deputy Minister and Chief of Rear Services is responsible for the supply of general goods, such as fuel, equipment and clothing, provisions and medicaments;
- the chiefs of administrations of various branches of services, such as artillery and rocket troops, armour, motor transport, chemical services, engineers, construction etc., are responsible for supplying their troops and services with specialized goods.

The supply offices of the rear services and the specialized supply branches of services are subdivided down to the staffs of lower commands, including the battalions.

An important role in the supply system of the NPA is played, as in civil planning, by the *norm.* Consumption and reserves of ammunition and fuel are determined, and also ordered, by tactical control. The "principle of supply" has, according to the Soviet doctrine, to assure speed and flexibility of the entire supply system in the field of combat.

Service troops and the infrastructure

The personnel strength of the service troops of the NPA can be quickly increased by calling up the reservists. The civil personnel of nationalized enterprises, for example in haulage, is subject to mobilization and can thus strengthen the corresponding service troops. Such measures, supported by the law, enable the supply apparatus of the NPA to be speedily put into full gear in the event of crisis.

For the maintenance of motor vehicles and tanks the NPA uses, besides its own workshops, the nationalized enterprises of the armaments industry and smaller local enterprises.

The transport system is regarded by the NPA as especially important for operational efficiency of the armed forces. It has to secure the transport of supplies by rail, water or pipes even in the difficult conditions of war. Thus the soldiers of the land forces and the conscientious objectors, who are doing their military service in the construction units, are used for repairing the railways, bridges and roads. The units for the construction of pipelines are trained in laying mobile fuel pipelines for speedy supply to the armoured and mechanized troops.

All improvements in the *road network* are planned from the military standpoint with the aim of increasing the capacity of roads for carrying military traffic. With 100 km of roads per 100 square kilometres East Germany has the highest road density in the Soviet bloc. The rail network of East Germany has the same density as that of the Federal Republic. An *inland waterways system* of canals and rivers spreads through East Germany from east to west and from north to south enabling the army to keep large stocks of supplies on water, to transport large quantities, to secure quick distribution and, at the same time, to relieve the heavy traffic on roads.

Modernization of military and postal communications offers the armed forces a diversified system of wire, radio and radio relay communications for military operations. The equipment of the communications service with systems for processing and transmission of data, which has now begun, will further increase its efficiency.

The air transport capacity is comparatively small (one transport group and one helicopter group) but it is sufficient for operational actions and for important supply transport. The helicopters can transport nuclear warheads from storage depots to launching positions.

Reserves of the NPA

Here one has to differentiate between
– mobile reserves of ammunition and fuel transported by the units of

the land forces in their own carriers or those available to the air
force in the depots at the airfields and to the navy on board ships;
– military and civil reserves of mass consumption goods and specialized goods which are stored in large depots of the NPA and industry.

These reserves are sufficient for the land, air and naval forces in the
first phase of war.

Material dependence of the NPA on the Soviet Army

In peacetime, the armed forces of East Germany are responsible
for their own supplies and the entire supply system is under East
German command.

At the present time, within the general military structure of the
Warsaw Pact there are neither any integrated command staffs for the
rear services nor integrated units of service troops. The almost total
dependence in weapons on the Soviet Army and Soviet armaments
industry forces the NPA to rely on the Soviet supply system.

Close cooperation between the NPA and the Soviet Army is also
manifested in the presence of Soviet advisers and in the resemblance
of its supply commands to the Soviet model. The dependence on the
Soviet armed forces is facilitated by the almost identical structure of
tactical units and rear services and by a suitable command system.

The widespread standardization of weapons, instruments and vehicles within the Warsaw Pact enables the communist armies to exchange
not only such mass consumption goods as ammunition or fuel but also
components and similar specialized goods.

Thus there already exists, in peacetime, the basis for an expansion
of the supply system in war.

PART THREE

THE PERSONNEL POTENTIAL

CHAPTER 8

THE RECRUITMENT
OF THE
ARMED FORCES

All Soviet bloc states have had from the very beginning universal conscription – only the Soviet Zone had been an exception until 1962. There were several reasons for this.

In the first years after World War II the Soviets had to take world opinion into account, among other things, and could not at once introduce compulsory military service for the population which was to remain – according to the Potsdam Agreement – unarmed forever. The Soviets also knew that the Germans were not in sympathy with the enforced communist regime. And besides, they had first to select and prepare politically reliable cadres for the new army, the establishment of which was decided by the Soviets beforehand. Regard for German antipathies against rearmament after the bad experience of the lost war was for the Soviets of only minor importance. The same was true for the antipathies of the Czechs and Poles against building any large army consisting of Germans even though they were under Soviet communist command. Also the economic potential of East Germany was in the first post-war years more important for the Soviets than its military potential. Even when in 1949 East Germany was given its "sovereignty" and when in 1956 the "People's Army" was established, the introduction of compulsory military service was still delayed for considerable time.

This delay did not create great difficulties for the SED regime, set up by the Soviets, since it thought it had sufficient power over the party and the mass organizations to enforce "voluntary" enlistment for the service in the armed forces.

At that time it was also possible to exert indirect pressure trough an amendment to the constitution which was approved by the People's Chamber in October 1955 and which said:

Service for the protection of the fatherland and the achievements of the workers is an honorary duty of the citizen of the GDR.[1]

This amendment also authorized the government to issue further decrees and directives since it said that

the organization of service for military protection of the fatherland and civil population is regulated by the decisions of the Council of Ministers.

Support by the party and the mass organizations

Members of the SED and the mass organizations were – and are still today – obliged, by the statutes, to join the armed forces when asked to, or to participate actively in recruitment. The Statute of the SED, approved by the Fourth Party Congress in 1954, explicitly stipulates the special role of the SED in this sphere:

The Party educates and organizes the workers for active defence of the fatherland, the workers' and peasants' state, against all aggression by its enemies.[2]

Similar stipulations – on the duty of their members to join the army and/or to assist in the recruitment of others – are contained in the statutes of the SED subsidiary organizations such as the FDJ and the trade unions.

The FDJ (Free German Youth) laid down the military obligations of its members in May 1955:

The members of the FDJ regard the acquisition of premilitary knowledge and efficiency as their honour and duty. Service in the armed organs of the GDR is an honourable duty for every member of the FDJ.[3]

Also the Statute of the Federation of Free German Trade Unions

1 "Gesetzblatt der DDR I" (Law Gazette of the GDR I), No. 82, 6 October 1955, p. 653.

2 *Dokumente der SED* (Documents of the SED), Vol. 5, Dietz-Verlag, East Berlin, 1956, p 92.

3 "Junge Welt" (Young World), East Berlin, No. 134, 8 June 1955, p 3.

(FDGB) has contained, since 1955, passages on military obligations:

> The trade unions educate the workers to patriotism, love of the fatherland, vigilance against saboteurs and agents, and to conscious fulfilment of their duty to protect the socialist achievements of the workers' and peasants' state.[4]

The trade unionists were, above all, asked to join the *Combat Groups.*

Since the SED had achieved, through its widespread and massive pressure, that almost everybody was in some way or other "organized", practically all men in the age classes liable to military service were under pressure and an obligation to join the armed forces.

Increasing difficulties in the recruitment of "volunteers"

Until 1951, in the first phase of rearmament, it was comparatively simple to win over the necessary personnel for the armed forces disguised as police units.

The much better food rations and higher remuneration were the main attractions. Thus while the members of the armed units received a daily ration of 120 g (a quarter of pound) of butter or lard, the civil population had only 29.5 g. Besides, the young workers wanted, by joining the police, to avoid the enforced work in the uranium mines and other dangerous industries.

A that time pressure was also exerted especially on the former members of the Wehrmacht, above all on professional soldiers, to put at the disposal of the regime their military experience. Great assistance was rendered to the regime in this respect by the *National Democratic Party of Germany* which was founded in the summer of 1948, at the time when the first barracked units of the People's Police were established. This party was appealing, in its own words, to the "middle classes, former members of the National Socialist German Workers' Party (NSDAP), professional soldiers and officers". Many former

4 "Die Arbeit" (Labour), monthly for the theory and practice of the German trade unions. Published by the Presidium of the FDGB, East Berlin, No. 6, June 1955.

officers and soldiers who had joined as prisoners of war in the Soviet Union the *National Committee "Free Germany"* and/or participated in the *Anti-fascist Schools* organized by the Soviets were delegated, after their release, into this party which taught them that they had previously served the "criminal militarism" and now they could redeem their guilt by joining the police units of East Germany.

The defects of this recruitment system, however, became apparent by the end of 1951 when the regime started to transform the existing cadre units into fully fledged military formations and when workmen became scarce. The recruitment commissions established by the SED could not find enough military personnel. It became clear that the personnel requirements of the new army demanded a new system for listing all young people in the military age classes as well as reservists.

On 1 October 1952 recruitment was transferred to the newly established *District Recruiting Departments* which were subordinated to the *Regional Recruitment Administrations*. The highest office of listing was the *Recruitment Administration* within the Staff of the *Barracked People's Police*. In 1956 the local recruiting offices were renamed *Regional* and *District Commands* and a *Recruitment and Enrolment Administration* was created within the new *Ministry of National Defence*.

In 1959 the districts and municipalities were given targets for the recruitment of "volunteers"; these could be, however, fulfilled only through considerably increased political pressure on all able-bodied youths and men. Students of high (grammar-type) schools were alloweed to enrol at the universities only after having served in the army. Young workers were threatened with transfer into lower wage groups; skilled workers had no prospect of promotion if they did not report "voluntarily for the honour of serving in the armed forces". To others it was hinted that "impending political investigation" against their parents would be suspended if they joined the NPA.

It was difficult to evade recruitment in the schools and factories. Usually the campaign began with lectures expounding the necessity of military service with ideological arguments. A great stress was put in these lectures on the alleged threat to the "achievements of the Workers and Peasants Power in the GDR" by the capitalist West and by the allegedly "reawakened German militarism" in the Federal Republic. At the same time the military service in East Germany was depicted in the brightest colours. After the lectures the campaigners from the SED or mass organizations concentrated their efforts on individual young men; in the schools the teachers were used for this work.

In the factories

The recruitment campaigns in factories created considerable tensions because the sudden departure of several skilled workers prevented the enterprise from fulfilling production targets. The managements of enterprises had no interest in losing for two or three years their skilled workers who were so scarce. They often tried to send to the army less useful workers whose loss would not be so painful.

The SED tried to counteract these tendencies by instructing the trade unions to include in the notorious "collective factory contracts" (which the workers councils concluded each year with the managements) not only such unpopular directives as the production norms and targets but also the explicit duty of the management to "assist actively" in the recruitment of soldiers. The enterprises were given quotas of "volunteers" whom they had to "delegate" to the NPA.

The few genuine volunteers could be divided into two groups:

In the first group were the young men who were convinced of the "political necessity of military service". They were a comparatively small group of youths educated by the FDJ and by the one-sided influence of the official political atmosphere.

In the second, larger, group the motives for joining the army were quite different. Good pay and the wish "to have some adventure" or "to see something of the world" brought into the army particularly the young men from the villages and the unskilled workers with lower wages. Among the volunteers were also young men who wanted to become seamen or pilots; others wanted to learn such highly skilled trades (otherwise almost inaccessible) as aircraft mechanics, radar technicians, radio operators etc.

"Large-scale recruiting campaigns" and their consequencies

In the years from 1950 until the introduction of universal conscription in 1962 the SED and the FDJ increasingly organized "large-scale recruiting campaigns". Like all other enforcement measures, these actions were reflected in the refugee statistics. A considerable part of the military age classes tried to evade the service by fleeing to the West. Between 4 February 1952 and 31 December 1959 a total of 234 154 men 18 to 24 years old reported as refugees in West Berlin and in the Federal Republic.

The largest recruiting campaign started on 28 August 1961, two weeks after East Germany had been almost hermetically closed against West Berlin and control on the the demarcation line with the Federal Republic of Germany had been tightened. Then, only six month before the introduction of compulsory military service, the regime tried through a "combat mission of the FDJ" to win over "volunteers" for the service in the NPA with a pathetic slogan "The Fatherland Calls – Protect the Socialist Republic". The "Combat Call of the FDJ" was read in all schools, universities, enterprises, villages and smaller towns. This campaign resembled mobilization for war and the press, radio and television were daily reporting in great detail the progress of the campaign.

All district towns organized farewell parties for the recruited "volunters" at which there were always young girls with flowers and officially encouraged "jubilation".

The SED regime deliberately used this campaign to prepare the population for the intended introduction of universal conscription. The press began, towards the end of 1961, to publish reports that the "working population" had repeatedly asked government finally to introduce conscription because it was the duty of every citizen to defend the "socialist achievemens and the fatherland".

The Act on Universal Conscription

The People's Chamber approved on 24 January 1962 the *Act on Universal Conscription*. Among the decisive reasons for the act were:
- the pressure by the Soviet Union and other members of the Warsaw Pact,
- the economic dificulties in the enterprises caused by the recruitment of skilled workers,
- a considerable financial saving by paying the conscripts less than the "volunteers",

– the possibility of building-up a large reserve.

The introduction of universal conscription had another advantage – it also enabled the regime to indoctrinate all young men in the "political school of the nation" which they, unlike in civil life, could not evade.

Communist propaganda now had a very difficult task to justify ideologically the about-turn from the claim that in the GDR, in contrast to the Federal Republic of Germany where military service was enforced on the population, the young men were joining the army "voluntarily". The propagandists tried to justify the new policy by claiming that universal conscription in a communist state is something quite different· Thus the central organ of the SED "Neues Deutschland" wrote on 26 January 1962:

> The military policy of our state consistently serves the peace because it is the policy of a socialist state. Conscription is not always the same thing. To be obliged to serve in the imperialist army of our sworn enemy – that always was and still is shameful, regardless of whether the individual does or does not understand it. That means serving one's own enemy. That is the road to ruin ... To be obliged to defend with our army socialism and peace – that is the highest honour. To serve ourselves and the working people – that is the road to a secure future of the nation.

(A few weeks later food rationing had to be re-introduced.)

Paragraph 3 of the Act subjected to compulsory service "all male citizens of the GDR aged 18 to 50, officers until 60. During a state of defence all male citizens from 18 to 60 are subject to compulsory service."

In part 5 – *Special regulations for the state of defence* – the Act states:

> When the defence of the state requires it, women from 18 to 50 can be subject to compulsory medical, veterinary, dental, technical or any other special service in the National People's Army. (Paragraph 31)

Under the provisions of the Act GDR citizens living abroad are also liable to military service (paragraph 4) and so are stateless persons living in the GDR (paragraph 3) as well as young men who moved to the GDR from the Federal Republic.

The *basic military service* is of 18 months' duration (paragraph 21).

Called up for this service are all mustered men aged 18 to 26; in cases when the citizen "maliciously" evaded military service, he can be called up until his 35th year. This provision, contained in paragraph 22, also applies for the cases when the citizens are temporarily dispensed from service.

The Act also provides for voluntary service (paragraph 1). Voluntary service as "short service soldier" or "career soldier", however, begins only after the basic service of 18 months. The minimum period of voluntary service for the "short soldier" is three years, for the "career soldier" – twelve years (paragraph 23).

After active service the soldiers are transferred into reserve. *Reserve I* includes all men and non-commissioned officers up to their 35th year of age, officers from major upward to the 60th year; in *Reserve II* are all reservists from 36 to 50 and officers up to the rank of captain to 60 (paragraph 26). The reservists can be called up, on the instruction of the National Defence Council, for short periods for training (paragraph 28) and exercises (paragraph 29) as well as for examination of their combat efficiency or readiness for action (paragraph 30). Previous release from the NPA can be "in state of defence or during international tension" annulled by a decision of the National Defence Council (paragraph 31).

The GDR does not recognize the right of conscientious objectors to refuse military service while the Federal Republic recognizes it. But the National Defence Council has established on 7 September 1964 *construction units* of the NPA for such objectors; they are, however, still subject to all military laws and have the status of regular soldiers.

Paragraph 4 of the Act states that those who "refuse military service with weapons because of their religion or similar views" are to be drafted into the construction units. The regime had apparently taken this decision not only to display its humanitarianism and legal order but also to eliminate from combats units unreliable elements and to subject them to heavy manual work.

Problems of universal conscription

The call-up of young men of all social strata had, outwardly, created the impression of bringing closer the population and the army.

Guided missile patrol boat "Osa"-class.

Mine layer and mine sweeper "Habicht"-class.

Coastal defence boat "Sperber"-class.

Mine sweeping boat "Schwalbe"-class.

Coastal defence ship "Riga"-class.

Mine layer and Mine sweeper "Krake"-class.

Submarine chaser "Hai"-class.

Submarine chaser "SO-1"-class.

Above: Motor torpedo boat
"Iltis"-class.

Left: Motor torpedo boat
"P-VI"-class.

Landing craft.

Since now almost every family had someone in the NPA, nobody would, it was thought, despise it. The drawback was, however, that young men of similar views banded together in the units and, despite increased control and supervision, found means to express their anti-communist attitude. The command of the NPA reacted to this by issuing a number of orders designed to strengthen SED control over both the non-communists and party members.

As references from the army are decisive for the civil careers of young men, the masses of soldiers display pseudo-activity and show zealousness in acquiring military efficiency trying thus to protect themselves from intensive political indoctrination.

This poses a difficult problem for the SED to differentiate between purely military efficiency and purposeful political activity. To a very large extent the party is not able to discern clearly between the genuine and pretended political conviction and has to be satisfied with military efficiency only. Thus the young men leaving the NPA are not as well indoctrinated as Defence Minister Hoffmann had expected and they are taking up, on the strength of army references based on their good service record, positions in civil life which the SED wanted to reserve only for proven communists.

CHAPTER 9

THE PERSONNEL RESERVES OF THE NPA

On 24 January 1962, simultaneously with the Act on Universal Conscription, the National Defence Council issued the so-called *Order of Reservists*[1] which laid down basic instructions for a systematic build-up of adequate reserves ready for action.

Until then the reserve, despite the relatively high number of men who had served in the armed forces for shorter or longer periods, practically did not exist. True, the military training was continuously extended to include not only all men serving in all branches of the armed forces but also the members of paramilitary organizations – the *Combat Groups*, the *Sport and Technology Association* and the youth organizations – and even large numbers of the civil population. Yet it was not clearly stated who was to be called up, in time of need, as a reservist. The reason for this was that there was possibly no clear idea on how the personnel replacement and further build-up of the army should proceed in detail.

As long as the NPA was a "volunteer" army, the "reserve" was increased each year by those soldiers who completed their two or three-year service, unless they did not decide to continue with their active service. The number of the latter was by no means small because the campaigns for further "recruitment" of serving soldiers were very intensive, due to constant manpower shortage in the army. Decisive for many of the "volunteers" was the perspective of becoming officer or NCO instead of starting again at the bottom in an agricultural cooperative.

The reservists of that time are, in quality, below the present level and may now play hardly any role in military planning. Since 1962 the situation has, however, changed. Twice each year, with the change

1 *Order of the National Defence Council on military service of the reservists (Order of Reservists).* Full text in "Volksarmee", Appendix 3/1962, p. 9–11.

of army personnel in the spring and autumn, the reserves are increased by 30 000 to 40 000 well-trained men. In the ten to fifteen years after their release from active service, the army authorities keep them combat ready by regularly calling them up for exercises and by encouraging them to have voluntary training in the so-called reservists' collectives.

Reservists with short-term training

To the former regular soldiers is to be added a second group of reservists who had only short-term training in the so-called *instruction courses for reservists* consisting of *basic courses* and *repetition courses* of four to six months duration. For training such reservists the NPA had established several regiments. They conduct training programmes for all services and branches as far as it is possible to train reservists in such short terms.

The genuine volunteers among these short-term servicemen are the *functionaries of the party* and mass organizations who are assisted in improving their basic military knowledge and acquiring a military rank corresponding to their party function. To this group belong also *members of the state administration, of other state organs such as courts and functionaries of economic organs.* They are given military ranks with the intention of tying them even closer to the regime.

Another strong group among the short-term servicemen are the *skilled workers and other specialists* who are, on the one hand, needed by industry and, on the other hand, also necessary for the troops in the event of military conflict. Specialist units have been established for military and technical training of these men so that they are not taken out of the production process for too long.

The numerically strongest group of those called up for short-term service are the *students from universities and technical colleges.* Even if these young men succeeded in avoiding the pitfalls of intensive recruiting campaigns in their schools for a voluntary service of two to three years, they still have to attend the short-term courses with the specialist troop units either before starting their studies or during school vacations. Students with serious physical deformities or illnesses are now practically the only ones able to avoid military service.

The army puts particular stress on the enlistment and training of these "intellectuals". Apparently it is important for the authorities to tie together the potential future leading strata and the armed forces at an early stage. In addition, the communist regime regards the training of these men in short-term courses as economically more advantageous as the economy is not deprived, for a longer period, of these valuable "productive forces".

Among the participants in the short-term courses there are also very many foremen, workshop managers, technicians, teachers and others who appear to be suitable to pass on the acquired knowledge or, at least, to influence favourably all men in the factories during the recruiting campaigns or in the Combat Groups, as well as in the organizations for training men before and after their military service.

These additional training duties must have taxed to the utmost the resources of the NPA which had, in the past, suffered – and because of weaker age classes even today still suffers – from shortage of personnel. Therefore the "reservists", that is the short-term servicemen, were used already in repetition courses as trainers in the basic courses.

Reserve officers and non-commissioned officers

The building up of reserves of officers and non-commissioned officers has been meeting with great difficulties.

The NPA is very short of good and "serviceable" reserve officers. The reason for this is that reserve officers are mainly civil functionaries who would in the event of war be almost indispensable in civil sphere; also the number of NPA officers transferred from regular service into reserve was rather small and in most cases the transfers were based on professional or political deficiencies.

The situation is not much better among the non-commissioned officers because those with the best training records – mostly soldiers with longer service – had to form, more or less voluntarily, the cadres for the factory Combat Groups and the Sport and Technology Association. The *collectives of reservists,* particularly in large enterprises, are important links in the apparatus designed not only to influence the citizens but also to keep up the spirit of the former servicemen, especially the officers and non-commissioned officers.

The Order of Reservists

In East Germany all men between eighteen and fifty are subject to compulsory military service; officers until sixty. The Order of Reservists states that all men of these age groups who are not in regular service have to belong to the NPA reserve; during a state of defence the reserve comprises all men until sixty.

The reserve is divided into two groups:

Group I – Reservists with the ranks of privates and non-commissioned officers as well as all men up to their 35th year of age who did not serve in the army; further all officers up to the rank of captain as long as they did not pass their 35th year, and officers with higher ranks until their 60th year.

Group II – Reservists with the rank of privates and non-commissioned officers as well as all men who did not serve in the army from thirty five to fifty (during a state of defence, until sixty); further all officers up to the rank of captain from thirty six to sixty.

The Reserve Group I comprises the best age classes and thus forms the actual reservoir of combat units of the NPA.

Reserve Group II will, on the other hand, form in the event of war the rear troops and organizations. Since supply to the troops and the cover of home territory and of the eventually occupied enemy territories is regarded as of paramount importance, it cannot be assumed that Group II is neglected.

The aim of the general reserve training to which the reservists are called up every three or four years is to preserve and improve the military efficiency of men. In Reserve Group I the duration of the training is one to three months, in Group II it is limited to two months. The maximum of reserve training for privates and non-commissioned officers is twenty one months, for the officers twenty four months.

If these directives are in the future consequently fulfilled the NPA will be considerably changed. Yet it would impose great strain on the army personnel, it was calculated that in the future some 5000 to 10 000 reservists with previous active service mainly officers and non commissioned officers would have to be called up all the time if every reservist were to do every three or four years the reserve training or exercises of the prescribed duration. And this number would even increase with time.

But in the years with weak influx of new recruits this would considerably alleviate the manpower shortage.

As these reservists are only partially trained in special courses, it can be assumed that the reservists may form about ten per cent of the actual strength of the formations. Thus the chronic shortage of non-commissioned officers could be less acute, though the reservists called up for exercises could not remove it completely because the reservist who is with the unit for only a short time not only helps but also demands attention for his military improvement. Anyway, the cadres of the NPA have been complaining that they are overburdened.

The NPA clearly differentiates in the military service of reservists between the *reserve exercises* and the *training of reservists*.

A reserve exercise is a two to three-month qualification service for soldiers released from basic military service.

The training of reservists is, on the other hand, the basic military training of men who are liable to service but did not actively serve. These are the men of the age classes which are no longer called up for regular active service of eighteen months and the men of the so-called surplus in the age classes which arises from the difference between the need for recruits and the actual strength of the class concerned. Their total varies, but from the later sixties on it is so considerable that the NPA will not be able, for many years, to train properly all those liable to service.

To enable that men of both these groups go through a basic military training, the NPA can call them up for a period of up to three months.

After basic training the soldiers are given the rank of reserve and from then on they are subject to training in reserve exercises to the same extent as the reservists with regular service - that is at least eighteen months. The time limit for the service of reservists is, however, more or less only on paper. In paragraph 9 of the Order of Reservists the regime has a loop-hole saying:

> The Defence Council can call up the reservists not only for regular reserve training and exercises but also for examining their combat readiness.

The reservists of East Germany will, like their colleagues in the other communist states, have to get used to being often taken from their enterprises or at night from their beds for hours, days or even weeks to take part in troop exercises, manoeuvres or mobilization exercises.

The *reserve officers* are also trained within the framework of the training of the reservists. The Order of Reservists explicitly enumerates the groups of persons for this training lasting up to six months:
– former active non-commissioned officers,
– non-commissioned officers of the reserve after several reserve exercises,
– soldiers and non-commissioned officers of the reserve after university or technical college final examinations,
– functionaries of the party, state administration and economic organs.

This comprises not only the reservists who had actively served before but also those who had received their basic training in the so-called training of reservists.

Even more important is the *social origin of the reserve officer candidates*. As the practice of training the reserve officers has shown the regime chooses for these functions only certain reliable people. A hint of this is contained in paragraph 7 of the Order according to which during a state of defence the army can immediately appoint as commissioned officers those reservists "who have through their professional activities or other qualifications the necessary personal and expert capability for commission".

In accordance with the needs of a communist state the corps of reserve officers is a mixture of:
– masters of military craft – the former active officers and non-commissioned officers,
– militarily educated intellectuals – the militarily trained men with university education,
– militarily trained general leading cadres – the functionaries of state and industry,
– political control organs – the militarily trained or untrained party cadres.

The military value of the corps of reserve officers will remain limited; their incorporation in the troops in time of need will not improve their value.

The training of reservists, which is a substitute service for men not called for active service, will also be conducted in the future in the same way as the training of short-term servicemen in the training units of the NPA. Former active servicemen are called up for exercises partially in the active (regular) units and partially in the training units.

The *reserve officer candidates* receive their training in separate courses at the officer schools of the NPA. *Reserve officers* do their training and exercises in the regular army units.

The existing training units consist basically of three training regiments of the NPA and some special units; they are able to train only a limited contingent of men – in the best case about 40 000 each year. The training of reservists is conducted especially by the land forces; the air force and the navy have only a limited interest in the reservists. With a population of 17 million and the Act on Universal Conscription hundreds of thousands of men are each year available for reserve exercises and training so the manpower potential of the reserve is practically limitless; an insurmountable obstacle is, however, the present size of the NPA.

The *promotion* of reservists depends on the acquisition of necessary qualifications for future commissions and ranks during the exercises.

Reserve officers can be promoted to majors and higher ranks only in cases of particular experience or efficiency. As the reserve officers of higher ranks are trained rather for tasks outside the NPA than for troop commands, the political qualifications are more relevant than the military ones.

The officers transferred from active service into reserve have hardly any chances of further promotion, unless they were released not because the army wanted to get rid of them but because they were given important posts outside the NPA.

The pay of reservists

The reservists of the NPA have not only special duties but also special rights. Among their duties – apart from that of regular reporting – is above all cooperation in the Combat Groups in factories and the Sport and Technology Association.

Some of the special rights are remarkable. In principle, the reservists should not suffer in any way because of their participation in the training or exercises. Non-commissioned officers with more than

10 years of active service and all reserve officers have the right to wear their uniforms on certain solemn occasions. Officers whose membership in the reserve had ended retain their rank with the addition (retd.). They have the same rights as reserve officers.

Economic problems of the reservists are dealt with in the *Pay Regulations*[2]. Enterprises, cooperatives etc. have to pay the reservists during the exercises or training their last salaries less 20 per cent. In addition they receive the military pay according to their ranks so that, on balance, nobody suffers financial loss. It is interesting that such a high proportion of military expenditure, namely 80 per cent of regular salaries and wages of the reservists, is imposed on the economy.

Military listing organization and total potential

The directives issued at the beginning of 1962 have created the basis of the build-up of sufficient reserves. In addition, they also form the legal framework for total militarization of the population. The decree of the National Defence Council on the military reserves has provisions extending widely over the present size of the army and the paramilitary organizations – especially the Combat Groups – will in time profit from them.

Since 1962, the basis of a purposeful review, administration and deployment of the entire military manpower potential is systematically being established. Listing of all men liable to military service and calling them up for training or exercises now come under the *regional and district military commands*. In the districts the so-called *district commissions for socialist military education* are assisting the district military commands.

It has to be assumed that the basis for successful mobilization in the personnel sphere has been completed. Thus East Germany would be now able to give its armed forces the necessary personnel backing in the event of need which the other communist states have had for many years. The NPA can now be regarded as an equal partner in the Warsaw Pact.

2 *The Pay Regulations* were issued on 24 January 1962 and published in "Volksarmee", Appendix 3/1962, p. 11–13.

Until the introduction of universal conscription and compulsory service the reserves, that is the number of more or less trained men, had grown to about 400 000. Since 1962 this number has been steadily growing. It can be assumed that in each year about 100 000 trained men are added to Reserve I and Reserve II. Even if this number has not been reached in recent years because of the weak age classes and of the mass fleeing of young men, the strong age classes of the coming years will overstep this number.

With about three quarters of a million men trained for active deployment within the armed forces the NPA now has at its disposal a potential which can cover all requirements.

PART FOUR

TRAINING AND SERVICE IN THE NPA

CHAPTER 10

POLITICAL EDUCATION, INDOCTRINATION AND CONTROL IN THE NPA

The practice of political indoctrination in the NPA clearly shows that the SED wants to educate, lead and use its military tool only as a communist "party-army", as an "army of a new, progressive type". The aims of political education, indoctrination and control of the troops and staffs, as well as their gradual strengthening, can be seen from a lecture delivered by the Minister of Defence, Army General Hoffmann, at a conference of the Institute of German Military History of East Germany and entitled "Ten years of the NPA":

> In accordance with the class character of our army, the leadership of the party and government were mainly concerned, in the basic and higher training of the cadres, with securing the unity of political and military qualifications. The training of so-called "only-specialists" was therefore inconsistent with the political character of our army as well as with the military requirements...
>
> Using the most diversified methods, the party guided the process which led to the establishment of a new, socialist German officers' corps. I am recalling the years 1956 and 1957 when hundreds of tried party workers joined the army as a party mission; I am recalling such fundamental documents as the decision of the Politburo of 14 January 1958 which represents an important milestone in the increased political and class education of the cadres...[1]

Taking priority before all the other purposes of training is, according to the tasks formulated by the party, that of forming a socialist

[1] *Ten years of the National People's Army — ten years of protecting peace and socialist construction in the GDR.* A lecture by the Minister of National Defence, Army General Heinz Hoffmann, at the conference of the Institute of German Military History, 16–17 September 1965 in Brandenburg-Havel. Translated from "Volksarmee", Documentation November 1965, p. 2.

fighter. Training schedules and utilization of soldiers' leisure confirm this priority. Political education, indoctrination and control, as "central factors", serve only one aim – to make soldiers of all ranks "weapon bearers of socialist thinking in the party way, feeling in the party way and acting in the party way" and thus to transform them into fanatical fighters for communist ideology:

> Political education is the main part of military training and its aim is to acquaint the soldiers with the teaching of Marxism-Leninism. In the course of political indoctrination the soldiers of the NPA are educated to be faihtful to, and to love, their workers' and peasants' state, the workers, the Socialist Unity Party of Germany and proletarian internationalism . . .[2]

Incessant surveillance, sharp criticism and self-critism are supposed to help in the acquisition of the desired political qualification. The supreme organs of the party are constantly concerned with the state of "development of consciousness, thinking of the men and their attitude to our policy". This is said in the report of the Politbüro delivered to the 9th plenum of the Central Committee of the SED:

> Generalized and partially superficial evaluation of the population's mood and opinion is often the reason that some arguments hold for a long time and that they are not always aggressively answered and definitely cleared.[3]

Since the political apparatus and all members of the party are entitled to control all soldiers of the NPA regardless of rank, the enforcement of purely military reliability and discipline would not be so difficult even in war, as long as the power of the party was not undermined. Political education is not, however, satisfied with only military reliability and discipline. It wants to, and also has to, achieve more: it must help to convince and persuade, to change the consciousness, and, finally, to communicate to all soldiers guiding

2 *Deutsches Militärlexikon* (German Military Encyclopaedia). Compiled by a team of the Military Academy of the National People's Army "Friedrich Engels". Published by the German Military Publishing House, East Berlin 1961, p. 51.

3 *Report of the Politburo to the 9th plenum of the Central Committee* "Volksarmee", special reprint 1965/6, p. 29.

models and behaviour norms of binding force so that political reliability becomes the end-product of the incessant persuasion during the re-formation process.

> We can claim, without exaggeration, that on no other category of the leaders of the party and state apparatus are placed such high demands as on the officers ...
>
> The majority of our soldiers are young workers from nationalized industries ... They have, to a great degree, a socialist attitude to work and have acquired a certain number of habits typical of our society.
>
> Despite this favourable prospect for socialist education of the members of the army, there are still many problems in this sphere. They are rooted in the insufficient socialist military indoctrination of our youth before military service, as well as in the weaknesses of political-ideological work in the army. In addition, military service in the conditions of a divided country demands from the conscripts political and human decisions such as they were never, in this respect, posed during the previous period of their lives. The readiness to defend his socialist fatherland, with weapon in hand, against any enemy while consciously taking up privations, burdens and physical hardships, and to be willing to sacrifice his life for the people and the socialist state, demands from the soldier a high degree of political conviction, moral attitude and military virtues.[4]

A cautionary statement by the Minister of Defence on the occasion of the 10th anniversary of the NPA's foundation shows that the leaders of East Germany and the top officers of the army are not very much satisfied with the results of indoctrination:

> ... our political work is ... not a purpose in itself but the means for a purpose ...
>
> This does not, at any rate, mean that we would not need to pay in the future less attention to the socialist education of soldiers. On the contrary, it must be increased because, firstly, the grade of political consciousness of the soldiers is a substantial factor in their readiness for action, and, secondly, we have not yet by far succeeded in giving the last soldier full clarity on the socialist military policy of our party and government and its consequencies.[5]

4 *Ten years of the National People's Army*, op. cit., p. 3.
5 Ibid., p. 4.

Commanders and party organizations have, in future, to pay more attention to ensure that our journals and information materials ... are even better used for the development of thinking ...[6]

In order to obtain objective clarity on the results of political education and indoctrination, the SED even applies modern scientific methods of opinion research within the NPA:

Sociological investigations of the Military Academy "Friedrich Engels" show, however, that some of our soldiers underestimate the war danger emanating from West German militarism and do not yet fully recognize the real danger of an imperialist aggression.[7]

Enlarged task: political indoctrination of the nation

Until the beginning of 1962 the NPA, as a volunteer army, concentrated in its political agitation mainly on its own ranks, trying to deepen and increase the soldiers readiness to serve, and also to create a proper image of the enemy; outside its ranks, the army mainly tried to influence the party and trade union functionaries to help in recruiting "volunteers". Since then, however, the style, art and methods of its political work have considerably changed.

The new syllabuses and training plans for political education and indoctrination, which are separate for officers, NCOs and privates, confirm, together with the directives for the work of the NPA among the population, that the party wants to make the army "a political school of the nation" within the framework of the communist "national mission".

The task of influencing the population was mentioned by Admiral Verner in his function as Head of the Chief Political Administration:

Our army's public work extends from cooperation of our officers in the sphere of agitation and propaganda among the population, to cooperation of commissions for socialist military education, links between the troops and units with the parents and factories of the conscripts, and to support of pre-military training for youth. And it also includes active participation in socio-political local life.

6 Ibid., p. 3.
7 Ibid., p. 4.

Herein we place great hopes in the officers' corps of our army, which bears a high degree of responsibility for socialist military education among the population. The officer of the National People's Army is especially able to explain to our workers the military balance in the world ... the fundamental difference in the character of armies existing on German soil and (to prove) that NPA is the bearer of the best military traditions in the history of the German people.[8]

Some of the reasons, important for the leadership of the SED and the NPA, why the NPA has to become an effective political school for the nation, were explained by Colonel Dr. Hübner on the 10th anniversary of the army:

1. The experience of the generation which had witnessed two world wars but had learnt to know personally only the armies of German imperialism, is still exerting its influence. This generation is that of the fathers of our present conscripts.

2. The thinking of our citiziens is also influenced by the not-yet-removed remnants of the pacifist illusions of the post-war years.

3. A certain role is played also by the fact that we must prepare, first of all, for a possible clash with the West German army. This puts especially high demands on the political and moral maturity of our soldiers.

4. The thinking of the population is to a considerable degree influenced today by the qualitative, new features of a potential war, as the result of the revolution in military technique (anxiety caused by the dangers of missile and nuclear warfare). Also widespread are the ideas of the existing "balance of deterrence" that is supposed to guarantee security, in some way.

5. And finally, one has to take into consideration the fact that in the conditions of the class struggle in Germany. West German imperialism is trying, through its mass media acting upon the population of the GDR, to present its aggressive preparations as harmless and to undermine our military morale.[9]

8 *Party decisions – the basis of party work in the NPA.* From the closing speech of the Deputy Minister of National Defence and Head of the Chief Political Administration Admiral Verner. "Volksarmee", Documentation, November 1965, p. 8.

9 *On some problems of military education.* Colonel Dr. Hübner at the conference of the Institute of German Military History on 15-17 September 1965. "Volksarmee", Documentation, November 1962, p. 22.

The official enumeration of reasons why the NPA must become the political school for the nation shows, between the lines, that the SED strongly reproaches the family, schools, teachers, the Pioneers' Organization for the children, the FDJ, the Sport and Technology Association, the trade unions etc. for having done unsatisfactory preparatory work for the strengthening of a higher military morale. And thus the aim of the party, the application of its ideology in the total sphere of life, can be realized only with the help of the army.

Target: creating a proper image of the enemy and hatred

As the NPA leadership itself admits, it is difficult to make its military intentions plausible. Many soldiers do not feel endangered. The majority of the population does not believe that the West will stage an attack against them. The Minister of National Defence, Hoffmann formulated this in the following way:

> The majority of the young soldiers did not know German imperialism and militarism from personal experience and has learnt about its anti-human policy, its aggressivness and adventurism only from history books. At the same time, their knowledge of the military exploits of the German working class against German imperialism is particularly weak. Therefore many young conscripts are not aware that German imperialism never in its history had any scruples about using its armies against its own countrymen . . .
>
> Where else, however, exept in the history of the class struggle of the German workers, can our soldiers learn to understand, with their hearts and reason, that the dividing line between friend and foe, especially in Germany, is a class line? In the military showdown the question "Who is my friend and who is my foe?" can be solely answered by pointing out the class, the state and the policy for which the soldier uses his weapons.
>
> . . . (we must) take earnestly the illusions about the Bundeswehr existing with some of our soldiers because they are slowing down the formation of conscious readiness to fight the enemy, in case of war, without compromise until his total annihilation in the positions from which he started his aggression.[10]

10 *Ten years of the National People's Army*, op. cit., p. 4.

The Political Chief Administration of the NPA insists, without any concessions, on education for hatred:

> Ardent love of the fatherland and limitless hatred against the enemy are for the socialist soldier indispensable qualities enabling him to remain always, and with his last breath, faithful to the oath of allegiance. These qualities cannot be created to order; nor are they created automatically. They are the results and the emotional expressions of deep conviction . . .[11]

Conscious of traditions through a new image of history

The basis of traditions in the NPA is to be the socialist consciousness of history and socialist partiotism. In political instruction, in indoctrination, in the controlled leisure of soldiers, in the syllabuses for obligatory education of officers and NCOs, "German military history" takes a constantly expanding place. Who and what is to be regarded as worthy of tradition was for a long time hotly disputed because the veteran communists could not put up with Scharnhorst, Gneisenau, Prussian military marches or Wehrmacht uniforms as symbols of the "military tradition of the working class". The dispute was taken as high as the Central Committee and was there decided, together with other military tasks.

> The great importance of consciousness of history in the fight between imperialism and socialism for peace and democracy in Germany was again stressed at the 10th session of the CC SED. The historians were given the binding task to communicate (to the people) the knowledge of the past so that the present could be properly assessed and the future mastered . . .
>
> The military historians have, with the publication of their new works, begun to contribute to the formation of a national image of history, a Marxist-Leninist analysis of German military history, and at the same time to develop the military policy of the workers' movement. Important materials for the teaching and propagation of military history in the NPA were elaborated.[12]

11 *Party decisions – the basis of party work in the NPA*, op. cit., p. 7.
12 Ibid., p. 8–9.

A typical example of devious methods used in political education for falsifying history are the statements made on the occasion of introduction of new uniforms. The then Minister of Defence Stoph argued for their introduction in a speech before the People's Chamber on 18 January 1956:

> There are important progressive traditions in the military history of our people which found their expression in the uniform. German imperialism and fascism, however, degraded the uniform as a symbol of military and national honour ... In the National People's Army, the German uniform will have a true patriotic meaning as an expression of a resolute readiness for the defence of our democratic achievements.

The illogicality of this argument is apparent. In reality, the "German uniform" was introduced in order to cover up the fact that the military forces of East Germany are a communist army under Soviet supreme command, for which there is no precedent in German history. The fact that millions of German soldiers in this "German uniform" gave, in the two world wars, excellent proof of personal bravery should be forgotten. Another remembrance, reshaped from the party's viewpoint, should be – according to Stoph – preferred in connection with this uniform:

> In these uniforms, but with red armbands, the armed workers in 1918 chased out the Kaiser; the Hamburg workers, miners from the Ruhr, workers and peasants from Saxony and Thuringia fought against the nationalist Freikorps and the reactionary Reichswehr. In these uniforms, in the Second World War, many officers and soldiers came forward in the National Committee "Free Germany" against the Hitler-fascist army.

For several months before the introduction of the new uniform the Central Committee had long discussions. It was decided to wait and see how the population would react to the new uniform of the police, which was also modelled closely on the old uniform. The new uniform brought, allegedly, an increase in the authority of the police among the population. Afterwards the CC decided to give back, to the NPA also, the uniform in the old style and colour.

After the issue of the directives of the 10th plenum of the CC SED, the army leadership celebrated the 10th anniversary of the NPA with festivals and meetings connected with giving new names

to the troops, ships and barracks, with the establishment of the
"Scharnhorst Order" and with the publication of battle songs and
numerous studies on military history. The new image of history now
presents as traditional the following events:

- 1525 the Great German Peasants' War,
- 1808 the Prussian history insofar as it can be connected with the
  reforms introduced by the Reichsfreiherr vom und zum Stein and
  the army reforms by Scharnhorst;
- 1813 the Wars of Liberation,
- 1919 the Bavarian Soviet Republic,
- 1919–1923 "the defensive battles of the German proletariat",
- 1936–1939 the fight of the International Brigades in the Spanish
  Civil War,
- 1939–1945 during World War II:
- the "fight of German anti-fascists" for the Soviet Union on the
  side of the Soviet military forces,
- the foundation of the National Committe "Free Germany" and
  the use of its members on the Soviet-German front,
- from 1949 deaths of members of the People's Police and NPA/
  Frontier Troops in the "defence of the state frontier of the GDR",
- 13 August 1961 "the saving of peace through the building of the
  anti-fascist protection wall (in Berlin) by the NPA".

Traditional links and a "military family tree" are cultivated,
especially in connection with the "alliance of brothers in arms" with
the Soviet Union. The Liberation Wars with the Battle of Leipzig
in 1813 are handled with this special view; they are examples *par
excellence* of the anti-Western, German-Russian alliance.

It is interesting to follow the changes in dealing with the National
Committee "Free Germany" in the course of time. While the Committee himself was declaring during the war that it was a movement
above party politics, aiming at the liberation of Germany from rule
by Hitler, the communists now deem it right to stress who had the
leadership of the National Committee.

> The foundation of the National Committee "Free Germany" was
> prepared, under the leadership of Wilhelm Pieck and Walter Ulbricht,
> by the Communist Party of Germany politically, programmatically
> and organizationally. Walter Ulbricht as member of the executive
> commission of the National Committee held the function of chair-

man of the operational section. He was proposed for this function by the Politburo because it was decisive for the proper orientation of the entire activity of the National Committee.[13]

Also the German Officers' League, which was founded in Lunovo near Moscow on 12 September 1943, that is 8 weeks after the National Committee, and which was expected to attract to the National Committee a number of opponents of Hitler within the officers' corps and the bourgeois camp, is today often presented in political instruction as an organization which came into being not so much on the initiative of the captive German officers as through the activity of the communist Ulbricht:

> By his convincing arguments, his revolutionary impatience, his open and fighting character, comrade Ulbricht was able to create for himself respect and authority in these cricles. Thus he came back to Moscow from Gorki with 25 delegates for the foundation conference of the German Officers' League.[14]

Props for thinking and conscience

Political instruction and indoctrination try to give numerous props for the development and strengthening of ideology. Among them are definitions on the "just and unjust wars" and the "ten commandments of socialist morale".

The war doctrine makes a basic differentiation between "just" and "unjust" wars. It is contained in the textbook *History of the CPSU(B)* which was based on Stalin's authority and regarded as official and binding until 1956. The *Military Encyclopaedia*, published by the NPA in 1961, still takes the same line in its entry on "just, progressive wars" which are defined as:

> wars of oppressed classes against the oppressor classes; national and colonial liberation wars; wars of nations against the threatening national subjugation; wars of the victorious proletariat for the defence

13 Major Willy Wolff: *For the life interests of the German nation – on the role of Comrade Walter Ulbricht in the National Committee "Free Germany"*. "Volksarmee", special reprint 1963/3, 20 July, p. 2.

14 Ibid.

of socialism against imperialist states. – Various categories of just wars can be united into one war for common aim.

There were just wars in the old social orders; they are, however, particularly common in the present time. Just wars are resolutely supported by the international working class and by the communist and workers' parties.[15]

On the other hand, the "unjust wars", according to the same definition, are:

> wars of imperialist conquest, wars for the suppression of revolutionary movements of the oppressed and exploited classes; wars for the suppression of national and colonial liberation movements; wars for the strenghtening of exploitation; wars against the workers' and peasants' power, against socialist states.

> The international working class and communist and workers' parties resolutely fight against unjust wars when they could not prevent their start.[16]

While the war is generally defined as the "continuation of policies of certain classes by force", the "war for the defence of the socialist fatherland" is regarded as the "highest form, a new quality of the just war".[17]

With these definitions any war started by communists can be declared a "just war". The aggressive war by North Korea against noncommunist South Korea in the summer of 1950 is also termed as a "just war"; the defence by the South Koreans and the aid given to them by the United Nations were, on the other hand, an "unjust war".

In this way, any other war, which would for example start with an attack on the defenceles population of a parliamentary democracy by the armoured units of a "people's democracy", would be defined as a "just war". "Unjust", on the other hand, would be declared the defence by that nation. The axiom of the communist doctrine is that the "socialist state, true to its nature, can conduct only

---

15 *Deutsches Militärlexikon* (German Military Encyclopaedia), op. cit., p. 227.

16 Ibid., p. 234.

17 Ibid., p. 222 and 234.

just wars"[18]. Thus the Soviet attack on Finland in 1939 was a "just war"; and thus also the suppression of the Hungarian popular rising in the autumn of 1956 by Soviet troops was "just".

Political instruction is trying to help the soldiers on their "road to become new, socialist men" by such props as the "ten commandments of socialist morale" proclaimed by Ulbricht at the Fifth Congress of the SED in 1958 and incorporated in the new party programme in January 1963

1. Thou shalt always stand for the international solidarity of the working class and all workers, as well as for the unbreakable alliance of all socialist countries.

2. Thou shalt love thy fatherland and always be ready to put all thy strength and capabilities for the defence of workers' and peasants' power.

3. Thou shalt help to do away with the exploitation of man by man.

4. Thou shalt do good deeds for socialism because it leads to a better life for all workers.

5. Thou shalt act in the construction of socialism in the spirit of mutual help and comradely cooperation, respect the collective and heed its criticism.

6. Thou shalt protect and increase people's property.

7. Thou shalt always strive for the improvement of thy performance, be thrifty and strengthen socialist work discipline.

8. Thou shalt bring up thy children in the spirit of peace and socialism as all-rounded, educated people of firm character, and physically steeled.

9. Thou shalt lead a clean and decent life and respect thy family.

10. Thou shalt practise solidarity with the peoples fighting for their national liberation and defending their national independence.[19]

With these ten commandments of socialist morale the SED wanted to replace the Christian Ten Commandments which, allegedly, are only a tool to support the slave-owners, feudal lords, capitalists and imperialists.

Open attacks against religion, such as the article *Religion – the opiate of the people* in "Volksarmee" in 1958 are now rarer. Then

18 *The Large Soviet Encyclopaedia*, 2nd edition 1951, p. 533.
19 Quoted from "Volksarmee", Appendix 15/1962, p. 21.

for instance the FDJ organization in one army unit formed a „Youth Forum"

> in which some 40 soldiers participated in order to acquire clarity on the role of religion in present time. The numerous questions showed that many comrades did not yet recognize the essence of religion. Hence they do not understand, either that religion is the opiate of the people, as Karl Marx teaches us. But he who wants to become a real young socialist must clearly understand this.[20]

The NPA is also eagerly helping to replace church weddings through a "socialist form of conclusion of marriage".

Means and ways of influencing and controlling

The everyday life in the NPA offers the party organs and organizations wide possibilities – corresponding to the "social role" assigned to them by the party – to form the consciousness and change it as well as to control the mood of soldiers. On the occasion of the 10th anniversary of the NPA the division of tasks in this sphere was defined in the following way:

> ... in the military sphere (there is) as before an increase in the consciousness, a strengthening of the will to victory and a trust in victory, a development of initiative of soldiers and of their conscious efforts for military mastery as the foremost task of the party and FDJ organizations.[21]
> ... (it is) the task of political organs to enable the basic party organizations to put through party decisions, to influence more effec-

20 First Lieutenant Kramer: *Religion – the opiate of the people – A good form of propaganda – Other units should follow this example.* "Volksarmee", 17 April 1958.

21 *To educate the members of the NPA to conscious striving for military mastery.* Colonel Teller, Deputy Head of the Chief Political Administration of the NPA at the conference of the Institute of German Military History 15–17 September 1965. "Volksarmee", Documentation, November 1965, p. 14.

tively the development of socialist consciousness of all members of
the army . . .[22]

The dogma of the leading role of the party is valid also in the
armed forces and this provides the most important means of influencing and controlling all troops, staffs and individual soldiers without
interruption. Foremost among them are the special rights of political
organs, SED and FDJ funcionaries (i. e. rights of interference and
objection) and the recklessly practised principle of "education by the
collective". Then come the candidature and membership in the SED
and FDJ basic organizations within the NPA, the appointments to
functions in their apparatus, and army commissions and posts of
authority and power. They are the driving force of the collectives;
they dictate the norms and enforce, through psychological terror in the
collective, censures for defects and public repentance, the subordination of the unpopular officers, NCOs or privates.

There are further means in this sophisticated system, essential
in influencing and controlling the army, which may not be discussed
in East Germany but which are known from the NPA soldiers
who have fled to the West. Among them are:
- party secretaries in troops and staffs have their own channels of
  communication;
- heads of security sections in party regions outside the NPA have
  the right to control officers and soldiers in the barracks; they report
  directly to the Central Committee;
- the Ministry of State Security MSS has its own liaison officers
  down to the battalions. Though they wear the NPA uniform, they
  execute orders of the MSS;
- agents of the State Security Service have in the units secret
  informers among the soldiers who submit written reports on their
  observation of the personnel of all ranks.

The reports and control measures include systematic surveillance
of soldiers' behaviour as well as the effects of all educational steps,
above all:
- the influence of political views brought by soldiers from their
  families;
- outward attitude, behaviour, eagerness in service, military morale;

22 Ibid., p. 15.

- private political conversations with positive or negative views;
- participation in the SED and FDJ activities;
- purchase of newspapers, reading of books and publications, obligatory communist reading;
- attitude to church;
- listening to Western radio and television broadcasts;
- friends and acquaintances outside barracks;
- participation, through self-commitments, in the socialist emulation movements.

Political education as the most important measure, from the military-pedagogic point of view, is in full accord with the Soviet model. It is conducted methodically with the aim to turn the soldiers into fanatical fighters as required by the communist army. A closer analysis shows that the system of political education has been transplanted from the Soviet Union without proper regard to specific German conditions and that it is – even when compared with agitation and propaganda in civil life – considered by the young soldiers to be too comprehensive, too hard and alien. The ordinary soldier is in many ways suffering from the enforced persuasion which may seem quite natural to a functionary to whom it is justified by the communist monopoly of "correct cognition of objective laws of nature and society".

The soldiers react very sharply against constant repetition of "old truths". The political officers are, on the other hand, mostly convinced that only incessant repetition leads to qualitative changes in the consciousness of those to be influenced.

Extremely exaggerated, almost continuously conducted campaigns of self-commitment lead near to breaking point in the soldiers' will to give a good performance and show enthusiasm. The enforced emulation system with its rewards and awards seduces soldiers to falsification because nobody wants to reverse the once-started road to higher performance, whether it be privates, NCOs or officers. Even the Minister of Defence, Army General Hoffmann gave vent to his surprise that almost every second soldier now bears the proud title of the "Best". The military press often attacks the fact that even non-swimmers have the silver badge of all-round sportsmen. In this system of rather primitive dictatorship in education and thinking, it seems almost impossible to avoid the danger of over-saturation. The results are tendencies to ideological disillusionment, strong defensive reactions, increasing mistrust because models are often artificially created and are known to be false.

The schedules include political instruction, topical political information, party schooling and study circles on given themes. In addition, there are schooling courses, seminars, evening universities of Marxism-Leninism etc.

Basically the political schooling is separate for officers, NCOs and privates, for party members and non-communists. It is only natural that generals also take part in the schooling.

Off duty, the political schooling of soldiers, separated from the party schooling for party members and candidates, is organized by the basic organizations of the FDJ for each unit. The level of this schooling in the soldiers' leisure is still (and often) criticized by the Chief Political Administration of the NPA. The criticism is, above all, aimed against the "hunt for figures" by the FDJ functionaries:

> One of the defects in the work of the FDJ was – and partially is still – that the organizations tackle the problem of assisting in education mainly from the purely organizing standpoint, by creating too many circles, taking over various youth institutions, hunting for self-commitments without combining these activities in a satisfactory way with the political-ideological education of their members.[23]

Political instruction for officers takes eight hours monthly; it is conducted by the political deputy of the regiment commander or his assistant. Eight hours are, however the minimum study required by the party. The officers have also been obliged, since 1963, to study social sciences in their spare-time. Their study is divided into two semesters during the training year and it requires much time and energy since the obligatory lectures and syllabuses are very comprehensive. For the ambitious officers there is also a host of additional literature to be read. The officers have to pass two examinations every year and the results of these exminations form an integral part of cadre files, playing a very important role in their promotion.

Political instruction for the NCOs and privates includes four hours weekly; instruction for the NCOs is conducted by the assistant of the political deputy or by the company commander. The

23 *To educate the members of the NPA to conscious striving for military mastery,* op cit., p. 19.

NCOs – generally platoon leaders – who are used as leaders of instruction groups for the privates are obliged to study privately and have to present their written reports on given themes to their officers. Since 1964 also the NCOs have had to pass every year an examination in political instruction.

The Chief Political Administration publishes, at the beginning of each school year, prescribed standard themes and puts down in detail the current political line, in accordance with the decisions of the party congress. Besides this the administration constantly works on directives and suggestions for dealing with new political problems and themes for short lectures within the framework of "political information".

In the present phase the following main themes are obligatory for political instruction:
– the transition period from socialism to communism,
– the national mission of the GDR,
– the peace offensive of the socialist camp,
– the aggressive policy of West Germany,
– Vietnam and our solidarity,
– the inevitability of the decline of capitalism and U. S. imperialism,
– "Who is thy friend and who the foe?"
– the Warsaw Pact – the socialist coalition,
– report on the study of the military press,
– discussion on the films of the NPA Film Studio,
– the socialist military tradition of the NPA,
– the oath of allegiance and loyalty to the banner,
– connection between the Hitler Wehrmacht and the Bundeswehr.

Political instruction is unpopular with the privates in general, and also many of the NCOs do not like it. Current demands in the military press to make the instruction more interesting show that the leadership is not satisfied. Dullness does not sell well.

The style and principles of political instruction are apparently not able to exclude critical comparisons between theory and practice and satisfactorily to explain, in favour of the SED, the contradiction between promises and reality, between the pipe dreams and the sober reality of everyday life. Even the powerful and accomplished apparatus is not able to prevent the young people in East Germany from independent thinking. The leadership knows this handicap but – in a typical communist way of thinking – sees the remedy only in more intensified political instruction. The final result must, therefore, be very doubtful.

Military-political literature

In an effort to apply Soviet experience the SED began early, with the support of the Soviet Military Administration in Germany, to produce military and military-political literature as well as reading materials for soldiers to bolster their morale. As early as 1952, when rearmament started, the most important Soviet works had been translated. Originally the military literature – including newspapers and periodicals for the various "armed forces" – grew rampantly, but from 1956 on, the production has been systematically expanded and has reached a considerable volume.

In 1962 the bibliography of the *Deutscher Militärverlag* (German Military Publishing House)[24] showed more than 800 titles. This publishing concern was founded in 1956 as the Publishing House of the Ministry of National Defence and later changed to its present name. In its entire activity, including the printing plant, it is directed by the Ministry of National Defence; its head is Colonel W. Lauterbach, member of the Central Revision Commission of the SED. In its first ten years the German Military Publishing House had published, according to its own data[25], 1339 titles in 41 479 450 copies.

Among the newspapers and periodicals of the German Military Publishing House which are available to the general public are:

– *Volksarmee* (People's Army), a weekly newspaper. (Its slogan is: "For our Workers' and Peasants' Power".) At least once a month it publishes a documentation appendix containing mainly the decisions and announcements of the SED. – In 1961 it was awarded the golden Merit Medal of the NPA and in 1966 the Battle Order of Merit "For the People and the Fatherland" in bronze.

– *Armeerundschau* – *Magazin des Soldaten* (Army Review – Soldier's

24 *Bibliographie des Deutschen Militärverlages (Bibliography of the German Military Publishing House)*, compiled by Fritz Becker, complete up to 31 November 1962, East Berlin, 160 pages.

25 "Neues Deutschland", 25 May 1966.

Magazine), illustrated, partly multi-coloured monthly magazine with about 100 pages.
- *Sport und Technik* (Sport and Technology), monthly newspaper, organ of the Sport and Technology Association (STA). Awarded the silver Merit Medal of the NPA.
- *Zeitschrift für Militärgeschichte* (Journal of Military History), published every two months (120 pages) by the Institute of German Military History.
- *Funkamateur* (Radio Amateur), a monthly publication, with about 50 pages; deals with electronics and is designated for general readership.
- *Aero-Sport,* a monthly for air sports and parachuting.
- *Poseidon,* a monthly for diving sports, underwater photography.

Apart from these publications available to the general public there are many periodicals for army use only, such as *Militärwesen* (Military Affairs), a journal for military politics and theory; *Marinewesen* (Naval Affairs), *Gefechtsausbildung,* (Combat Training); *Rückwärtige Dienste* (Rear Services) etc.

The paramilitary organizations placed under the Ministry of Interior also have their own newspapers or periodicals published by the Publishing House of the Ministry of Interior.

The "Marxist- Leninist military literature" is addressed – as the publishers state – not only to the "commanders and political workers of the NPA" but also to the "activists of political parties and mass organizations, members of the police, commanders of the Combat Groups, university teachers and students, librarians, booksellers, journalists and all other persons connected with our literature". Military training should be "supported and deepened" by reading good novels.

The literature of the German Military Publishing House is to be displayed, according to a recommendation of the Free German Trade Union Congress (FDGB) (Information Gazette of the FDGB, Nr. 17/1963), in the trade union and factory libraries "so that it can be used by the basic organizations of the STA, units of the Combat Groups, order groups of the FDJ, groups of reservists and young conscripts in general".

Among the authors of the 800 titles published by 1962 were at least 225 Russians and 90 of unknown, but not German, nationality. Among the 1339 titles published in the first ten years, i.e. until May

1966, there were 385 translations. In addition, the works of most German military writers are almost entirely based on Soviet sources. The Russian authors prevail not only in general and specialized literature but also in other publishing spheres.

In the entire bibliography there is hardly a book, apart from the works of Clausewitz, which could give those who are interested an understanding of western military thinking and planning. This is not surprising in view of the attitude of the party. (However, the works on the experiences of German and other non-communist armies in the World War II as well as the latest American war experiences are studied at the "Friedrich Engels" Military Academy in Dresden.)

It is interesting that in the libraries of the NPA there is apparently no place for such a military writer as Mao Tse-tung. In the section "History of Wars" there is no work which evaluates the important military campaigns of Mao. A Russian description of the "glorious Chinese People's Liberation Army" is "out of print".

The NPA appears to have some difficulties also with the Soviet standard work *Military Strategy* edited by Marshal Sokolovskiy. This book takes a relatively realistic stand in the evaluation of the strength of western armies; it was published in the Soviet Union for the first time in 1962 (since then a total of 60 000 copies have been printed), but the NPA edition was published in the GDR only in 1966 (a West German edition was published in 1965).

It is also worthy to note that all books and publications are inexpensive.

CHAPTER 11

MILITARY TRAINING OF THE NPA

Theoretical basis of training

The "Deutsches Militärlexikon" (German Military Encyclopaedia) edited by a group of the *"Friedrich Engels" Military Academy of the National People's Army* in Dresden, defines military training as

> Entirety of all measures which are systematically organized in the socialist armies for the formation of socialist fighters (units, troops, forces and staffs), their equipment with a system of scientific-technical, political and military knowledge, capabilities and skills, as well as formation of their socialist consciousness and behaviour, among other things also their military discipline. The aims of training are decided by the demands of defending the socialist fatherland under the conditions of rocket and nuclear warfare.
>
> The process of training comprises education and instruction. Important parts of military training are political training, tactical training, physical training and rifle training.[1]

In training as in all other matters the Soviet Army is the teacher and model. The first cadres of the East German army originated in the Red Army or were trained by it. Soviet assistance is still plentiful either in the form of training the NPA officers in specialist units or military academies, or in the specialist training of entire special units; in addition there are Soviet liaison officers in all higher staffs of the NPA. Also important in this connection are the joint exercises of the NPA and the Soviet Army, land, air and naval forces.

The closeness of relations between the NPA and the Soviet Army can also be seen from the publications of the *Deutscher Militärverlag* (German Military Publishing House) subordinated to the Ministry of National Defence (earlier it was called the Publishing House of the Ministry of National Defence). A considerable number of its publications are unchanged reprints of Soviet originals.

1 *Deutsches Militärlexikon*, op. cit. p. 50/51.

The examples and models presented to the NPA soldiers are always based on Soviet experiences and reports. Thus, for example, the publication "Stratagems and Resources" says:

> In the Great Patriotic War, the Soviet soldiers were able to trick the enemy cleverly, to confuse him, to bluff him by the surprise and speed of their operations and to mar his plans and measures.
> It is the task of every soldier to study these numerous combat experiences and to evaluate them.[2]

The textbooks for the officers of the NPA are generally only extracts from the vast Soviet military literature. They were, however, taken over without any changes and thus they try to apply on the men of an industrially and technically developed country the ideas and practices tailored for the mentality of the Soviet people, a product of typical agrarian society.

In the ten years of the existence of the NPA, several problems came to the fore in the training of young Germans which are typical for the GDR and which do not exist in the Soviet Army or in other communist armies. The most difficult problem is the attitude of the NPA soldiers to their employment against Germans whether they are citizens of East Germany, inhabitants of Berlin or West Germany, members of the police or frontier guards or of the Bundeswehr. This is not only a theoretical question – in the popular rising in June 1953 the armed forces, supposed to be the shield of the Ulbricht regime, partly failed. The question especially acute for the NPA/Frontier Troops is whether they should shoot at their own countrymen.[3]

The SED leadership knows only too well that the question of willingness of the soldiers to fight against the Germans is the touchstone of the usefulness of the NPA. This, however, shows to what a great extent the NPA is not an ordinary army but one to be used for civil war:

> Through the body and blood of every member of the NPA must penetrate the realisation that every soldier of NATO, even if he is of German origin, who raises arms against the socialist camp, is not his brother but his foe.

2 *Kriegslist und Findigkeit* (Stratagems and Resources), Publishing House of the Ministry of National Defence, East Berlin, 1956, p. 23.

3 Compare the "firing order" on page 220.

Our brothers in West Germany are the patriots fighting under the leadership of the illegal Communist Party of Germany ...[4]

The theoretical basis of the training of the NPA units are the *Service Regulations* and other so-called *Training Principles* such as directives, orders, programmes etc. They are very detailed, lay down the training for inter-connected spheres (branches, troops, forces) and tie the training instructors with prescribed time limits and themes.

Permanent political persuasion, coupled with technical-tactical training based almost entirely on Soviet methods, is supposed to help the NPA leadership in
– turning the soldiers into convinced communists,
– educating them to iron discipline and unconditional obedience,
– training excellent weapons specialists,
– amalgamating units ready for employment,
– closely coordinating formations for combat and
– assuring constant and high readiness for action.

To achieve these targets the personnel conducting the training have to show
– purposefulness in political work,
– strong military discipline,
– purposeful planning,
– good preparatory work,
– personal initiative and
– uncompromising attitude.

Planning and preparation of training

The uniform principles for training are laid down by the Deputy Minister of National Defence charged with training.

The *Administration of Training* in the Ministry of National Defence is not the only organ responsible for training. The leaders of special troops also have their say, for example the chiefs of administrations of armour, motor transport service or rear services and the com-

4 Götz Scharf, *Über den moralischen Faktor im modernen Krieg* (On the moral factor in the modern war). The Publishing House of the Ministry of National Defence, East Berlin, 1959.

mands of the NPA/Air Force and Air Defence as well as NPA/People's Navy.

Though the ministry has already laid down the details of the training, the troops are nevertheless required to go even further in planning the training of their units.

According to the principle of the so-called *one-man command* the commanders and leaders of the units are fully responsible for the preparation and conduct of their soldiers' training. Thus unsatisfactory results in the training of a unit or troop leads to disciplinary action against the leader or commander. Inspections and surprise visits by superiors and by special commissions are therefore received with great anxiety.

Meetings and instruction courses are used for the preparation of the training. In addition all superiors and training officers are requested to use their leisure for studying the training instructions. General service and obligatory study during the leisure lead to the exhaustion of the NPA cadres. The volume of obligatory study literature is a great brake on the proper preparation and conduct of the training.

The *Soviet advisers* attached to the higher staffs of the NPA are active not only in the planning and preparation of training but also in the control and surveillance. The advisers have always at least the same rank as the commanders of the formations to which they are attached; the possess special qualifications for their office and are regarded as authorities in their sphere. They are further proof of the *Gleichschaltung* of the NPA training with that of the Soviet Army.

During the preparatory time for the new training year the unit is often spurred to overfulfil the existing instructions or to create new installations. With great inventiveness, and also very economically, installations are constructed for combat training, firing practice, driving instruction and physical training which create nearly real combat conditions.

Besides the systematic preparation and construction of useful training installations the responsible leaders of units are faced with the problem of planning the employment of the training instructors since the permanent shortage of NCOs forces them to emergency solutions.

The course of training

The introduction of compulsory military service in January 1962 led to the shortening of active service from 24 to 18 months. This necessitated changes in the course and system of training; these however had their effect only from the autumn of 1962. Thus the *basic training* was reduced from six to four weeks and the training year now begins at the beginning of December instead of 1st of January.

The basis of the new training programme now is the basic military service of eighteen months, prescribed by the law, and the change of personnel which takes place regularly every six months.

The training was divided into three yearly periods. In the spring and autumn enlistments and releases about a third of the NPA personnel are always changed. The newly enlisted soldiers of the first half-year are mostly incorporated in their parent units but for the purposes of training they are for four weeks concentrated in *recruit units*.

Apart from political indoctrination the greatest part of the available time is used for
– military physical training,
– drill training,
– instruction in the use of weapons, firing practice,
– field training, combat training, combat drill,
– special training of troops,
– technical motor transport training,
– specialist training such as protection against the ABC weapons, engineer training etc.

Night training is given particular attention within the total training. Between one third and one half of the training in the terrain, combat training, special training, firing practice, driving training and specialist training takes place during the night.

A special part of the training is the stay in *camps* which are occupied by all troops in winter and summer. In these camps, mostly located in the training areas, the soldiers live, under war conditions, in tents for two or four weeks. Also food supplies are, during this time, very much like in war. Training in the camps is as realistic as possible and comprises training of companies, battalions and partly also regiments as well as firing practice. Every soldier has to attend, during his basic military service, three training camps.

Service in barracks is strict but restricted in time.

The *administration, maintenance and care of weapons, instruments and vehicles* as well as of other equipment and clothing take a larger proportion of time. Special *reconditioning days,* mainly after larger exercises, are used both for technical training and instruction of the cadre personnel.

The training schedules leave only little time for learning service regulations, instructions and data for tactical (terrain), technical and political training and education. These has to be studied mainly in the off-duty time.

Military basic training

In the first four weeks, the recruits are trained, in many formations, within their own units but in special sections or platoons. During this time the young soldiers have to get used to – as in all other armies in the world – military discipline and order. They are also given a basic knowledge of the various branches of military training.

In this early stage, the future specialists and – so far this did not happen before enlistment – also the future non-commissioned officers are selected.

Physical and mental demands on the recruits are high and the basic training does not give the soldiers much leisure. They have to spend eight hours daily in training and in addition there are duties in barracks such as cleaning of the sick quarters and living quarters, cleaning of equipment and maintenance of clothing which has to be done in leisure time. Only on Saturday is there more alleviation from service and Sundays are mostly free.

The entire time of the basic training is on average divided in the following way:

– drill	15 per cent
– terrain (tactical) training	10 per cent
– military physical training	12 per cent
– weapons training and firing practice	20 per cent
– special training	18 per cent
– political education and instruction on behaviour on and off duty	25 per cent

Service during basic training is thus different from that in the western armies. The stress on political education and a firm connection between political and military instruction are quite obvious.

Some themes of the individual training branches are:

a) drill: close order drill, saluting with or without cap, with or without arms, individually or in close order, "attention!" posture, turns and marching and also parade step.

Close order drill and other parts of the drill are practised every day.

b) terrain training: behaviour and movements of soldiers in the terrain. Observation of field of combat and reporting to the commanding officer. Cover, camouflage and construction of field fortifications.

Generally the recruits are given, in the very early stage of their basic training, a demonstration on the deployment of their unit or even of a larger formation of their service. It is not unusual for the combat formations to conduct these exercises with live ammunition.

c) Military physical training: exercises facilitating relaxation, mobility and flexibility as well as endurance; exercises with partners and combat games. At the end of the military basic training the recruits have to prove their physical fitness in a test.

d) Weapons training and firing: weapons knowledge on small arms such as carbines, pistols and submachine guns, including ammunition. Firing practice, firing positions and taking part in one training and combat firing exercise with small arms.

e) Special training: included herein is a knowledge of the ABC weapons and protection against them, basic medical training with personal hygiene and first aid.

f) The barracks routine training includes the following themes:
– disciplinary and complaints procedure regulations,
– behaviour on and off duty,
– duties and rights of the soldiers,
– soldiers' rights in connection with leave of absence, rations and pay,
– garrison and guard duties. (The soldiers on basic training are relieved of guard duties.)

The recruits are rarely allowed to leave the barracks or given leave of absence. The length of duty and the high demands as well as the aims of the training do not permit this.

Individual training

In the individual training the soldiers are trained specially for the functions which they have to fulfil in the current half year of service.

Training in the use of weapons in the terrain and other terrain training is based on drill which is regarded as especially important. The individual stages of the drill are drill in forming ranks, saluting, turns, and marching, drill with the weapons, combat drill. The "German Military Encyclopaedia" defines drill as

> a method of military training. Included in the drill is the uniform repetition of basic military action until this leads to a corresponding skill in performing the action automatically, even under most difficult conditions of rocket and nuclear warfare. In the socialist armies the drill is confined to military training and is related to training the soldiers to a conscious performance of tasks and to developing the creative initiative of the masses ... [5]

In the second or third service half-year the individual training of the soldiers differs from the first or second service half-year insofar as:

a) the instruction schedules of the first or second service half-years are repeated, deepened and completed,

b) a *mutual exchangeability* is reached.

That means that the soldiers receive in the second and/or third service half-year additional training in one or two other functions. Thus the gun ammunition handlers are trained also as gun loaders, gun loaders as gun pointers, gun pointers as drivers, drivers as radio operators etc.

In addition all soldiers who did not receive any training in *communications* are, in their individual training during the second service half-year, acquainted with the principles of modern communications systems. They must be qualified so that they could, if need arises, operate a wireless set.

The training hours in the second and third service half-year of the individual training are practically the same as in the first half year.

---

5 *Deutsches Militärlexikon* (German Military Encyclopaedia) op. cit., p. 99.

Main stress is given here, too, on training in the terrain, equally by day as by night.

Training in the sections or crews

Already during the stage of the individual training in the first half-year exercises of larger formations are carried out. These are not only instruction exercises in which the recruits are acquainted with the deployment and efficiency of the weapons of their services but also formation exercises in which the recruits, too, participate.

After the conclusion of individual training begins the cooperation of soldiers in the smallest units, i. e. in sections and in the crews. Now, for the first time, the older soldiers are trained with the new conscripts in the same units. The training in sections now takes more than half of the available training time.

The themes of the section training correspond to those of other armies, apart from the political education. Night training takes almost the same time as day training; also firing practice is conducted at day and at night. Combat in towns, combat with the unexpectedly appearing enemy and surmounting water obstacles are among the important training themes in all units. A frequent feature of the training programme ist also the technical service under field conditions and combat drill.

Training in the platoons (platoon training)

Platoon training belongs to the same training phase as training in the sections and they merge together. Platoon training, too, is conducted mainly in the terrain.

The units spend part of the time in the training areas and camps or carry out their training near their garrisons.

Apart from combat training the schedules also provide for repetition of individual and section training. Weapons and combat drill has to be finished before the start of company or battery training.

In this phase, for the first time, cooperation of different arms is practised; also the radio operators and other communications experts are included.

Political education is, however, continued even during the prolonged training in the camps.

Military physical training now aims at sports supporting physical efficiency and includes training for individual and "collective records" in cross-country running, swimming in uniform of entire units (platoons) etc.

Platoon training, which still affords close attention to the individual, is a kind of a finishing school for the individual soldier before he starts his next training phase within a larger framework.

Training in the companies, battalions and regiments

Training in companies (batteries), battalions and regiments – corresponding perhaps to the formation training in the western sense – is the longest and most important phase. In each service half-year, two or three months are allocated for it. During this phase divisional exercises and manoeuvres on the military regional level are also carried out. They conclude each training half-year and they are, in the last years, done increasingly in cooperation with the Soviet troops. After these exercises the units always return to their company (battery) training.

This phase is divided in approximately the following way:
– combat training including formation training   50 per cent
– political education   10 per cent
– physical training   8 per cent
– drill   5 per cent

The remaining 27 per cent can be divided into the repetition of individual, section and platoon training and also include a reserve for special employment of the units (help with the harvest, labour service, larger manoeuvres etc.).

The main stress in this phase of the training is put on *warlike field training*.

The following training schedules are prescribed for the infantry, armoured troops and artillery.

a) The combat training of the *infantry units*. i. e. also of the motorized infantry companies, reconnaissance companies etc. includes:

- movements of the company in extended order with or without combat vehicles in the terrain,
- attack, from the approach to the enemy to the charge; combat in depth; behaviour under atomic attack; pursuit of the enemy;
- attack after concentration in an organized position; camouflage of an intended attack; preparation; charge; fight for positions, defence against counter-attacks; attack on the flanks and in the rear of the enemy; use of combat vehicles and going over to pursuit or penetration by assault;
- attack over a water obstacle, with preparation of weapons and vehicles for fording (wading); thrust in depth;
- engagements with parachutists and "counter-revolutionaries"; reconnaissance; encirclement; assault and destruction;
- defence with occupying a defensive position; construction of the position; coordination of fire plans; preparation of the combat and going over to assault;
- reconnaissance and cover by the company;
- construction of, and life in, a camp;
- behaviour during railway, sea and air transport.

An important part of this training is also field firing with differentiated points of impact.

b) The *armoured troops*

Particularly important in the training of the *armoured troops* are the following items of the schedule for an armoured company:
- attack from the concentration area through the section of deployment up to the assault; repulsing of counter-attacks and pursuit of the evading enemy;
- attack over a water obstacle and difficult terrain with anti-tank defences; preparation of tanks; approach; "forcing the main obstacles"; construction of bridgeheads and penetration;
- fire and counter thrust power in defence with digging in; fire plans; plans for the cooperation and terrain preparation for the thrust attack;
- march, transport and camping;
- field firing.

c) On the training schedule of the *artillery units* are the following items (specially designed for battery training):

— movements in extended order;
— attack under the artillery preparation fire and under the support of armoured and motorized infantry units;
— repulsing of enemy counter-attacks; defence against tanks and aircraft;
— deployment in defence, cover and as reserve;
— march, transport and camping;
— field firing.

It has to be added that night training is intensively practised and that weather conditions are ignored.

A comparison of the training schedules shows that the main stress in the entire combat training is put on *offensive* actions. A military deployment can become a success – also according to the NPA regulations on the combat training – only through the attack.

Military physical training in the phase of the company training has nothing in common with sport. A certain connection with sport can be found only in the cross-country races with obstacles from two to six miles (longest races are for the infantry units); all other physical training activities are aimed only at proper preparation of soldiers for combat conditions.

In drill training, the stress is on strict discipline and behaviour which is not impaired either by the frequent periods in camps or in terrain exercises and manoeuvres. Close order drill is also supplemented on the company level with drill movements with or without vehicles.

In the phase of the training of companies, battalions and regiments the units belonging to the operational and supporting troops strive for frequent contact with the trained tank and motorized infantry units and with their artillery batteries. They not only participate in the battalion, regimental and divisional exercises, which often take place in this phase, but they also often train in cooperation with larger formations with other training companies and batteries.

Thus the training of an infantry company is conducted in coope-ration with the communications units, armoured units, artillery, staff units, rear services and even air force liaison units. The mixing of ser-vices and arms on the regimental level and their often common quartering in garrisons and training areas favourably influence this procedure.

Training within the tactical/operational framework

Systematical transition to formation training is effected regularly in March and April and then again in summer during the period of company training. From then on the number of exercises increases within a larger framework and within the participating troop formations.

The NPA does not know the term "formation training" (under "formation" are understood: brigades, divisions and corps, tactical troops and army-military-operational troops).

The Administration of Training in the Defence Ministry issues detailled directives for tactical operational training in the same way as it does for individual, section and platoon training. The reason for this apparent standardization of training tasks is not only the communist system of schematic planning; practical considerations, too, force the Ministry to plan and direct centrally all exercises.

Since the end of the war strong Soviet forces have been stationed in the GDR. *The Group of the Soviet Troops in Germany* represents the strongest concentration of Soviet forces in a narrow space anywhere. Its twenty divisions and numerous supporting units fill the Soviet Zone to overspilling. To this is to be added the NPA with its six divisions, strong Frontier Troops, People's Navy, Air Force and Air Defence troops and also the – partly barracked – security troops. Thus there are concentrated here so many troops that their movements and exercises have to be carefully and centrally planned and directed to avoid any inconvenience or unexpected congestion.

The ministerial central authority, competent for the conduct of exercises, also lays down well in advance the training and exercise schedules and designates the troops which have to take part; it also issues general directives for training. The plans designating time limits and type of exercises are only partly communicated to the commanders in advance; the commanders cannot, however, display any initiative in their planning. Many exercises begin with an alert which surprises also the commanders.

The aim of creating warlike conditions in the exercises is easily recognizable. Generally, all soldiers have to take part and only a very small number of soldiers are left for garrison duties; all leaves are practically cancelled. The exercising troops are subjected to field conditions even during a prolonged exercise or a series of exercise tasks.

Camps, lacking in any comfort, are used both in summer and in winter. During the training period in the exercise areas the troops sometimes live in barracks, but mostly they build their own tent camps, using in some cases the canvas covers for vehicles or other makeshifts. The camps are covered and camouflaged as if in wartime.

The exercises are very exacting. Thus one battalion had to take part in four exercises in one year and, in addition, was sent five times to training areas for two weeks each time.

The exercising units take with them their war equipment and outfit so that their mobility and deployment readiness can be tested.

The main stress is laid on the *manoeuvrability* of the troops, i. e. the capability of the troop and its command to carry out movements and combat actions speedily and in good order.

Long marches, on foot or on vehicles, combat actions in large sections, uninterrupted day and night and under all weather conditions – these are the characteristic features of exercises up to the level of divisions and military regions.

In its training schedules the NPA is guided by the war experiences of the Soviet Army. According to these experiences the independent, imaginative activity of commanders on all levels is regarded as the decisive factor in fighting. Therefore, the stress in the training of formations is laid on the greatest possible mental and technical flexibility and mobility. On the other hand, the love for schemas, inherent in the communist system, undoubtedly seriously impairs the "manoeuvrability and joy in manoeuvring".

Themes of exercises and "tactical manoeuvres"

The exercises of battalions and regiments are carried out according to the training schedules within the framework of the units. The main stress is on attack in all forms, in any terrain including uplands, in any season, at any time of the day or night. March exercises, taking and organizing defence positions and covering tasks regularly lead to final phases containing attack or preparation for attack.

Drill takes a prominent place in the training of the NPA-soldiers.

Training often takes place during night: overcoming barbed-wire obstacles.
River-crossing on rope under war-like conditions.

Right page, top: Soldiers of a reconnaissance group of the Frontier Troops in winter training; bottom: Parachuting is not only part of service training of the paratroopers; it is also practised during off-duty time.

The Soviet influence in the training of the NPA is very great. NPA-officers participating in a course at a military school in the Soviet Union, meet West German journalists at the Red Square in Karkow.

Joint training of Soviet and NPA-soldiers in a Soviet battery equipped with 112 mm FH M-1938 howitzers.

In recent years the NPA had been increasingly conducting joint exercises[6] with the Soviet troops stationed in the GDR; these exercises are, by all accounts, under Soviet command and may also be used to check on and compare the NPA's efficiency.

Since 1961 the NPA has also been taking part in the large-scale manoeuvres of the *United Armed Forces* of the Warsaw Pact.

A review of all known details of the exercises and manoeuvres of the NPA shows that the main themes are practically always the same:
– parrying hostile attack across the "state border" (demarcation line with the Federal Republic),
– counter-attack over the "state border" into the "aggressor's land",
– destruction of enemy troops and airborne units.

In the exercises of the operational troops the parrying of enemy attack at the beginning of an armed conflict appears to be more of a psychological nature ("We are attacked and thus we must defend ourselves"). The (counter) attack is the proper tactical task ("Only through attack operations can an armed conflict be decided").

Peculiarities in the training of the NPA/Frontier Troops

The training of the NPA/Frontier Troops is aimed at their main task: to guard the demarcation lines with West Germany and West Berlin and prevent the inhabitants of East Germany from fleeing.

The main problem of the Frontier Troops is therefore to preserve politically reliable personnel and educate the soldiers, who could, in the course of their frontier service, easily flee to the West, to unconditional obedience and fulfilment of their duties. Constant political indoctrination and strictest discipline are supposed to achieve this aim.

The recruits are called up, as in the land, naval and air forces, each spring and autumn. They remain, however, for six months in special training units where they receive basic training, special training for their service on the demarcation line ("border training") and intensive political indoctrination. During this time they are very carefully screened and checked, also by the state security organs, for political reliability. Then the recruits are transferred to the indi-

6 See Chapter 14, The NPA in Manoeuvres.

vidual frontier companies and special units, such as engineering or communication units, where they take part in normal service.

The military training of the Frontier Troops, which were incorporated into the NPA in 1961 (until then they were – as the German Frontier Police – under the Ministry of Interior), is basically the same as that of the land forces.

A special difficulty in training is the problem of how to force the frontier soldiers to obey blindly the strict "fire orders"[7].

Specialized training for special units

Certain special units, such as the airborne troops (parachutists), undergo a specialized training. The training of the NPA parachutists appears, however, to be aimed less at preparing closed formations of airborne troops rather than at training small units and individuals for espionage and sabotage activities.

Specialized training is also given to the transport and technical troops and guard units. It is adjusted to their special requirements and thus does not need detailed explanation.

Training of the Air Force and Air Defence soldiers

The Air Force (AF) and Air Defence (AD) units of the NPA are placed under their own command which also takes over from the Defence Ministry a number of tasks connected with their administration; among them is their training.

The department of training directs the education and training of soldiers and units and regulates the training schedules.

Since the soldiers of the AF and AD have to serve at least three years, a special training rotation system has been evolved for them. The general military basic training is the same as for all other conscripts but added to it are strongly specialized schedules for the training of individuals in different branches.

Flying training is given to soldiers in the flying training groups of the Officers' School of the AF/AD. Here are also trained the mem-

7 See Chapter 15, The NPA / Frontier Troops on the Demarcation Line and the Berlin Wall.

bers of the technical personnel. Communication personnel are trained in the special units, the *radio engineering regiments and battalions* or in the *radar school*. Included in the training system are special tasks for the *flying technical battalions and companies*.

The equipment of the relatively small and for a long time unimportant air force and air defence units has now been considerably improved. A corresponding progress has also been made in the training of soldiers which had earlier not been too good.

The AF of East Germany is designated mainly for defence and its training is adapted to this purpose. Tactical support of land forces is only of secondary importance.

Training of the People's Navy

The People's Navy (PN), too, is placed under its own command which has also taken over some duties of the Defence Ministry. Among them is training.

The largest units among the 300 odd ships and boats are the frigates. In the last years the PN has received missile patrol boats and coastal defence missiles.

It can be assumed that the PN has, within the framework of the Warsaw Pact, the following tasks:
– defence of the East German coast,
– fighting the naval forces of the enemy,
– protection and preservation of own sea routes,
– support of the land forces in their operations in coastal areas.

Naval and weapons training as well as political education are especially intensive and in many respects resemble that of the Frontier Troops.

The Command of the PN has at its disposal for the training of units the *Fleet Schools* in Parrow and Kühlungsborn and the *Officers' School of the PN "Karl Liebknecht"* in Stralsund.

The training and general demands on the PN are very hard; in addition, the crews are often required to participate in emulations and "self-commitments". The level of the training is good and the PN can thus join, as an equal, the navies of the other Warsaw Pact members in common exercises.

Among the tasks of the PN which are often performed are provocative incidents such as molesting of western ships in the Baltic Sea, disregard of international regulations for sea routes and training attacks on the vessels of the Bundeswehr. They are also proof of the intensive political indoctrination.

Main stress – on drill

The training of the NPA soldiers in the use of weapons, vehicles and instruments is very intensive. Intelligence and technical preparedness of conscripts facilitate the training.

The main stress is laid on combat training and this together with the thorough and systematic approach to the training of the actions of the individual and the cooperation of the units, enables the NPA to use its equipment efficiently under most difficult conditions and show good results.

Great effort is made to teach the commanders at all levels how to deploy purposefully and flexibly their units which have mastered the military craft. The existing successes in the *training of commanders* (see Chapter 12) at all levels are, undoubtedly, not yet absolute, but they are constantly improved on. The sore point of the NPA remains, as before, the problem of the non-commissioned officers. Several measures undertaken by the authorities with the aim of winning over the necessary number of able men for the career of non-commissioned officers have not, as yet, shown good results.

The main stress in training is laid on:
– technical training in the use of weapons, vehicles and instruments,
– combat training under warlike conditions,
– training of commanders.

The system of drill in each branch of training, in physical, mental and moral aspect, is the main feature of the NPA.

This is understandable because it is the only means of inculcating discipline to the soldiers who are mostly against the regime and cannot be brought by persuasion to become willing and ready fighters for the communist cause. Drill is also regarded by the SED regime to be the only means of keeping the NPA soldiers obedient in the event of war or tension. Hard training and drill are supposed to make the soldier a willing tool in the hands of his superiors. The fighting morale of soldiers is not yet sufficiently based on the feeling of team spirit, comradeship and willingness to action, but almost entirely on drill and subordination.

As in civil life in the communist countries the whip of the so-called self-commitment to higher perfomances, which is more or less forced on the troops, hangs over the heads of the NPA soldiers.

The level of NPA training has been in recent years constantly improving and is now hardly distinguishable from the level of the Soviet troops stationed in the East Germany.

The success of the training efforts depends on the quality of available equipment, efficiency of the trainers and the number and readiness of the soldiers.

The material equipment of the NPA is basically the same as that of the Soviet Army and the armed forces of other communist states.

The trainers, i. e. the officers and NCOs, have mastered the military craft. They are capable of training properly their soldiers and lead, in some cases excellently, their formations, units, subunits and combat teams.

The difficulties concerning the NCOs are mainly caused by the fact that only a few men are willing to serve as professional soldiers for a prolonged time. The available non-commissioned officers are, in general, up to the necessary standard.

The soldiers of the NPA fulfil their duties in the same way as is usual with people who are doing what they do not like but cannot avoid doing. They like some aspects of their service without, however, inwardly participating in the "defence of the socialist fatherland". Thus they have mastered their weapons, know how to use them and sometimes even display sport-like ambitions. But the regime is not yet able to create the type of soldier which it would like to have and which it is trying to create by intensive weapons training and constant political indoctrination.

CHAPTER 12

TRAINING OF THE CADRES

The SED is well aware of the fact that the army cadres are one of the most important links in the all-embracing chain of command and control organs of the communist state. According to Walter Ulbricht[1], the training of the NPA officers must, therefore, produce reliable, politically and professionally highly skilled *military functionaries*.

The command cadres of the armed forces were originally formed from
— veteran communists with or without military knowledge,
— former members of the Wehrmacht,
— enthusiastic young communists and
— fellow-travellers.

What this heterogeneous cadre personnel lacked in military knowledge, it made good in short instruction courses, mostly in Soviet military schools. This has created a basis for future development of the armed forces, but not a uniform, closed body of officers.

Each of these groups of persons reacted differently to controls, demands, burdens and tests. Amalgamation was not possible and, apparently, it was not even intended by the SED regime as far as the former Wehrmacht officers were concerned. In the first phase of the army build-up they were indispensable experts and, therefore, regarded as an inevitable evil.

Yet even the relations between the veteran and young communists did not develop in the direction which could have been expected in view of their common ideology. The shortcomings in military and general knowledge of the veteran communists stood out crassly against their "socialist merit"; there were only a few exceptions among

1 In a speech made on the occasion of the opening of the "Friedrich Engels" Military Academy in Dresden on 5 January 1959. The speech was published in "Einheit" (Unity), op. cit.

stronger personalities who had a longer training in the Soviet Army. The young communists, occupying subordinate posts but having better education and military training, were well aware of their superiors' weaknesses. It is therefore understandable that the regime laid the main stress on younger officers without, however, ceasing to tie to itself the existing body of officers by privileges, personal and professional favours, controls and ideological indoctrination.

Conditions, methods and successes of both of these efforts will be shown in the following passages. But before this, it is necessary to give some background information concerning the higher officers of the NPA.

The higher officers

Among the higher officers of the NPA two groups can be clearly distinguished:

1. The smaller group of the former officers of the German Wehrmacht who were won over in the Soviet prisoner-of-war camps and, after proper "reorientation" in the Soviet political and military schools, were used mainly in the first phase of building the armed forces in East Germany.

2. The large and decisive group of party functionaries who as veteran communists – with military experience in the Spanish Civil War in 1936–38 and in the Soviet partisan units in World War II – or as young apparatchiks made a rapid career, after having received good training in the Soviet military schools.

The former Wehrmacht officers presented many difficulties for the communist publicists. On the one hand, the publicists had to claim: "No officers of Hitler in the armed forces of the First Workers' and Peasants' State on German soil!"; on the other, the apparently prominent names of "the former", as they are called, had to be used as an attraction for the other former career officers who possessed military experience so necessary for the build-up of the new army. Thus there are enough publications on those who as "the former" held high ranks in the new communist armed forces; they came particularly from the National Democratic Party of Germany which has been appealing ever since its foundation in the summer of 1948, according to its declaration, to the middle classes, former members of the NSDAP

(Hitler's National Socialist Workers' Party of Germany), career soldiers and officers.

The fact that "the former" have been, since 1956, disappearing more and more from NPA has a simple explanation: they have reached the retiring age. Most of them, even those who did not participate in the build-up of the NPA, continue to serve the regime in the Working Circle of the Former Officers (Arbeitsgemeinschaft ehemaliger Offiziere) which was founded in January 1958.

The Circle is, as its statute shows, not an organization for the protection of the interests of "the former" but an instrument of communist propaganda.

Some of "the former" are also active outside the Circle. Wehrmacht Major General von Lenski, now 74 years old, a "Junker", was retained, after his retirement as major general of the NPA, as member of the Military Council of the Government of the GDR and also as first chairman of the Olympic Committee for Equestrian Sport in East Germany. Walter Freytag, now 75 years old, former major general of the Wehrmacht and later major general of the NPA, received in 1962 "as a token of the recognition of excellent services in the construction of socialism and in the strengthening of the GDR" the Fatherland Merit Order in bronze. The rulers of the GDR saw nothing wrong in the fact that Freytag was commander of the Danzig Fortress and "chief of one of the largest war tribunals passing sometimes weekly 6–8 death sentences in the cases of the People's List III", that is against the Poles, and that he recommended himself (in vain) on 15 October 1944 in a personal letter to the head of the army's Personnel Office for promotion to lieutenant general.

Even today there are still some former Wehrmacht officers in the leading posts in the NPA. Commander of the "Friedrich Engels" Military Academy in Dresden in 1963 was an NPA major general and former Wehrmacht major, Heinrich Heitsch. The son of a manufacturer and former Wehrmacht major, Bernhard Bechler, is, as major general of the NPA, head of the Operations and Tactics Department in the same academy. For many years the post of the chief of staff in the NPA/Frontier Command has been held by a former career soldier in the Wehrmacht, now Major General Helmut Borufka.

It can be assumed that these former Wehrmacht officers have been fully amalgamated with the ruling communist clique, that they try, as experts, to give the regime their best services and identify themselves with the regime more than is necessary – even though the most prominent among them, Lieutenant General Vincenz Müller, committed suicide in 1958.

It is necessary to point out the earlier and present activities of the former Wehrmacht officers in the NPA since the communist rulers prefer to show to the general public only one side of their officers' corps:

> The NPA is led by an officers' corps consisting in 85 per cent of former industrial and agricultural workers. Among the generals and admirals of the National People's Army eight defended the Spanish Republic in the International Brigades, seven were held in prisons and concentration camps for their fight against Hitler-fascism and fourteen fought bravely against fascism in World War II in the resistance movements in various countries.[2]

The proven communists in the NPA leadership who allegedly were never in conflict with the party line, are often presented as models to all soldiers. Their life stories are published, on special occasions, in the newspapers and journals of the People's Army. A veteran like NPA-General (retd.) Sepp Gutsche then proudly talks of his exploits as a German "Red Guard" in the Civil War 1918–21 on the side of the Bolsheviks against the "White Guards".

Praise is lavished particularly on the participants in the Spanish Civil War 1936–38, members of the International Brigades. Of course, they are not allowed to mention that many of their comrades who as non-communists refused to toe the Moscow line were executed on the Spanish soil by special commandos of the Soviet secret service. (Walter Ulbricht collaborated with these firing squads.) Neither can they mention that the defeated remnants of the International Brigades had to undergo, during their emigration in the Soviet Union, another purge by Stalin. Nobody mentions today the ace of the Interbrigadists, the legendary "General Gomez", Wilhelm Zaisser because on 17 June 1953, as Minister of State Security, he had taken a "defeatist attitude" to the popular rising.

2 *Im Dienste der Nation* (Serving the nation). From a speech delivered by Army General Heinz Hoffmann, Minister of National Defence, on the occasion of the 6th anniversary of the NPA. "Volksarmee", Appendix 4/1962, p.8.

Biographies of communist fuctionaries are always full of gaps. Thus there is anxious silence about a period in the life of the former Defence Minister, Army General Willi Stoph who is now practically the head of the government in the GDR. When the "illegal resistance fighter in the Nazi period" served in 1937 in the German Wehrmacht, he wrote in the newspaper of Hitler's "German Labour Front" an enthusiastic report on his army life. Under the headline "From the construction site to the barracks – by Willi Stoph, brick-layer" he wrote among other things: "He who once served in the army and took part in a manouevre understands what the true *Volks-gemeinschaft* means." (Volksgemeinschaft was a term very popular with the Nazi leaders and to them it meant a community of Germans bound together by the feeling of racial kinship and Nazi ideology – translator's note.) And further he wrote in elation: "An experience of permanent value was the birthday parade before the Führer."

There are certainly more damaging facts in the lives of the commu-nist generals-functionaries. Some of these generals are even almost unknown to the army outside the small circle of their collaborators, and their past is kept secret.

Officers' careers

The decree of the State Council regulating the affairs of commission-ed and non-commissioned officers of the NPA[3] distinguishes the following careers of officers:
- officers of the *operational service* (included in this category, accor-ding to German language, are commanding officers and officers of the main staff unless they belong to the rear service or foreign ser-vice),
- *political* officers,
- officers of the *technical service*,
- officers of the *rear service*,
- officers of the *medical service*,

3 *The Decree of the State Council of the GDR on the New Version of the Decree on Active Military Service in the NPA*, issued on 14 January 1966. Published in *"Gesetzblatt der Deutschen Demokratischen Republik"* (Law Gazette of the German Democratie Republic), part I, 1 February 1966.

- officers of the *administrative service,*
- officers of the *judicial service,*
- officers of the *foreign service* (military attachés and liaison officers),
- officers of the *military music service.*

All officers, and even the cadets, are regarded as career officers. They have to sign for at least 10 years. Generally, they remain in service until they reach the age limit which is for:

- captains   35 years,
- majors   40 years,
- lieutenant colonels 45 years,
- colonels   50 years,
- major generals   65 years.

Training and efficiency of officers are furthered by numerous qualification examinations which force them constantly to improve political, scienitific-technical and general knowledge necessary for their present and future posts. If they lack in talent or industry they are transferred into *reserve* or *released* from the service.

Normally, the officers are transferred into reserve after they have finished their active service. A special "Assistance Order"[4] helps the officers, released from active service, to find corresponding posts in the state administration, economy or "social organizations".

Sometimes, the officers with special qualifications are transferred into reserve in order "to take over important state or social tasks". On the other hand, the regulations provide that not only the graduates from military schools can get commissions but also – after having passed special instruction courses – other "citizens of the GDR" who have distinguished themselves by outstanding actions or performance in civil life or, rarely, because they have certain qualifications or special knowledge.

Commissions and promotions of NPA officers are thus dependent on how the "higher placed" evaluate their political reliability and professional capabilities. This, however, opens the door for political career-hunting, mistrust and envy, and also creates a tense and unpleasant atmosphere. Yet an considerable number of young men

---

4 *Order on the assistance for the members of the NPA released from active service (Assistance Order)* issued on 24 January 1962. Published in "Volksarmee", Appendix 3/1962, p. 14–16.

decide on an officer career since it gives them one of the rare chances to climb quickly and high on the social ladder and hold tight to the acquired social status.

Who can become an officer?

The change-over to universal conscription also influenced the selection and training of the officers. Today, the officer career is open to young men who have passed their final examinations at higher secondary schools of a general type or at polytechnical secondary schools, or to soldiers and non-commissioned officers who have distinguished themselves in active service. The candidates have to be, of course, physically able and politically reliable and active; the latter means that they must have proved themselves in some function in mass organizations.

The candidate who fulfills these conditions is trained in basic instruction courses at the officer school of his service and branch.

In the past, the greater part of candidates came from the troop. Suitable soldiers were intensively influenced to choose the officer career. The different educational levels of such candidates, however, created considerable difficulties in training. Since 1962 all officer candidates from higher secondary schools have the level of education required for prospective university students.

Officer schools

Towards the end of 1963, the numerous, widely dispersed officer schools of the individual branches of the land forces were united in the *Officer School of the Land Forces "Ernst Thälmann"* in Löbau.

For the NPA/Frontier Troops the *Officer School of the Frontier Troops "Rosa Luxemburg"* was established in Plauen, and the *Officer School of the Air Force "Franz Mehring"* came into being in the district of Dresden. The *Officer School of the People's Navy* in Stralsund was named *"Karl Liebknecht"*.

The cadets remain in the school for the whole time of their training which lasts in the schools of the land forces and of the People's Navy for four years, and in the school of the Frontier Troops for three years. They leave the school with the rank of sub-lieutenant or lieutenant.

The training schedule follows the Soviet model. The extent of the theoretical knowledge to be mastered in considerable. Technique and natural sciences take much time. In tactical training the cadets learn the essentials for commanding the first unit – platoon – which they will take over.

Prominent place in the schedule is taken by political education since the party wants the officers to be true "military functionaries". As from 1961, the extent of cadets' "socio-scientific" instruction is equal to the instruction given to party functionaries at the SED regional party schools.

The reports of final examinations at the officers' schools are on the same level as the reports of pupils from specialized higher educational institutions; they also qualify the officers for corresponding functions in the state administration, economy and other branches of civil life. Thus the officers can qualify for scientific, technical or teaching careers in civil life.

In practice, things are different

The sub-lieutenants and lieutenants leaving the army schools have a considerable amount of theoretical specialist knowledge. But they also bring with them a certain amount of arrogance so that their involvement in army life is not so simple. The young officers often find in difficult to cooperate with older officers, especially when the latter are of different social origin, education and efficiency.

It is also often difficult to apply in practice the large amount of theoretical knowledge of pedagogy, psychology and leadership because the young officers are not expertly guided by regimental officers and commanders. Intensive political education of the young officers often makes their fellow officers and soldiers suspect and mistrust them. This leads to situations in which the newcomers are ridiculed in political discussions.

It is characteristic that, despite the vast flood of literature on how to train and lead the soldiers, the practical results of training are not very good. The daily service routine is very exacting on the regimental officer whose working day is long since he is expected to order and inspect everything and to evaluate the results. There is not enough time for service training of the officers or for independent study.

The possibilities for theoretical officers' training with the troops are rather small when one considers the fact that a large proportion of time is spent, day and night, in the terrain, in makeshift shelters, in training areas. It is a lot if, during the training year, the battalion commander assembles his officers three or four times for training, i. e. sometimes not even once in a quarter. The regimental commanders have no greater opportunities to come together with their battalion commanders and leaders of regimental units – they meet about once in a quarter. The divisional commander is in a similar position.

Thus the officer is left with independent study as the main means of improving his qualifications. For this he has at his disposal good, rich and not expensive literature. The "Deutscher Militärverlag" (German Military Publishing House, belonging to the NPA) publishes a host of material, not only of ideological character, but also military studies which are, when one disregards the obligatory communist phraseology, a real treasure trove for the leaders of units. The officers are, however, overburdened and do not have enough time for independent study.

Further training before new appointments is principally done in the instruction courses at the corresponding school. By 1962, about 80 per cent of regimental and 90 per cent of divisional commanders were said to have graduated from military academy.

Many NPA officers, and particularly those belonging to the "unschooled cadres", base their service activities on what they have learnt in practice and on common sense. Their results are not, perhaps, first-class but they understand how to get on with their men and fulfil the training targets.

The officers who try to base their work on scientific foundations appear to be in a minority. The same may be the case in the Soviet Army. There, too, is a wide gap between theoretical knowledge and practical application. It would be, therefore, wrong to view the contents of the East German military literature as generally valid and applied principles of combat methods and warfare.

Since it is important to know the ideas and principles influencing the officers and soldiers of the NPA, a typical formulation of commander's capabilities may be useful:

> Every operation and the war in general demand a strict centrali-
> zation of command, discipline, organization, purposefulness in ac-
> tions ... these are, however, possible only when the troops are led
> by resolute commanders who are experts in their craft ... Marxism-
> Leninism designates military affairs as a system of scientific know-
> ledge and laws, requiring thorough learning and highly rational,
> sometimes even mathematically precise, calculations of numerous
> characteristic features, factors etc. This does not mean that Marxism-
> Leninism underestimates the fact that the art and talent of the mili-
> tary commanders is of greatest importance ... The talent of a com-
> mander is developed in a lengthy and all-round study of military
> affairs.[5]

The sobering everyday life in the NPA is hindering the development
of officers' corps filled with high professional ethos. The "transfor-
mation of officers' schools into socialist military educational and training institutions"[6] envisages the officer as

> first of all, a political functionary who, closely tied to the working
> class, carries out his work on orders from the party of the working
> class ... The officer must be guided in his activities by socialist
> principles of work and must strive to fulfil his duties in the collective
> in a socialist way, to learn and live in the collective.

This creates many difficulties. Though 88 per cent of the officers
of the NPA are allegedly workers and peasants (the remaining 12 per
cent are classed as "employees")[7], there "are still many things in the
relations between the officers and soldiers which need straightening".[8]
There are still, in the words of the Politburo member Erich Honecker,

> here and there comrade officers who do not see in the rank-and-file
> soldier their class comrade and an equal fighter for the cause of social-

---

5 *Man and technology in the modern war, op cit.*

6 Major general Siegfried Weiss in the journal of military politics and
theory "Militärwesen" (Military Affairs), No. 6/1959, Publishing House
of the Ministry of National Defence.

7 "Neues Deutschland", 1 March 1963 – In April 1966, 82.7 per cent
of the officers were allegedly members of the working class and 17.3 per
cent employees, craftsmen, peasants and intellectuals.

8 *Protocols of the Fifth Party Congress of the SED*, op cit., p 729.

ism and peace, who do not consider his personal worries and troubles and treat him haughtily, even when off duty.

On the other hand, the officers are warned not to be too friendly with the soldiers and display any signs of favouritism, and thus they often find it difficult so strike the right note in their relations with their subordinates.

To reduce the danger of the separation of the officers' corps from the other functionaries, the party closed the "Cadet School of the National People's Army" which was opened on 1 September 1956.

In the service with troops the officer gains a considerable skill in his craft. He knows the regulations, carries out precisely all the prescribed duties, is able to use the weapons and instruments technically and tactically, and drills his men. In his military life there is, however, no room for the creative imagination which is required from him by the theory.

The military literature claims that the large number of units, the large distances and the varied weapons require an independent leadership by the officers of all ranks. The speed and intensity of modern operations necessarily call for quick, brief and clear orders.

Yet the reality in the leadership of units is different. Against the theory of a highly developed military science, based on the Soviet model, stands the sobering practice of the system, as in many other spheres of the communist regime.

Special branches

To deal in detail with the officers' training in the various special branches would take too much space. Insofar as technology and natural sciences are involved, the training is good and in line with its aims. The officers' cadre is also replenished by graduates from universities and technical colleges who have expert education in the disciplines necessary for the NPA.

Since 1962 a large number of officers have been studying at the College of Heavy and Electrical Engineering in Berlin-Lichtenberg. Officer candidates with such specialist degrees are immediately commissioned, usually as sub-lieutenants. The graduates of the department of military medicine at the Greifswald University are commissioned with the rank of lieutenants. Among the medical officers there are sometimes women and also some who did not graduate.

Especially intensive and long is the training of naval officers. First, they have to serve one or two years as naval ratings. Only then, after thorough testing in which political reliability and activity are also important, can they become officer candidates. The training at the naval officers' school, with service on board ship and examinations, lasts four years. Only after five or six years of service is the officer candidate granted his first commission (sub-lieutenant).

Officers of the Frontier Troops

In addition to the general infantry officers' training the officer candidates of the Frontier Troops have to go through frontier service training in which, besides the defence of the frontier, a certain role is played by frontier police duties.

Political education and reliability are more decisive than in any other branch, with the exception of the People's Navy and the Air Force. Yet still too many officers of the Frontier Troops defect to West Berlin or West Germany. This only proves how difficult it is to discover the real attitudes of many officers.

In this connection it is worthy of note that the officers' cadre of the Frontier Troops shows the greatest number of veteran communists and also the highest average age in comparison with the other services.

Special demands are made on the officers' cadre of the Frontier Troops – as was shown in a very critical speech by Defence Minister Hoffmann. Speaking at a meeting of the officers of the Frontier Troops, Hoffmann said among other things:

> In all your military activities you must always bear in mind that the Frontier Troops have to be an elite troop of the National People's Army. The comrades of the Frontier Troops who stand guard on the dividing line between socialism and capitalism are every day exposed to ideological influence of the enemy . . .
>
> In the showdown with the class enemy our political work must radiate such a strength that every soldier shall become convinced that socialism will be victorious and that anyone who bets on capitalism is preparing his own downfall. For this work one needs great political experience and knowledge. When one has chosen the career

of officer of the Frontier Troops then he must stand for socialism with all his strength and against all difficulties.

What is, however, wrong in our work?

I have been commander for a long time and everywhere I have had the experience that political work is effective only when everything is in order. Therefore the commander must, besides political work, pay full attention to military discipline. This is the key problem of leadership:

The commander of the unit who had spoken before me said that orders were not carried out satisfactorily mainly because the officers were not ideologically clear on the importance of the given order ... Yet despite all the importance of consciousness one must not forget that the main problem in carrying out orders is a discipline that makes it impossible not to carry out an order without objection, exactly and in the ordered time.[9]

Political officers

Position, education and tasks of the political officers in the communist armies have often undergone changes which were determined by political developments.

The present function of political officer has its origin in that of *commissar* in the Red Army of the Soviet Union. During the years of Civil War 1917–1921 the *military specialist*, who usually came from the Czarist army, was subordinated to the commissar. Later, the commissar was put on the same level as the commander. In 1942 the commissar was given the title of *deputy commander for political matters* and explicitly subordinated to the commander. This relationship has been maintained ever since.

After Marshal Zhukov became Soviet Defence Minister in 1955 and after the Twentieth Congress of the Soviet Communist Party in 1956, party organizations in the Soviet Army were shorn of some of their powers and the unlimited authority of commanders in all spheres strongly stressed. Even after Zhukov's fall in 1957 the principle of *one-man command*, that is of the commander alone, has been retained. The political deputy is now only the first assistant of the commander in political questions which, however, deeply penetrate the entire military sphere.

9 "Volksarmee", No. 20/1963, p. 4.

Even the relatively young armed forces of the East Germany had to go through similar developments, especially as the number of former Wehrmacht officers was comparable with the originally high number of Czarist officers in the Red Army.

Until 1961 the *Political School* in Treptow was the centre for the training of political officers of the NPA responsible for political education, internal order and surveillance of the cadres and the ranks.

Volunteers who wanted to become political officers first received a three-year political schooling and then went to the officers' schools of their branches where they were militarily trained in special courses. The Treptow school also organized two-year political training courses for officers commissioned from the ranks.

After several years of service with troops the political officers were again sent to the school for qualification courses.

Since 1961, in order to increase the efficiency of political organs, only proved officers commissioned from the ranks have been appointed political officers. The separate training of political officers was then replaced by specialist and other instruction courses.

Soviet aid in training

In the first years, practically all cadres of the East German armed forces were trained in the Soviet Union. Today, Soviet aid in training is limited only to specialist training of officers of the lower and medium ranks.

The training of higher officers of the People's Navy and the Air Force/Air Defence, of divisional commanders and generals of the land forces, however, still takes place in the USSR.

The NPA officers attend the military schools in other communist countries only on an exchange basis and such exchanges are negligible.

The "Friedrich Engels" Military Academy

On 5 January 1959 the foundation of the "first socialist military academy in Germany's history" was celebrated. On this occasion

Ulbricht himself made the main speech and explained that the school was honoured by Engels' name because this

> name of the co-founder of Marxism and first military theoretician of the working class is the embodiment of unity of creative military analysis and passionate revolutionary action. With Engels the German working class has taken over the heritage of the progressive bourgeois military science and its greatest theoretician Clausewitz.[10]

The Academy was given the following main tasks:
- to educate and train, under the leadership of the party, military functionaries;
- to develop, in research and theory, the most modern methods of the employment of troops and their equipment under complicated conditions;
- to become the forge of highly qualified cadres.

The Academy is expected to unite theory and practice in its work. It should attract and employ as teachers the most experienced officers from the troops, staffs and the ministry, to maintain constant liaison with troops and thus to make the graduates of this highest military school the elite of the NPA.

The Academy trains the higher commanders of the entire NPA, not only of the land forces. Thus it does not correspond to a western general staff academy; it is also a commanders' school. The NPA, as the other communist armies, does not have a general staff service of the western type. In practice the higher commanders and their staff chiefs receive the same training; the functions corresponding to those of the general staff are performed by specialist staff officers.

Training at the Academy is on the regimental and, later, divisional level. The curriculum and level, so far as is known today, correspond to those of the *Frunze Academy* in Moscow at which not only Soviet commanders but also numerous officers of the communist and non-communist countries were carefully trained.

The first graduates of the Academy were released in September 1962. There is no doubt that the leadership of the SED expects very much from the military functionaries trained at the Academy. The diploma of the Academy is equal to the diplomas of universities and technical colleges of the same level.

10 Quoted from "Einheit", op cit.

There is no separate educational institute for the NPA generals. The officers of the land forces, Air Force/Air Defence and the People's Navy, selected for the rank of general, are usually trained for 2 to 3 years in the Soviet Union.

Summary evaluation of the officers' cadre of the NPA

The NPA has no possibility of reorganizing thoroughly its officers' cadre or even only to sift it to some degree. For some time it has to make with the available and only slowly retiring older officers of varying origin and efficiency.

There is no doubt that the level of the medium and higher commanders is steadily improving. Among the staff officers in the age group 30 to 60 there is a sufficient number of intelligent and able men who grow with their tasks and can train and lead their units and formations. Some evidence, however, makes it doubtful whether their peacetime loyalty would also guarantee an enthusiastic leadership in combat actions.

Only a few of the broad stratum of subaltern officers are up to the minimum requirements. Many of the older officers perform their duties negligently, they lack most of the leadership qualities and are a serious obstacle to the general improvement of the army.

Especially conspicuous is the number of mentally inflexible, uneducated and insufficiently trained officers among the company and platoon leaders.

Very difficult is the situation in the replacement of the battalion commanders, chiefs of staffs of units etc. There is a gap which can be filled only in the course of years as the number of younger, qualified officers increases.

Only a part of the younger officers who graduated from the military schools in recent years fulfil the demands made on the ideal type of military functionary.

The creation of an *esprit de corps* among the young officers is hampered by widespread careerist tendencies, overburdening with duties, political fanaticism on the one hand, and political indifference, lack of professional ethos and differences in the educational level on the other.

When, however, the education and training of the officers' cadre is not able to create unity of knowledge, skill and will and inculcate it in the army, then its value is limited.

Training of non-commissioned officers

In comparison with the western armies the non-commissioned officers of the NPA play only a minor role.

According to the new army regulations of 14 January 1966 there are:

– non-commissioned officers of the operational service,
– non-commissioned officers of the technical service,
– non-commissioned officers of the rear service,
– non-commissioned officers of the medical service,
– non-commissioned officers of the administrative service,
– non-commissioned officers of the judicial service,
– non-commissioned officers of the military music service.

After basic military service non-commissioned officers can continue to serve as short service soldiers or as career soldiers. The highest grade the short service soldiers can reach is that of sergeant (Feldwebel or Wachtmeister). Career soldiers signing for ten years of service, can become sergeant majors or warrant officers (Hauptfeldwebel or Stabs-feldwebel). As short service soldiers can sign non-commissioned officers or privates (after basic military service of 18 months); the latter must, however, reach within three service years one of the grades of the non-commissioned officer or leave the army. As career soldiers can sign only those who are already non-commissioned officers.

Soldiers suitable for the NCO career are selected during basic training and then go through an instruction course for NCOs.

In the past, the training of the NCOs was carried out in the units which had prepared the course lasting about six months. The soldiers joined these courses after having finished individual and section training and afterwards returned to their units and took the corresponding posts.

Both military regions of the land forces now have a regiment for training the NCOs; also the Air Force/Air Defence and the People's Navy train their NCOs (petty officers). The capacity of these training institutions is not sufficient and therefore the troops, too, have their own training courses. Thus for example a motorized infantry regiment has its own training company for NCOs.

The training in the central institutions is specialized according to branches and special services. The aim is to prepare section leaders, tank commanders, gun commanders and NCOs for other posts. Vocational qualification from civil life is usually, especially in the technical units, taken into consideration, and vice-versa, vocational examinations (such as for motor transport sergeant) are recognized in civil life. In 1962 79.9 per cent of all non-commissioned officers had allegedly gone through some trade training.

A military foreman

The training of future non-commissioned officers is strict and limited to well defined task spheres. It appears that no great efforts are made to raise the level of general education of candidates. Even political instruction is not very much above the level of that for the ranks. Taken all together, the aim of technical and mental drill is to produce a kind of military foremen.

While the level of the non-specialized NCOs, for example of the infantry section leaders, is generally below the average, the NCOs in many technical branches – in motor transport, in armouries (ordnance shops) etc. – are highly skilled men. They themselves pay greatest attention to their specialized training because later, in civil life, they profit from their skill.

The NPA, too is normally exposed to the campaigns of socialist self-commitments which are supposed to be made on various political occasions and are expected to lead to the improvement of performance. Yet in practice they have little, if any, effect on the efficiency of the NCOs or ranks.

Normally the other constant high demands on the soldiers and material equipment are the stimuli for intensive activity. The non-commissioned officer is responsible more for the equipment than for his men; he was always taught that "the least negligence in the maintenance and handling of equipment means wasting the property of the working people and treason of the socialist cause". Thus he makes great efforts not to lag in this trade. More cannot be, and apparently is not, asked from him. Textbooks for the NCOs usually contain admonitions like this:

> Success or failure depend on mastering the technical means of combat and on unconditional obedience to orders.

This seems aptly to describe the limited tasks and responsibilities of the NPA non-commissioned officers.

The non-commissioned officers serving today in the NPA are – with all their strong and weak points – the product of the NPA's own training.

The most active NCOs leave the army after a comparatively short service. The NCOs with long service are, in the opinion of the thousands of the NPA soldiers who fled to West Germany, mostly of lower quality both in their level of training and human behaviour. Even if the views of the refugees are not always objective, their unanimity is striking. These views appear to be confirmed by the criticism of the behaviour, knowledge and efficiency of the non-commissioned officers often made by the SED.

A summary evaluation of the level of the training and efficiency of the NPA non-commissioned officers must also note the fact that – at least in the past – a large number of the officer candidates came from the ranks of the non-commissioned officers. This prolonged depleting of the NCOs ranks had, of course, a bad effect on the general level of those who remained in their posts. Thus the general impression made by the NPA non-commissioned officers, who are not – in their training and attitudes – a uniform corps, is rather weak.

CHAPTER 13

BARRACKS DUTIES AND ORDER

Responsibility for carrying out barracks duties in the units of the NPA lies with *Hauptfeldwebels* (sergeant majors). To this function non-commissioned officers of all grades can be appointed. The Hauptfeldwebel is responsible for punctual *conduct of duties,* state of *barracks accomodation, discipline* and for the completeness and maintenance of *weapons, ammunition, equipment* and *clothing* of his unit. In the absence of all officers he represents the unit leader. He is also superior in disciplinary matters to all non-commissioned officers and privates.

The *daily duty* begins at 06.00 hours with *physical exercise.* Before breakfast, the Hauptfeldwebel carries out the *morning roll call* and inspection parade and receives sickness reports. After breakfast and announcement of the daily programme, the unit leaves barracks. Usually there are eleven hours of duty daily, not including one hour for cleaning and repairing clothing, obligatory participation in various political lectures and similar activities, but including the ninety-minute break for lunch. On Sundays and holidays duty ends at 13.00 hours. The curfew signal is sounded at 21.45 hours and the *non-commisioned officer on duty* goes through the rooms and takes reports; rest starts at 22.00 hours.

There are four to thirty men (each man should have 4 square metres) and up to four officers or NCOs to a *room.* Married men live with their families; single officers and NCOs can also live, with special permission, outside barracks.

Accomodation is mostly in older barracks; the NPA accomodates in them more personnel than the Wehrmacht did previously.

In *domestic offices* the *messing* is done separately for officers, NCOs and privates. Meals – breakfast, lunch and supper – are the same for all. They are, according to the type of meal, either served by men on table duty or collected individually. Officers and NCOs are served by civil personnel. *Officer on mess duty* is in charge, for 24 hours, of all cooks and their assistants.

Sick quarters provide out-patient service. Doctors can give up to three days sick leave. The soldiers are medically examined every three months. Preventive inoculations are given at the beginning of military service.

Once a week the whole unit takes *baths.*

For *leisure* the soldiers have the necessary rooms in barracks – libraries, cinemas and club-rooms. During the daily duty time the rooms are used for political education and as installations for furthering the "formation of class consciousness". The off-duty time of soldiers is mostly "organized" by the FDJ organization.

Television sets may be installed only in club-rooms and in the rooms of career soldiers with commander's permission.

In the rooms of the privates there are usually only loudspeakers for listening to the *radio programmes* which are switched on and off by an appointed functionary. The new regulations, however, permit the NCOs and soldiers their own radio sets in their rooms but, again, only with the commander's explicit consent. Listening to western radio and television broadcasts is forbidden.

In their leisure the soldiers can receive *visits* in barracks. Most units have a reception room for this purpose. Visitors have to report to the guard who examines their identification cards and then conducts them to the reception room or calls the visited soldier.

Soldiers must *salute* all superiors and equal ranks of the NPA and all other armed forces of the GDR as well as of all armies of the Soviet bloc.

On and off duty, soldiers must wear *uniforms;* special permission to wear civilian clothing may be given to soldiers when they are on leave. Career and short service soldiers from the rank of sergeant upwards have the right to wear civilian clothing when off duty. The same regulations are valid for officers from captain upwards. Special regulations exist for the officers of the Ministry of State Security in the NPA for whom civilian clothing, when they are surveilling soldiers in their off-duty activities, is, so to say, service uniform.

The NPA has the following types of *leave:* recreation leave, short leave, festive days leave, special leave, relief of duty, convalescent leave and sojourn in spa.

The right to grant leave is given to immediate superiors starting from the company commander. Permission for convalescent leave and sojourn in spa is given by regimental commanders and higher ranks.

Only 50 per cent of the soldiers of a unit may be on leave at the same time.

Soldiers of all grades in basic military service have to be in barracks at curfew time; on pass, they may stay out until midnight. After their third year of service the NCOs and corporals usually have full night leave. For the officers there are no limitations.

Men on leave, with the exception of men on pass, have to report within 24 hours after arrival, and at least 24 hours before return, at the regional command of the NPA or at the local police station. Special regulations are in force for all soldiers who are spending their leave in the 5 km (3 miles) zone along the frontiers – they have to report to the frontier companies.

Soldiers, with the exception of officers, receive four free travel warrants each year; three of them from the garrison to the homes of their families, one to any holiday resort in East Germany.

Uniforms, branch colours and insignia of rank

All services of the NPA, except the People's Navy, wear a "stone grey" uniform; the People's Navy has a dark blue uniform. The Minister of National Defence can order other suitable colours of uniform for special branches.

The NPA has the following types of uniform:
- *service uniform:* boots, belt, clothing, field cap or helmet;
- *dress uniform:* laced shoe, long trousers, clothing, sleeve patches, belt, peaked cap;
- *parade uniform:* as the dress uniform but with boots and helmet;
- *combat uniform:* in two parts, of canvas;
- *work uniform:* (canvas material) training uniform and special equipment objects;
- *private dress uniform:* all soldiers can have tailored, at their own cost, a double breasted dress uniform with aslant pockets. They can wear it, without belt, instead of the dress uniform issued by the army.

The NPA has no metal badges for individual branches as the Soviet army and other armed forces of the Warsaw Pact have; thus the colours of the branches displayed on the uniform are of great importance. The branch colour is distinctively displayed on shoulder straps or loops, collar and sleeve patches. Motorized infantry men wear white, artillery brick-red etc.

Members of different branches assigned to the formation of another branch wear the colour of the branch to which the formation belongs.

Peaked caps, parade or dress jackets and long trousers (these only for the officers) have piping which is for

– land forces white,
– Air Force/Air Defence light-blue,
– Frontier Troops light-green.

Sailors and leading ratings of the People's Navy wear cornflower-blue shoulder straps, petty officers, officers and admirals have shoulder loops superimposed on a dark-blue background.

Speciality insignia are worn very much in the same way as in the western armies.

Officers wear a *dagger* with the *dress uniform;* officers in honour-guard companies a *sword.*

The officers of the NPA wear, as did the officers of the Wehrmacht, insignia of rank on the shoulder loops, NCOs and privates on the shoulder straps. The members of the People's Navy wear the insignia of rank also on the sleeves.

Disciplinary regulations

To maintain military order and discipline the NPA has intro-duced a comprehensive *system of punishments and commendations.* It is characteristic that even here the party has a decisive influence though the "commanders have the full responsibility" for maintaining and strengthening military discipline and order.[1]

Since 1 January 1963 breaches of discipline can be dealt with in a "collective". This corresponds to the "criticism and self-criticism method" practised in party organizations. The procedure wears down the "culprit" since all the soldiers of the "collective" are incited against him. In some cases even civilians are allowed to take part in

1 *Second Act Complementing the Penal Code – Military Penal Law,* adopted on 24 January 1962. Quoted from "Volksarmee", Appendix 4/1962, p. 14–16.

these actions, for example when they complain of soldiers' behaviour in public.

First differentiation is between light and serious breaches of discipline. For light breaches only disciplinary punishments are provided in the regulations while serious breaches are dealt with by military courts. "Collective punishments" are forbidden.

Disciplinary punishments range from reprimand to dismissal from the NPA with or without degradation.

Officers' honour councils have to preserve the "honour and dignity" of the officers' corps. They have to examine whether the behaviour of an officer is a breach of officer's honour and thus also a violation of the *Ten commandments of socialist morale*. Paragraph 7 of the Act on Universal Conscription obliges every soldier to observe these "commandments"[2]. The decision to put a matter before the council is made by the superior who has authority over the honour council.

Disciplinary punishments can be imposed only by *immediate superiors*.

Disciplinary punishments against officers can be decided only by company commanders and higher ranks, against generals and admirals only by the chiefs of military regions or the chiefs of services.

Disciplinary punishments must be imposed within five days, but not sooner than one day after the breach has become known.

One breach can be punished by only *one* punishment. If there are more breaches, they have to be dealt with in one punishment. The accused must have an opportunity to state his case.

A disciplinary punishment does not preclude a judicial punishment. For the execution of the disciplinary punishment, the superior who imposed it, is responsible.

In some cases *disciplinary punishments can be rescinded* by higher superiors.

Each soldier has the right to raise a *complaint* against the imposed disciplinary punishment if:

– he has had no opportunity to state his case,
– the punishment is in his opinion unjust,
– the disciplinary superior has transgressed his powers,
– regulations were violated in the execution of the punishment.

2 The Ten commandments of socialist morale, see p. 149.

Each disciplinary superior can *commend* his soldiers for prominent performance or brave behaviour.

The disciplinary regulations of the NPA have the unusual provision that even the *non-commissioned officers* have – as immediate superiors – the right to impose disciplinary punishments and pronounce commendations. This does not, however, give them any special status since it is the SED which makes, through its organizations in the units, the decisions on the punishments and commendations.

The actions of the *party organizations* have much greater weight than the military disciplinary punishments. Party meetings with public accusation, self-criticism and repentence are more efficient than the punishments or commendations which are often pronounced with commanders bearing in mind that they will damage or improve the prestige of the unit. Thus many unit leaders make commendations to show off in the numerous competitions and self-commitments. And vice-versa, many punishments are omitted because the commanders want to shift the antipathy of their soldiers on to the party (party organizations and political officers) rather than to themelves.

The punishments and commendations have considerable consequences for the released soldiers. In many cases the NPA forewards "cadre references" containing details of punishments and commendations of the soldiers to the party organizations in their factories, institutions, villages etc. This greatly influences the civil careers of the released soldiers.

Military courts

Parallel with universal conscription the *Second Act Completing the Penal Code – Military Penal Law* was passed on 24 January 1962. The *First Act Completing the Penal Code*, adopted on 11 December 1957, was at the same time cancelled in its third part on *Crimes against military discipline*. The new law is valid for the entire NPA and other armed formations and is used in all cases of military crimes. Civilians accused of instigation of and complicity in military crimes (espionage, sabotage) are also tried by military courts.

The military penal law, too, follows the communist party line and strictly serves the party aims in the armed forces. It threatens with draconian punishments and its main features correspond to the principles of the general penal code of the GDR. Death sentences can be imposed in "particularly serious cases" for certain crimes even in peacetime.

The following crimes are punishable:

- *desertion* – penal servitude up to eight years or death during a state of defence;
- *non-reporting of desertion* – prison;
- *absence without leave* – prison up to three years or penal servitude up to eight years during a state of defence;
- *avoidance of service or refusal of service* – prison, during a state of defence not less than three years' penal servitude or death;
- *cowardice in the face of the enemy* – not less than three years' penal servitude or death;
- *refusal to obey an order* – in minor cases, detention or prison; when two or more soldiers participate in the crime two to ten years' penal servitude; during a state of defence death sentences can be imposed. (The refusal to obey an order is not punishable "when the execution of the order violates the recognized norms of international criminal law".[3])
- *non-execution of an order* – in minor cases, detention or prison up to three years; during a state of defence, minimum three years' penal servitude;
- *attack on superiors, guards, patrols* – prison; when two or more soldiers participate, two to eight years' penal servitude or death; during a state of defence not less than three years' penal servitude or death;
- *violation of guard duty regulations* – detention or prison; during a state of defence penal servitude or death;
- *violation of radio engineering and stand-by duty regulations* – detention or prison; during a state of defence two to eight years' penal servitude, in serious cases a minimum of three years' penal servitude or death;
- *violation of frontier duty regulations* – in light cases detention or prison; up to eight years' penal servitude "when strict security measures were ordered" or when the culprit was an officer.

Also punishable by penal servitude or death are the *desecration of*

3 The communists themselves decide in each case what are the "recogni- zed norms".

fallen soldiers and abuse of the situation of the wounded as well as the use of violence and looting in the combat area. (These provisions were also contained in Soviet military penal law during World War II – it is well known how the Soviet Army behaved.)

Also punishable are the *insults to superiors or subordinates, abuse of authority and duty, violation of the right of complaint, violation of military secrets, violation of flying regulations, impairing the serviceability of military equipment, violation of the rights of prisoners of war and misuse of the Red Cross sign.* Military penal law orders in paragraphs 22–25 the observation of part of the Geneva Red Cross Agreements, but the soldiers are not taught its provisions and international law; thus in case of need they would not know how to behave, i. e. they would have to rely on the interpretation of their fanatical superiors.

The jurisdiction in penal matters against military persons and against participants in crimes against military security is exercised by *military courts.* They were established on 24 January 1962 but only began to work on 1 July 1963; they are organs of the unified state machinery.

The military judges of the *Supreme Court of the GDR* are elected by the People's Chamber at the "recommendation" of the SED Central Committee. Judges of the *higher military courts* and *military courts* are appointed by the State Council.

The *military jurymen* are elected in staffs, formations and units of the NPA. The soldiers, NCOs and officers elected to act as military jurymen have to "possess adequate maturity and life experience (and) fulfil their military and social duties in a model way". This means that only those are elected who have the confidence of the SED.

The tasks of public prosecution are fulfilled in the NPA by *military prosecutors.* The *Chief Military Prosecutor* is subordinated to the *General Prosecutor* of the GDR.

Decorations

There are more than seventy state decorations in East Germany: orders, medals, prizes, honorary titles and proficiency badges. In addition, there are also "roving flags" awarded by the ministries and the Council of Ministers for a certain period to the winners in socialist emulation.

This cornucopia of decorations and their generous awarding[4] is in line with the general practice in all communist states.

There are the following decorations (they can also be awarded to non-soldiers):
- *Scharnhorst Order,*
- *Battle Order of Merit "For the People and the Fatherland"* (in gold, silver and bronze),
- *Medal of Comradeship in Arms* (in gold, silver and bronze),
- *Merit Medal of the NPA* (in gold, silver and bronze),
- *Medal for Faithful Service in the NPA* (in gold after 15, in silver after 10 and in bronze after 5 years of service),
- *Medal for Model Frontier Service,*
- *Proficiency Badge of the NPA* (three grades),
- *Proficiency Badge of the Frontier Troops,*
- *Marksmanship Cord* (four grades).

The Scharnhorst Order, with which goes a premium of 5000 DM-East, was established by a decree of the Council of Ministers of 17 February 1966. This highest military decoration was awarded for the first time on 1 March 1966, the anniversary of the NPA, by Walter Ulbricht to Army General Hoffmann and Admiral Verner.

The Battle Order of Merit "For the People and the Fatherland" and the Medal of Comradeship in Arms have also been introduced only recently.

The Merit Medal of the NPA in gold and the Medal for Faithful Service in the NPA in gold may be awarded only by the Minister of National Defence. The lower grades – in silver and bronze – are awarded by the chiefs of military regions and similar authorities.

The Proficiency Badge of the NPA is awarded by divisional commander; the Marksmanship Cord by regimental commander.

The Medal for Faithful Service in the NPA, the Medal for Model Frontier Service and the Marksmanship Cord can be awarded only to

---

4 In World War II, 10 940 persons were awarded the highest order, the Golden Star of the Hero of the Soviet Union. In contrast to this practice, the highest American decoration for heroism, the Medal of Honor, was awarded in the same time only to 269 soldiers. The highest German decoration, the Knight's Cross to the Iron Cross in its various forms was awarded in these numbers: Great Cross 1, Golden Oak Leaves 1, Oak Leaves with Swords and Brilliants 27, Oak Leaves with Swords 150, Oak Leaves 862, Knight's Cross about 6 160.

individuals; all other decorations can also be gained by military units.

Any of the decorations can be awarded only when the party organization does not raise any objections. Even in awarding the proficiency badges the political attitude of the soldier has to be taken into account. The generous awards of decorations, honorary titles and prizes is expected to spur the soldiers' ambition, to lead to higher efficiency and loyalty to the regime.

Pay

All soldiers who have been conscripted for active military service receive – according to their rank – monthly *pay* ranging from 80 to 330 DM-East.

Conscripts who, after their basic military service of 18 months, voluntarily remain in the NPA as *short service soldiers* receive a premium of 1500 DM-East. The NPA expects good recruiting results from this measure; volunteers have to provide 40 to 50 per cent of its manpower.

Conscripts drafted for *reservists' training* or *reservists' exercises* also receive pay. Students receive their scholarships reduced by the amount of the pay for privates.

Family members (wife, children and dependent persons) receive during the soldier's active service only a *small maintenance pay,* for example a working housewife 100 DM-East and 30 DM-East for each dependent child.

Short service soldiers and *career soldiers,* as well as *women* serving in the NPA, receive during their service monthly *salaries* ranging from 300 DM-East for soldiers (sailors, flyers) to 700 DM-East for warrant officers and from 300 DM-East for sub-lieutenants to 3000 DM-East for army generals.

In addition to these salaries they also receive remuneration for appointments such as:
- 75 DM-East for company or regimental sergeant-majors,
- 550 DM-East for company commanders,
- 650 DM-East for SED and FDJ secretaries in battalions,
- 800 DM-East for SED and FDJ secretaries in regiments and for political deputies of regimental commanders,
- 1000 DM-East for regimental commanders,

– 2000 DM-East for divisional commanders.

In certain cases the salaries are augmented by allowances for extra-ordinary physical or mental strain in the performance of duty; for example for frontier service (30 DM-East), for tank drivers, radio operators, flyers, sailors etc.

Seniority increases are accorded after 5, 10, 15 and 20 years.

Monthly *quarters allowance* is graded from 25 DM-East for privates to 100 DM-East for generals.

The regulations also contain provisions for assistance to the NPA members returning to civil life, but only for those released "with honour".

Civil employment of the conscripts is not terminated with their enlistment, it is only suspended for the duration of basic military service and the employer must not terminate the employment. The released conscripts do not have to suffer, after their return to civil employment, any material or other disadvantages.

The regional and city councils have to assist *soldiers with longer service,* returning to civil life, in finding suitable employment. The councils receive references on the released soldiers from the units with a suggestion where they should be employed. Thus the NPA decides even the civil careers of its soldiers. A soldier who receives on his release an unfavourable reference has great difficulties in finding employment corresponding to his knowledge and capabilities.

PART FIVE

THE NPA IN ACTION

CHAPTER 14

THE NPA IN MANOEUVRES

For every army the manoeuvres are the culmination of military training. They differ from the usual exercises, which are conducted in regular intervals in accordance with seasons and enlistment of conscripts, by a greater number of participating units and staffs as well as by the extent of space in which they take place. The manoeuvre areas in East Germany also include training areas and are usually out of bounds for the civil population.

A manoeuvre is for the NPA a "tactical or operational/tactical (mostly bilateral) exercise of higher level under combat conditions".[1]

The Deputy Defence Minister Admiral Verner defined the term "manoeuvre", in an article before the large-scale exercise *October Storm* in the autumn of 1965, in the following way:

> As a culmination of political and military education and training it serves not only to verify but also to increase the combat readiness of units, formations and staffs of our allied armies. At the same time, it will also contribute to closer comradeship in arms among the armed forces of our countries.
>
> This manoeuvre will demonstrate the military strength and power of the socialist defensive coalition; the high level of combat readiness and military mastery by soldiers, non-commissioned officers and officers; the striking power of our modern arms and equipment as well as the firm unity between the people and the army. All this will strengthen the citizens of our republic and of other socialist states in their conviction that the military protection of peace and socialism is in reliable and strong hands. The West German imperialists, however, will be given a clear lesson . . .[2]

These two quotations show that the manoeuvres of the NPA are, as a rule, of bilateral or even multilateral kind. They are also politically important in so far as they represent the culmination of political

1 *German Military Encyclopaedia*, op. cit., p. 260.
2 "Volksarmee", No. 42/1965.

education and training and, at the same time, also serve as a political demonstration to impress the population of East Germany and other countries of the Eastern bloc and as a "clear lesson" – that is threat – to the Federal Republic of Germany.

Manoeuvres require a high level of training from the participating units and commanders. The NPA must, therefore, take into consideration the enlistment terms and carry out the manoeuvres either in the spring or autumn. The latter term is internationally preferred for many reasons – mainly because the conclusion of harvest and field work allows for uninhibited movements in the terrain – as the most suitable time, and the NPA always conducts its largest manoeuvres in this season.

The manoeuvres on the East German territory are usually carried out by the land and air forces of the NPA, Soviet Army, Polish People's Army and Czechoslovak People's Army. On some occasions the Baltic naval forces of East Germany, Poland and the Soviet Union also participate.

The manoeuvres of the armed forces of the Warsaw Pact are offensive in nature though the starting point is represented – as in the manoeuvres in the West – by an enemy attack. But while the formations of NATO train, for the whole time of the manoeuvres, only in defence against an attack, for the forces of the Warsaw Pact the attack is only a pretext for the proper aim – to transfer their offensive actions to the territory of the supposed enemy and there to destroy him.

At the manoeuvres of the Warsaw Pact armies there is no uniform command language as English is in NATO. The problem is solved by the establishment of multi-lingual liaison organs attached to the commands. It is, however, recommended, to the NPA commanders and all officers to learn Russian. (Many Soviet officers speak German.)

Human relations among the various national units participating in the manoeuvres were originally reserved or even strained; in isolated cases there were brawls. Long political and psychological influencing has substantially improved these relations though even today considerable resentment remains. Therefore the demonstration of "comradeship in arms" is always an important part of the multi-lateral manoeuvres.

The NPA with all its divisions took part in the first large autumn manoeuvres of the United Forces of the Warsaw Pact in October 1961. Under the leadership of the United Supreme Command stood the largest part of the units stationed in Central and East Germany, Czechoslovakia, Poland and western military regions of the Soviet Union. These manoeuvres had a clear political character since they were held shortly after the building of the Berlin Wall and after the Berlin crisis and were intended as a threat against the West.

The starting point of the manoeuvres provided a "blue" thrust from northern Germany and northern Bavaria against Berlin. While in the north of East Germany a Soviet army fought delaying actions, a NPA army consisting of two motorized infantry divisions and one tank division of the Military Region III (Leipzig) repulsed the "blue" attack in South Thuringia. Then, without waiting for the reinforcements, the remaining armies of the Group of Soviet Troops in Germany concentrated and went, from the Thuringia Forest, into attack against the Rhein-Main area. After the arrival of reinforcements from the rear, the "blue" invaders were also attacked from the north. For this attack a special NPA corps[3] was formed of two divisions of the Military Region V (Neubrandenburg) and subordinated to the Soviet army penetrating through the North German Lowlands. Atomic weapons were used against the territory of the Federal Republic.

Next year, in 1962, came a series of manoeuvres of the Warsaw Pact armies in which the NPA participated only with small forces. Under the code name of *Odra* a crossing and covering exercise on the lower Oder took place with the aim of bringing the forces from the depth to the coastal front and deploying them as a second echelon formation. The manoeuvre *Vietre*, which also took place in 1962, had the task of mopping up the penetrating units on the northern flank.

In can be assumed that the training and exercise programmes of all Soviet bloc armed forces were considerably disorganized when in the Cuban crisis they were put in state of alert on 23 October 1962.[4]

In 1962, there also took place, under the leadership of the Command of the United Baltic Fleet, an exercise of the naval forces of

3 At present, the armed forces of the Warsaw Pact do not have army corps.

4 Tass. 23 October 1962.

East Germany, Soviet Union and Poland; the Peoples' Navy operated, for the first time, its own ships and coastal craft.

The manoeuvre *Quartet* held in Saxony in September 1963 was another important milestone in the development of the NPA.

The operational staffs, land and air forces of the armies of the Soviet Union, Poland, Czechoslovakia and East Germany with about 40 000 men, 760 tanks, more than 8000 vehicles and several hundred aircraft participated in this manoeuvre. The majority of participating land and air forces came from the NPA, but the other countries participated with larger units and formations which came thus, for the first time, under the leadership of an NPA general, Minister Hoffmann. The task of the Quartet manoeuvre was to stop an enemy penetration attempt and, through a counter-attack, restore the situation.

The People's Navy had to pass in 1963 another test in the manoeuvre *Flood* which was the culmination of joint operational/tactical and combat training of the United Baltic Fleet. The People's Navy had the task of covering the actions of the Soviet and Polish navies.

The training activities of the NPA Air Force/Air Defence, which always closely cooperates with the Soviet Air Force, culminated in the same year in the exercise *Zenit*.

The 1964 manoeuvres were not very important for the development of the NPA.

The joint manoeuvres of the NPA and the Soviet troops stationed in East Germany, held in April 1965 west of Berlin, were clearly meant as a political demonstration. They had the task of "testing the level of training achieved in the winter programme" in sealing off Berlin; the air space over West Berlin was included in the manoeuvres and Admiral Verner, head of the Chief Political Administration of the NPA, declared in this connection:

> To the clamouring of the excited West Berlin press that the illegal session of the Bundestag in West Berlin was disturbed, one has to make clear that the military exercise was important not only from the standpoint of testing the readiness of the armed forces.[5]

5 "Neues Deutschland", 9 April 1965.

Headlines in the official "Neues Deutschland" proudly proclaimed: "Aircraft in low flying over Kurfürstendamm", "All interzonal roads to Berlin closed".

Political character also had the "most important manoeuvre which until now has taken place on German soil"[6], namely the *October Storm* manoeuvre in the autumn of 1965. In the words of Army General Hoffmann it

> dots the i's and crosses the t's in our policy of safeguarding peace and mobilizing all peaceloving forces in West Germany ... At the same time, it also serves to verify the results of the training year 1964–1965 in the armies of the First Strategic Echelon. [7]

In this manoeuvre, which took place in the south of the GDR, the units of the armies of the Soviet Union, Poland and Czechoslovakia, also participated.

The October Storm started with a surprise attack by the forces of the "blues", that is the aggressors, on a fictional demarcation line running alongside the northern edge of the Thuringia Forest. The selection of the manoeuvre area was explained in these words:

> Our armies will test their superior military power in areas that are most similar to the conditions of a potential war with destruction of the aggressor on his own territory.[8]

The attack was waged by the armoured and motorized infantry formations supported by fighters and bombers. Estwards of the "border" combats flared up between the "blues" and "reds" in which the air force units on both sides also participated. The "reds", still losing, withdrew in delaying actions. On 21 October the "reds" were reinforced and new defensive actions and combats developed; "red" parachutists and airborne troops were landed in the rear areas of the "blues". The "blues" who by 22 October were in a difficult position, made several counter-attacks using nuclear weapons against the

6 *The mightiest military coalition of the world protects the socialist states.* Speech by comrade Walter Ulbricht at the mass meeting of comradeship in arms. "Volksarmee", Documentation – Manoeuvre October Storm, p 7.

7 "Volksarmee", No. 47/1965.

8 Broadcast by "Radio GDR", 18 October 1965, 22.00 hours.

attacking and constantly growing "red" troops. The latter immediately responded with nuclear weapons in larger quantities and higher yield, and finally they destroyed the "blue" aggressor on his territory.

The October Storm was led by the Supreme Commander of the Soviet troops stationed in East Germany, Army General Koshevoy. "Commander of the fighting sides", was chief of the Military Region III of the NPA, Major General Ernst. To his operational group belonged, besides one division of the NPA, among other units one Soviet guard division and one Soviet air corps. The chief umpire was another NPA commander, Major General Poppe.

The manoeuvre reports, stripped of their propagandist phrases, reveal two important aspects:
– the military cooperation of the NPA with its partners in the Warsaw Pact is closer than in the previous years,
– the leadership of the NPA was able to improve its position compared with that of the leaderships of the other armies of the Soviet bloc.

Speaking at the parade held in Erfurt at the end of the October Storm manoeuvre, the Supreme Commander of the United Forces of the Warsaw Pact, Marshal Grechko said:

> We are convinced that the members of the Warsaw Treaty will, in accordance with the instructions of our parties and governments, achieve even better results in combat and political training in the new training year 1966. Our comradeship in arms will become even closer and stronger. [9]

The NPA had shown in the manoeuvres that its training and equipment enable it to fight efficiently alongside the other armies of the Warsaw Pact. The evaluation of the manoeuvres makes credible the claim of the Defence Minister, Army General Hoffmann, that the NPA belongs to the First Strategic Echelon of the Warsaw Pact.

---

9 *Most useful and instructive for all.* The speech made by Marshal Grechko at the parade of the allied socialist armies. "Volksarmee", Documentation – Manoeuvre October Storm, p. 11.

CHAPTER 15

THE NPA/FRONTIER TROOPS
ON THE
DEMARCATION LINE AND THE BERLIN WALL

The Frontier Troops serving on the demarcation line and the Berlin Wall offer the best opportunity to observe the NPA in its actions and to learn to know its character, morale, discipline and, finally, political reliability. It is, of course, only part of the NPA and it is exposed to constant strain. It also has to be taken into consideration that the Frontier Troops have to fulfil, with military or police means, a mainly political task – to prevent the population from fleeing to West Berlin or West Germany. Thus the results of the observation of the Frontier Troops are not generally valid for the entire NPA; yet they are helpful in learning to know the NPA as a whole.

The task of the Frontier Troops, according to the official statements, is "to oppose with all means the aggression of the enemy who operates just below the threshold of the hot war". This allegedly means that the Frontier Troops are constantly exposed to danger of life. The reports of numerous military refugees, however, show that the frontier soldiers do not accept the image of the enemy as it is presented to them by political instructors.

The tasks and organization

The GDR is a sovereign state and has the right to protect its frontier against any enemy attack and to prevent any violation of its territory...

The politically wise and responsible behaviour of the frontier soldiers... wrecked all attempts of the adversary to make the border between the two German states a burning border. In fulfilling their combat orders to protect the border, the Frontier Troops of the NPA serve the cause of safeguarding peace in Germany and in the whole world...

The task of the Frontier Troops is

- to allow the traffic to cross the frontier only at the official crossing points;
- to maintain and enforce order in the protection zones established for the protection of the frontier between the GDR and the West German Federal Republic and the separate territory of West Berlin;
- to protect the lives of the population in the frontier areas, their personal and communal property;
- to cooperate closely with other armed organs in the frontier sector, to strengthen constantly cooperation with the local organs of the state power and population and to maintain socialist legal order.

The Frontier Troops must be always ready to nip in the bud all provocations on the frontier and to prevent their spreading into the territory of the GDR.[1]

Some 50 000 men of the Frontier Troops are now constantly deployed on the 1381 km (860 miles) demarcation line from the Baltic Sea to the Fichtelgebirge, on the 164 km (100 miles) Berlin demarcation line and Wall, on the 430 km (275 miles) frontier with Czechoslovakia and on the 460 km (290 miles) Oder-Neisse line which is now the "state frontier with the People's Republic of Poland". In this total strength of the Frontier Troops are included the training regiments and battalions, the staffs and the branch schools. There are 6000 officers (12 per cent of the total) and 8000 non-commissioned officers (16 per cent).

Six frontier brigades cover the sections from Lübeck to the Czechoslovak frontier, three brigades encircle Berlin, one brigade safeguards the Baltic coast from the Lübeck Bay to the Isle of Usedom and one frontier regiment each is stationed on the frontiers with Czechoslovakia and Poland.

Development of the Frontier Troops

The strength of the Frontier Troops and their efficiency in assuring the self-imposed seclusion of East Germany have been in the course of years constantly increasing.

1 *Taschenbuch für Wehrpflichtige* (Manual for conscripts). Prepared by a group of authors, edited by Colonel Karl Dittmar, Lieutenant Colonel Günter Frenzel and Siegfried Wieczorek. German Military Publishing House 1965, pp. 187, 192/193.

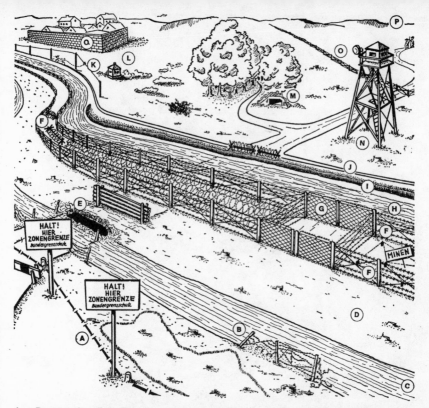

A = Demarcation line, B = Obsolete barbed-wire fence, C = First control strip (10 m wide), D = Security strip (without trees, bushes, houses), E = Street made impassable for vehicles by deep ditches, F = Double fence with mine belt and rolls of barbed wire, G = Passage through the double fence, H = Second control strip (circa 6 m wide), I = ditch (60–80 cm deep) to prevent the passage of vehicles, J = Road for vehicles, K = Dog on lead, L = Concrete bunker constructed from prefabricated parts, M = Ground observation post, N = Observation post with searchlight, O = 500 m wide closed zone with wire fence and road obstacles, P = 5 km wide closed zone controlled by the People's Police patrols, Q = Wall around farm (locality).

Additional security installations (not illustrated) include: trip wires, accoustic and electric signal systems, knife rests.

NPA-engineers fortifying the demarcation line. The depth-echeloned system of obstacles is from the military standpoint useless; its only aim is to prevent the people from fleeing to West Germany.

A frontier soldier receiving the report: "Frontier violated!"

"The pursuit begins."

Two pictures on the deployment of Frontier Troops reproduced from the East German book "Our National People's Army".

A scene from the frontier at Steinbachtal where a refugee was killed by an NPA-frontier soldier: 1) the presumed stand of the killer, 2) the presumed line of shooting, 3) the demarcation line, 4) the ten-meter strip.

The weekly newspaper of the NPA, "Volksarmee", is an important tool in the indoctrination of soldiers and as such serves the aims of propagating the final victory of world communism.

The NPA always takes part in the May Day parades and other party public parades and assemblies as the "guarantee of the victory of socialism".

The so-called *German Frontier Police* appeared for the first time on the zonal border, together with the Soviet troops, in 1946. It had only a small personnel and concentrated only on the crossing points and patrol duties in the vast space it had to watch.

In 1952 the regime in East Germany was strong enough to extend considerably its control over the frontier. At that time the Frontier Police closed 174 roads, among them three motorways, and thousands of public and private ways. The extensive network of waterways in the east-west direction, with the exception of goods transport on the Mittelland Canal and on the Elbe in both directions, was declared to be out of use.

The next great step was made when, after the proclamation of the German Democratic Republic, a treaty was signed on 20 September 1955 with the Soviet Union on mutual relations. According to this treaty the GDR, als a "fully sovereign state", took over the "surveillance and control of the state frontier including the personnel of the western occupation powers". (In fact, the Soviets have retained, until today, a decisive part of sovereignty functions.)

Further developments were depicted, on the occasion of the 10th anniversary of the NPA, by the Lieutenant Colonel Vogt in these words:

> In accordance with the task of preparing the units for combat actions, the Frontier Police was given, for the first time, a thorough military structure from the leading organs down to the units. It began to train its personnel on military principles and deployed forces for the safeguarding of the frontier according to the rules of field patrols.
>
> The Frontier Police was, to a great extent, relieved of duties connected with the control of the traffic passing through the state frontier with the West German Federal Republic and on the western ring around Berlin. Control on the crossing points was taken over by the then "Office for Customs and Control of Goods Transport".
>
> The deployment of the German Frontier Police in securing the state frontier in the autumn of 1961 proved to be a decisive test for the Frontier Troops.[2]

The action of the NPA on 13 August 1961, with the erection of the

2 Lieutenant Colonel Vogt, *On the development of the German Frontier Police to the Frontier Troops.* Article published in "Volksarmee", Documentation November 1965, p. 20.

Berlin Wall, completely cut off West Berlin as the "NATO base and the nest of revanchism". The order No. 1/1961 of the Defence Council of the GDR transferred the entire German Frontier Police, as from 15 September 1961, inte the National People's Army as the *Command Frontier Troops* and provided for its considerable expansion. The above mentioned Lieutenant Colonel Vogt commented these steps in the following way:

> The new subordination brought substantial changes for the Frontier Troops. The changes helped to establish fully their character and improved the protection of the frontier. The main new measures were:
> – The Frontier Troops were reinforced with the cadres from other branches of the NPA. The level of training of the Frontier Troops' officers was increased.
> – A uniform structure was introduced on the western frontier.
> – Frontier surveillance was started on the border with the People's Republic of Poland an the Czechoslovak Socialist Republic.
> – Equipment and technique for the protection of the frontier were modernized and measures for motorization (of the Frontier Troops) introduced.
> – The frontier with the West German Federal Republic was built by engineers and technicians.
> – Political and military regulations of the NPA were taken over.[3]

On 23 August 1962 the City Garrison Headquarters were officially established in East Berlin and the frontier brigades stationed there were subordinated to them. New weapons, concentrated training in specialized units, massive construction of protective frontier installations and finally the transition from the recruitment of volunteers to the careful selection of reliable conscripts enabled the Frontier Troops to achieve a high degree of outward perfection.

Special conditions

Compared with the land forces, Air Force/Air Defence and the People's Navy the Frontier Troops have retained, even after their inclusion in the NPA, a certain special status. Thus the Central Committee of the SED has a direct contact with the Frontier Troops' Com-

3 Ibid.

mand in Pätz, not through the Minister of Defence; also a large part of the Frontier Troops is subordinated to other commands – the three Berlin frontier brigades to the "City Commander of the Capital of the GDR, Major General Poppe", and the frontier brigade on the Baltic coast to the Command of the People's Navy. In addition, the units maintain close liaison with the organs of the Ministries of Interior and State Security which have numerous offices in the frontier zones.

The special status of the Frontier Troops is also stressed by a "frontier allowance" and better food for soldiers.

The SED wants the Frontier Troops to become an elite formation, at least in the political sense. The comparatively high number of frontier soldiers fleeing to the West (which began to rise steeply in the spring of 1966), however, shows that this aim has not yet been achieved despite all the efforts of the SED and the NPA leadership.

The flight statistics

According to the flight statistics there is not one frontier regiment which did not lose men through flights to West Germany. Almost every day, despite the extraordinarily difficult conditions, at least one frontier soldier flees in full uniform, often with weapons, and thus shows his aversion to service on the frontier. The strain of the firing order, the realization of the great difference between the promises and images of communist propaganda and the dullness of everyday life, make the watchers of the population think; then it often becomes unbearable to see civilian refugees, sometimes very old, risk their lives only to be able to get to the other part of Germany. Then, perhaps, they make the final decision to try the same. There are, however, also some young men who volunteered for frontier service and pretend to live as good communists until they find the long awaited opportunity to flee. Among the NPA soldiers who fled in 1965 and later are many non-commissioned officers; they are, more than the others, exposed to the psychological strain created by the firing order to kill.

Experience until now proves sufficiently that the frontier soldiers do not risk their lives in flight because of hard military life or because they were lured by the higher living standard in West Germany. Their life has mostly become unbearable because they were ordered to fire at the defenceless refugees who, in the view of most of the frontier soldiers, did not commit any crime by fleeing to the West. While for a fanatical communist the "flight from the republic" is a crime which has to be prevented by all available means, including a deadly shot, an independently thinking young man who is, like most of his contemporaries, sceptical and repelled by the lies of political instructors, cannot accept it. And yet even he may become a killer.

The firing order

The SED a the ruling party, the government of East Germany and the Ministry of National Defence have always maintained that there does not exist any firing order which would not be campatible with the normal functions of frontier organs of other nations. Defence Minister, Army General Hoffmann declared in May 1966:

> There is no special "firing order" for our Frontier Troops . . .[4]

The existence of a special firing order can be, however, seen in the "Manual for frontier soldiers". One passage in the chapter *Regulations on the use of firearms by guards, sentries and patrols of the National People's Army (DV – 10/4)* says:

> The guards and sentries of the Frontier Troops of the National People's Army on the state frontier with the West German Federal Republic and West Berlin have, in addition of the regulations, to use firearms for the protection of the frontier according to the instructions of DV–30/10, No. 114–124.[5]

Service regulation DV-30/10

The Central Committee of the SED thinks that – because the service regulation DV–30/10 has never been published – the existence of the firing order cannot be proved. The regulation is strictly secret and the

4 *From the discussion at the 12th meeting of the Central Committee Army General Heinz Hoffmann, member of the CC: The superior military power of the socialist camp.* Speech published in "Neues Deutschland" of 3 May 1966.

5 *Handbuch für Grenzsoldaten* (Manual for frontier soldiers), German Military Publishing House, East Berlin 1965, p. 43.

unit commanders have to keep it always locked. It was, however, preceded by Service Regulation III/2 of the German Frontier Police which was in force until 1962 and, according to reports by the refugee soldiers, was taken over by the NPA in DV–30/10. Paragraph 208 of Service Regulation III/2 said:

> The members of the German Frontier Police can, apart from the cases enumerated in paragraph 207 (self-defence or armed attack on state order and its institutions), use firearms:
> a) to safeguard the inviolability of the frontier and to protect the territory of the German Democratic Republic against armed attacks by individuals or groups of antistate or criminal elements;
> b) to arrest spies, saboteurs, provocateurs and similar criminals when they resist arrest with arms, try to flee, ignore a warning shot and when there is no possibility of seizing them by other qualified measures.

Paragraph 210 says this:

> When, by using the firearm, one or more persons are killed, the frontier guard lets them lie on the spot, without any change, secures the place of the incident and notifies the frontier company. If the place of the incident is in the immediate vicinity of the frontier and if there are signs of provocations or massing of people on the other side of the frontier, immediate measures are to be taken – without effacing any traces on the spot of the incident – to remove securely the killed person or persons.

The terms "provocateur" and "criminal" in the regulations mean that all refugees will be shot at unless they stop and remain still. The still valid NPA *Regulation 30/9 for frontier sentry service* instructs every soldier to ferret out persons suspected of the intention to "flee from the republic", encircle and seize them, and when necessary to shoot at them. Paragraph 5 of Article 2 says:

> Members of the frontier sentries have:
> – to wear their arms so that they are always ready, in accordance with the regulations on the use of firearms, to be used in aimed fire;
> – under all conditions, day or night, to find out the frontier violators, to arrest them, and if necessary to act, in accordance with the regulations on the use of firearms;
> – immediately to transfer to a cover frontier violators injured by the use of firearms, to give them first aid and report the incident to their superiors.

According to paragraph 49 of this regulation:

> The ambush sentry is a camouflaged, immobile frontier sentry ...
> It is posted at an ordered place which lies in the potential direction
> of the expected frontier violator. As sentry leaders are ... non-com-
> missioned officers or officers to be appointed.

Paragraph 52 explains the ordered manhunt in even greater detail:

> The searching sentry ... is employed in the search or pursuit with
> the aim of seizing the frontier violator. The searching sentry can be
> reinforced by a service dog and equipped with a wireless set.

The seizure of own citizens is explained in paragraph 64:

> The seizure of frontier violators is to be organized by the sentry
> leader in the following way:
> — the frontier violators who move in the direction of the neighbouring
> state and are discovered only before the line of the forward delimi-
> tation of the frontier sentry are to be requested to stop. When they
> do not comply with this request the sentry has to act in accordance
> with the regulations on the use of firearms and not to allow them
> to cross the frontier.[6]

Besides these official directives there is another proof of the existence
of the firing order and brutality of the regime — the reality. In the
period between 13 August 1961 and April 1966 alone at least 128
people were shot dead by the frontier soldiers of the GDR on
the Berlin Wall or on the demarcation line with the Federal Republic
or killed by exploding mines. A larger number of people was seriously
injured. The killers and their helpers were commended and rewarded.

The regime thinks it is right when it brazenly threatens that he who
"illegally crosses the frontier", that is in this case wants to go from one
part of Germany to the other, will forefeit "his life and soul".[7]

According to the law the "flight from the republic" is a crime
punishable by imprisonment. However this law, like many other laws
of the GDR, contradicts the Universal Declaration of Human

6 *Regulation for frontier sentry service, DV–30/9.* Issued on August
1st, 1963, by the Minister of National Defence, Army General Hoffmann.
7 Army General Hoffmann, *A sovereign state, normalcy on the frontier.*
Article published in "Volksarmee" No. 21/1966.

Rights the text of which was adopted by the United Nations. Article 13 of the Declaration states:

> Everyone has the right to freedom of movement and residence within the borders of each state.
>
> Everyone has the right to leave any country, including his own, and to return to his country.

The most important condition not fulfilled

According to the reports by refugees the majority of soldiers and a part of the non-commissioned officers of the Frontier Troops appear to be neither credulous adherents of communism nor its resolute opponents. This labile disposition means that the most important condition for the success of the task imposed on the Frontier Troops is not fulfilled. Without a party-like disposition, faithful adherence to the doctrine of the SED, the aims of the Frontier Troops cannot be achieved. The soldiers cannot be constantly forced to almost exclusively political actions when they are not convinced of their rightness. It is difficult to fully prove disobedience in cases of clever behaviour. And according to all signs the position of the SED will get even worse in the near future since the young people, who will soon join the world of the adults, now react even more critically to political problems than in the past.

Many of the officers and non-commissioned officers of the Frontier Troops are disillusioned, their idealism has been shattered by daily strains. Mistrust and rejection, which the majority of the people still alowed to live in the frontier zone display against the frontier soldiers, and the fact that they are made responsible for everything create a mood of resignation in many of them. In cases of successful "frontier provocations" the officers are made fully responsible; they are interrogated, investigated by special commissions of higher officers, military procurators and state security service until the guilt is properly apportioned and exemplary punishments meted out. In all cases a considerable part of the blame is put on political instructors who allegedly failed in creating a proper degree of consciousness. Among the punishments are suspension from service, ban on promotion, transfer, fines etc.

In summing up one can say that the soldiers of the Frontier Troops as a whole are under a constant strain which impairs their morale, makes it difficult to comply with orders and thus creates a feeling of insecurity among them. In long perspective insecurity, however, destroys the basis for soldierly behaviour.

Of course, this does not mean that the Frontier Troops of the NPA would one day, in peace time, stop fulfilling orders; it rather shows that their military value could be very small in a crisis when the power of the regime would be paralyzed.

CHAPTER 16

THE PSYCHOLOGICAL OFFENSIVE OF THE NPA AGAINST THE BUNDESWEHR

Communist efforts to subvert the armed forces of non-communist states and thus to facilitate the seizure of power have a long tradition. As early as 1920 the *Communist International* stipulated in the fourth of its 22 conditions for member parties:

> 4. A persistent and systematic propaganda is necessary in the army, where communist groups should be formed in every military unit. Wherever, owing to repressive legislation, agitation becomes legally impossible, it is necessary to conduct such agitation illegally. Refusal to carry out or participate in such work should be considered as treason to the revolutionary cause and incompatible with affiliation to the Third International.[1]

During the Weimar Republic the *Communist Party of Germany (CPG)* made great efforts to spread its slogans in the Reichswehr. In 1932 the CPG issued instructions for "military-political tasks" which said, among other things:

> – Soldier slogans and soldiers' demands are of revolutionary importance only in connection with the revolutionary defeatist programme against the bourgeois army and imperialist war.
> – Soldier slogans are always addressed to the masses of soldiers and not to the governments.
> – The content of the slogans depends on the actual political situation and the state of the class struggle.
> – First condition for appeals to soldiers: concreteness, reflection of mood. Therefore: winning over of soldier correspondents, establishing of liaisons, searching for and utilizing all incidents in barracks and in the life of soldiers.
> – It is important to find the best and safest ways for distributing the materials among the soldiers.

1 *Theses of the Communist International (complete)*, published by the Communist Party of Great Britain, London, 1921, p. 9.

The target of the offensive – the Bundeswehr

The Bundeswehr is not the only target of communist subversion. The trade unions, political parties, youth and farmers' organizations are also on the list. But as far as the intensity and extent of the offensive are concerned, the Bundeswehr is first; the explanation for this is simple – it protects, together with its NATO allies, the Federal Republic and an important part of the free world against an attack from the communist bloc. When the communist political strategists failed to prevent the build-up of the Bundeswehr and its integration in NATO, they strove to weaken it, at least.

The communists justify their attacks on the Bundeswehr by arguments based on "class standpoint". According to this, the Bundeswehr is a "revanchist army", a "reactionary instrument of power in the hands of the particularly aggressive West German imperialism" etc. A standard East German work on the Bundeswehr depicts it in the following way:

> In its character the Bundeswehr is an anti-national, anti-socialist military instrument of power of the Bonn state closely connected with the most reactionary group of West German monopolistic capital ... The Bundeswehr is the direct successor to the fascist Wehrmacht. Thus the West German armed forces combine in their character all the reactionary, anti-national, anti-democratic and anti-socialst features of former militaristic German armies in even greater intensity.[2]

Propaganda materials of the "Independent Department" of the NPA

The GDR has many institutions for propaganda and subversion in the Bundeswehr. The most important among them is the *Independent Department* of the NPA's Chief Political Administration.

This department works in a conspiratorial way, with its activities carefully camouflaged. In its numerous actions it never uses its own name of the Independent Department or of any other NPA organ,

2 *Bundeswehr – Armee der Revanche* (The Bundeswehr – A revanchist army), German Military Publishing House, East Berlin 1965, p. 11.

but figures under more or less imaginative titles such as School for Politics, Military Political Institute or Society for Military Politics.

The Independent Department began its work in 1956 and has since produced a number of varied materials and used various methods.

One of its most important activities is to produce and distribute *subversive publications* against the Bundeswehr. The titles and contents of these materials have considerably changed in the cours of years. It began with *Die Kaserne* (The Barracks), *Tabu* (Taboo) and *Soldatenfreund* (Soldiers' Friend); these small newspapers had sensational layout and their contents and pictures were often almost pornographic. In 1961–62 they were replaced by three new publications:

Wahre Information für die Truppe (True Information for the Troops) – This is a regularly appearing "journal for civic education and psychological rearmament". It mainly contains detailed articles on general political, military-political and topical themes. It imitates the "Information für die Truppe", published by the Bundeswehr, and appeals to a "higher" stratum of readers, officers and NCOs.

Soldatenheft (Soldiers' Journal) – It appears irregularly and is meant as supplement to the previous publication. It always deals with one theme in greater context and detail *(The secret of the war, A German army etc.)* and has good layout and print.

Wehrpolitik – Zeitschrift für den deutschen Offizier (Military Politics – A Journal for the German Officer) – Its first "publisher" was the non-existent League of German Officers; now only a "postbox organization" figures in its mast-head. It belongs to the "more serious" subversive publications. Numbers 5 and 6 of the 1965 volume had, for example, the following articles: *Geneva and the atomic demarche from Bonn, Theory and practice of escalation, France and NATO.*

Soldatenbriefe (Soldiers' Letters) This publication contains in each issue one letter addressed to "Dear Comrade" on a theme like *Behind the enemy line, The great chance, Do politics spoil the character?* From No. 3/1965 is reproduced the following passage:

> You, too, can avoid the evil. Pick your comrades among those who think in the same way as you do, who do not want to become cannon fodder for Erhard, Hassel and Trettner. Open your eyes and ears. Watch the men who are in your unit shouting loudest "Hurrah!". It is also good to know where the atomic mines and other lethal war

material are kept. And it is even better when one knows how to prevent these things from being used. And don't forget: Not one shot against the East remains unanswered.

How slightly the appeal to espionage and mutiny is veiled!

Contra – It describes itself as an "illustrated newspaper for all who are also against (contra) the Bonn policy of atomic armaments and war". Contra is published monthly and offers light reading – short articles, glosses, anecdotes, short stories, plenty of pictures, cartoons. But even under this light cover serious matters are hidden. Thus in No. 9/1965 a certain Walter Hausner replied to a "reader's letter" from the Federal Republic which asked for advice on what could be done against conscription:

> I, personally, think that standing aside does not help at all. Therefore, I would enlist without, however, changing my attitude ... I would follow with open eyes and ears everything that was going on around me. Because I think that it does not do any harm if one knows where are the places and accesses to ammunition and atomic mines depots.

Rührt Euch! (Rest!) – This is a "magazine for soldiers and all who are to become soldiers". It allegedly "tells the truth of the atomic war and how one can prevent it". The magazine is lavishly illustrated, contains glosses, short information, jokes, crosswords and conundrums and in each issue there is a full page picture of a nude woman.

Besides these periodicals the Chief Political Administration of the NPA also issues from time to time *special publications*.

Thus in the summer of 1965 a pamphlet was distributed which imitated the cover page of the well-known news magazine *Der Spiegel*. In it the NPA wanted to counteract the main feature in No. 23/1965 of the magazine on the "Ulbricht's People's Army". The pamphlet reproduced the cover page of the magazine with only one small change – it placed a question mark at the end of the headline "Armed for a war against own brothers". The NPA article in the pamphlet wanted to show that the NPA is not only a well armed and trained army but that it is also morally much superior to the Bundeswehr, exactly what the West German news magazine dared to doubt.

Various ways of distribution

The above mentioned publications are produced and partly also packed and posted in East Germany. For this purpose envelopes of non-existent firms are often used: It also happens that the envelopes are provided with false West German postmarks and then are circulated in the ordinary mail.

The Independent Department uses various methods for smuggling the published materials to West Germany. It has collaborators there who now and then visit the GDR and receive the propaganda materials ready for posting. If they travel by car they can easily hide the packets of envelopes. When travelling by train, they take the materials in trunks which they casually leave in the corridor so that during an inspection the owner of the trunk cannot be established. In other cases the materials are transported to West Germany by truck drivers or railwaymen and then taken over by other collaborators and put into postboxes.

The Independent Department is apparently short of standing collaborators and its officials have, therefore, to approach inhabitants of West Germany who come to East Germany to visit their relatives. Usually the visitors are first asked to "do a favour" or "render service to the cause of peace", that is to take with them "some letters" and post them in West Germany. They often do not know what they are, in fact, being asked to do, or they promise to cooperate because the officials make them understand that otherwise they would not be allowed to come again to the GDR. If the visitor has accepted such tasks on several occasions, then he has to cooperate in future because he is afraid that he could be prosecuted by the West German authorities if they learned in "some way" of his previous activities. A slightly veiled threat in this sense is made by the officials of the Independent Department to those West Germans who seem not to be too enthusiastic about their tasks.

The "editors" of the publications sometimes enter into correspondence whith some readers who appear approachable and invite them to visit the Soviet sector of Berlin. The posted publications are usually accompanied by up to four order forms for free subscriptions. However, the publications are mostly sent unsolicited. The addresses are provided by informants or taken from directories.

Rockets with broadsheets

In recent years rockets containing propaganda broadsheets have several times been shot near the barracks of the Bundeswehr. The rockets, provided with a pocket-watch time fuse, were made of cardboard; the fuel sent up a cardboard ball from which broadsheets were released and dropped to earth. The advantage of this method was that in this way propaganda material could be delivered into barracks and thus reach the soldiers directly. Either because of shortage of collaborators or because its effect was negligible, the NPA has for some time now not used the "rocket method" in West German cities. In several cases it had, however, shot similar rockets from the demarcation line into West Germany territory.

In some cases the NPA also used, apparently in experiments, plastic balls and covers for bringing propaganda materials to West Germany. They were thrown into rivers, lakes or canals in East Germany in the hope that they would be taken by the stream or wind to the Federal Republic's territory and there picked up by the population. The balls, containing around 100 small broadsheets or nine copies of the "Rest!" magazine, carried the instruction: "Open, read and pass on!". Rewards were also promised to the finders and distributors if they came to East Berlin and reported at a given address.

By these varied methods the NPA and other organizations of East Germany smuggle hundreds of thousands of propaganda materials into the Federal Republic each month.

The "German Soldier Radio Station 935"

The NPA also operates the *German Soldier Radio Station 935* which has been broadcasting its programmes since the beginning of October 1960. Previously the *German Freedom Station 904* also had a *Broadcast for the Bundeswehr* which is even today still on the air. The difference between them is that the Freedom Station conducts general propaganda and agitation on the lines of the Communist Party of Germany while the Soldier Station is directly aimed at the members of the Bundeswehr and young men. The programme is therefore arranged so that it contains not only political themes but also "pop" music appealing to the young. Thus in the request programme *Your popular melodies* the station also broadcasts songs which are strictly forbidden for the youth in the GDR. The station wants to make itself interesting also by broadcasting information on events in the units of the Bundeswehr mentioning details, names and garrisons.

The Soldier Station is located in Burg near Magdeburg from where the Freedom Station also transmits. Editorial offices are in Berlin-Köpenick, Regattastraße 267, yet it gives its address in the broadcasts as P. O. B. 116, Berlin W. 8.

It transmits three programmes daily: 12.30–13.30, 18.00–18.45 and 20.15–20.45 hours.

Other organizations for the subversion of the Bundeswehr

In the attempts to subvert the Bundeswehr all institutions and organizations charged with propaganda and agitation against the Federal Republic take part. Their arguments – "revanchist militarism", "Hitler's generals", "aggressive plans" etc. – are to a very great extent directed against the leadership of the Bundeswehr.

In the following paragraphs several of these organizations are enumerated.

The *Working Circle of Former Officers* was founded in January 1958 in East Berlin by a number of former officers of the Wehrmacht who were active during the war in the Moscow *National Committee "Free Germany"* or in the *League of German Officers*. Chairman of the Working Circle was, until his death in August 1964, Major General (retd.) Dr. Otto Korfes. He was succeeded by Major General Arno von Lenski.

The Circle has the task of winning over "the population of the Federal Republic for the fight against the atomic war policy of the Federal Government and for the reunification of both German states on a peaceful basis". It must also "convince the officers and soldiers in the Federal Republic of the rightness of the tasks and peaceful character as well as military superiority of the socialist armies".

The same aim is also pursued by the *Mitteilungsblatt der Arbeitsgemeinschaft ehemaliger Offiziere* (Gazette of the Working Circle of Former Officers) which is sent each month to a large number of addresses in West Germany, especially to former Wehrmacht officers.

The *Committee for German Unity*, placed under the Council of

Ministers of the GDR, is charged in the first place with propaganda on the problem of reunification, but it has also issued many subversive publications against the Bundeswehr, such as *Hitler's generals reach for atomic weapons* (1964). Its secretary is a functionary of the SED, Adolf Deter.

The *National Council of the National Front,* a sort of "holding company" for all political parties and organizations, is also strongly active in the infiltration of West Germany. It has published, among other material, *Brown books on war and Nazi criminals in the Federal Republic* and the *White book on war crimes of Inspector General of the Bundeswehr Heinz Trettner.*

The *German Institute for History* publishes, besides other materials, "documentation" on the problem of "militarism in the Federal Republic", on the "militarization" of West Germany and similar publications which are not based on scientific truth but on the SED propagandist slogans.

The Administration of Coordination

In its offensive against the Federal Republic the NPA does not rely only on propaganda and subversion. It also tries to acquire secret information by using agents.

The German Democratic Republic has two espionage and counterespionage services:
— the Ministry of State Security (MSS) and
— the Administration of Coordination (AC).

The MSS is larger and its task is not only to safeguard the security of the GDR and survey the population but also to conduct intelligence activities in the Federal Republik and other non-communist states. For the collection of such intelligence the *Chief Administration of Intelligence* of the MSS is responsible; it carries out military, political and economic espionage duties.

The NPA also has an espionage service of its own, the *Administration of Coordination.* It tries to collect, above all, military and military-political information as well as data and plans of production of arms and equipment.

How effective are the subversive activities?

Going through the numerous subversive publications one is struck by the constant repetition of a few basic themes and above all by the picture of extreme black and white.

The NPA – and, of course, also the other armies of the communist bloc – are excellently equipped, excellently led forces without any shortcomings and, in addition, they are "progressive and peaceloving". In contrast, the Bundeswehr is insufficiently equipped, uses "inhuman training methods", is torn by tensions and struggles of feuding cliques and, what is even worse, is aggressive and warmongering. The NPA, since it stands for a "just" cause, has a "high national mission" and is allied with the Soviet Army – cannot be defeated. The Bundeswehr – the last pillar of a doomed class – will inevitably be defeated. Thus the balance is: it is useless and contrary to common sense to rely on an army which cannot win but can only lose.

The white and black picture of the armies is also extended to social systems. Everything in East Germany and Soviet bloc is good and positive; in the West, there is only oppression, exploitation and decadence.

It is characteristic that the subversive literature almost entirely avoids mentioning communism as an ideology or political system. At best, here and there hints are made at the "progressive socialist order". Apparently the authors themselves do not think very high by of the attraction of ideological themes. They prefer to appeal to the nationalism and self-interest of the Bundeswehr soldiers, try to create fear and frustration, to undermine loyalty and feelings of closeness with the state and society and to replace them with new attachments.

To achieve this aim, all means are regarded as just. Black and white painting, distortions and lies, slanders and calumnies – general or concrete against individual officers and NCOs – pop music and sex, all this is used in order to
– create dissatisfaction and disturbances,
– increase tension,
– incite subordinates against their superiors, the civil population against the Bundeswehr,
– vilify generals, officers and the Bundeswehr in general,
– make the soldiers dislike military service and undermine their obedience.

To what extent have the communists been successful in these efforts?

Some propaganda elements contained in the subversive literature spoil their chances of success. The attempts often meet with rejection because they are too one-sided, violent and primitive.

Certainly it would be wrong to say that the population of the Federal Republic and the soldiers of the Bundeswehr are immune against any communist propaganda and agitation. The immunity is perhaps strongest when the communist try with open propaganda. It is weaker when the origin of the propaganda and agitation ist not known to the people. The communists apparently speculate on this. Their aim is first negative: to destroy the existing ties, loyalties and values. Only afterwards do they try to fill the vacuum with their own ideas. And herein lies the real danger of communist subversive attempts.

PART SIX

EVALUATION

CHAPTER 17

THE STRONG AND WEAK POINTS OF THE NPA

The previous chapters have shown the East German armed forces in their political and military organization, structure, equipment, training and activities. Before a concluding summary evaluation is made, a few notes appear to be necessary.

Standards for evaluation of modern armies

Armies are similar in their organization and structure, armament and equipment, tactics and strategy, recruitment and logistics because the experience of the last war and the demands of a possible showdown present certain similar basic suppositions.

Armies differ in their top level organization and structure of formations on their own territories, in the composition of their command organs, in their traditions, in the strength and stress on certain arms — partly because of historical reasons, partly because of military-political or purely political conceptions.

Armies are not worth more than the human substance, from which they can be recruited and replaced, can offer in fighting values.

They have, however, to be judged also by the coalition value which they represent within the framework of alliances. Important factors are also the level of their training, their usefulness in the most varied forms of war, their adaptability, their mastery of weapons and their capability of withstanding strain in periods of crisis.

Armies must have their soldiers under firm control. Such enforcement measures as orders and duty to obedience, disciplinary and military courts are of only limited value. All armies must strive to tie their soldiers inwardly to the principles of political and military leadership of their states; the soldiers must also be equipped to withstand psychological attacks.

These principles are valid for all armies and in the event of a defensive war they are strengthened by an additional power – the effort to protect and safeguard the homeland against the aggressor.

The principle of tying the soldiers politically is, however, even more necessary for the armies of states where the leadership are pursuing ideological, revolutionary aims. Political messianism of the regime has to be inculcated in the soldiers to make them useful for expansion outwardly and for holding in check a population not willingly toeing the political line. Thus the political ties and controls acquire a particular role in the armies of authoritarian states. From this angle the National People's Army, the armed forces of East Germany should be considered.

The role of the NPA in the state and society

When on 18 January 1956, the regime let fall the veil and gave the armed forces, until then camouflaged as the Barracked People's Police, the official name of the National People's Army, it was authoritatively stated that the NPA would

> protect the territory, independence and civil population of the Republic ... serve the interests of the entire German people ... (and) wear German uniforms reflecting thus the national traditions of our people.[1]

Outwardly the NPA was meant to be a symbol of sovereignty of the GDR and, at the same time, a counter-measure to the Bundeswehr which was at that time being set up. Inside East Germany it was to be accepted by the population as a continuation of traditions and to serve as a reliable support for the regime. In other words the NPA has:

1. to safeguard the dictatorship of the communist party in East Germany since the notions *"German Democratic Republic"* and the *"Workers' and Peasants' Government"* are a permanent part of the communist regime on German soil;

2. to contribute to the expansion of international communism since

---

1 *The speech of comrade Willi Stoph, Deputy Chairman of the Council of Ministers of the GDR, in the People's Chamber explaining the Bill on the foundation of the NPA and the Ministry of National Defence.* Published in "Neues Deutschland" on 19 January 1956.

socialism is, according to the doctrine, only a transitional stage to communism of the Soviet brand.

What matters in this conception is not so much the *defence of socialism* but rather the *conquest of the whole world*. This would be the meaning of the NPA soldiers' participation in any communist offensive war, irrespective of the part of the world where it would take place.

The members of the NPA who thus become soldiers of the world revolution are not allowed to think that they can decide on their own what *socialism* is or is not. Their personal participation is therefore tied to unconditional obedience to the communist regime in East Germany and the Soviet bloc as a whole.

The Oath of Allegiance states in its final version which was adopted after some changes in 1962:

> I swear:
> to serve always faithfully the German Democratic Republic, my fatherland, and to protect it, on the order of the Workers' and Peasants' Government, against all enemies.
>
> I swear:
> to be always ready, side by side with the Soviet Army and the armies of our socialist allies, to protect socialism against all enemies and to risk my life for the achievement of victory.
>
> I swear:
> to be an honest, brave, disciplined and watchful soldier, to obey unconditionally my military superiors, to fulfil resolutely the orders and always strictly to guard military and state secrets.
>
> I swear:
> to acquire conscientiously military knowledge, to observe military regulations and to safeguard always and everywhere the honour of our Republic and its National People's Army.
>
> Should I ever violate this solemn oath of allegiance, may a hard punishment by the laws of our Republic and the contempt of the working people hit me.[2]

2 *Decree of the State Council of the GDR on active military service in the National People's Army of 24 January 1962.* Quoted from "Volksarmee", No 3/1962, p. 4.

The name of this army is therefore deceptive. *National* may, in the best case, only mean that the army does not consist of members of various nations.

Some high officers of the NPA also have Soviet citizenship. Ulbricht who is sometimes called Supreme Commander, is a *Hero of the Soviet Union*. Some of the officers also wear, next to Soviet decorations, the foreign order *Victory over Germany*. All this reflects the character of the army which is a German contingent of the imperialist Soviet Union but not a "national army".

The designation *People's Army* is only justified in so far as now all men living in East Germany can be conscripted.

At the time when the NPA was an army of career soldiers, that is until 1962, its only important task, apart from representing the so-called sovereignty of the German Democratic Republic, was the protection of the regime against all international attacks, the closure of the country outwards and a limited cooperation in the event of war.

Since then an important change has been effected. The NPA has been incorporated into the First Strategic Echelon of the Warsaw Pact forces and into the Soviet military planning. It has thus become an integral part of the Warsaw Pact armed forces standing under Soviet leadership and designated, in case of need, for offensive operations.

The introduction of universal conscription had another advantage for the communist regime. The welcome opportunity to have the youth under strict control for another 18 months is used for intensive political indoctrination. The NPA has thus become an obligatory indoctrination institution of the SED.

The development of the NPA was, however, limited at the outset by certain factors. The Soviets did not intend to accord the GDR the right to develop fully its military power. This was not in the political plans of the Soviets who would not regard the 17 million Germans living in East Germany as reliable enough.

The armed forces which were allowed in East Germany are therefore not properly balanced as the defence of the country requires and they are relatively much weaker than the armies of their partners.[3]

3 Poland with 31 million inhabitants has 14 army divisions, Rumania with about 19 million inhabitants – 11 divisions, Czechoslovakia with about 14 million inhabitants – 14 divisions, Hungary with about 10 million inhabitants – 100 000 soldiers, Bulgaria with about 8 million inhabitants – 11 divisions. Even Albania with 1.9 million inhabitants has 6 army brigades

The limitation of the NPA to six army divisions and the relatively weak naval and air forces cannot be explained by the real potential of East Germany.

The NPA is tied to the United Supreme Command of the Warsaw Pact much closer than the forces of other partners; this again shows that political calculations and safety precautions have been decisive in the limitations of military power of the GDR.

Yet despite all this the NPA's prestige was considerably strengthened when the Soviet Union became convinced of the absolute loyalty of the Ulbricht regime and decided to build up East Germany as a communist strenghold on German territory. The Treaty of Friendship, Mutual Assistance and Cooperation concluded in Moscow on 12 June 1964 by the Soviet Union and the GDR is to be understood in this context. The NPA has become one of the most modern armies of the Warsaw Pact.

Personnel and the psychological situation

There cannot be any doubt that, despite all the successes in the organizational build-up, training and combat readiness, one aim has not been by far achieved – to make the NPA a reliable support of the communist system.

The leaders originally thought that this aim could be better achieved with volunteers than with conscripts but they were wrong. This has been proved not only by the NPA soldiers who fled in recent years to West Germany in such numbers that they could form a full division, but also by admissions of the highest military functionaries.

With the enlistment of the first conscripts after the introduction of compulsory military service in January 1962 the NPA was able to get rid of a great number of more or less unfit "volunteers". They were replaced by conscripts who changed the face of the NPA. In judging the personnel it is necessary to distinguish among the individual ranks.

The *officers' corps* is intensively trained, provided with privileges but also held in obedience by the threat of dismissal in case of dissatisfaction with the fulfilment of duties. The corps is the clamp tying the NPA to the communist regime. It must be assumed that the officers are to a relatively high degree reliable – whether out of opportunism or conviction, it is difficult to establish.

The *corps of the non-commissioned officers* is still the "cadre problem" of the NPA. This is clearly reflected in the high number of the NCOs constantly fleeing to the Federal Republic. As yet there are no signs of a change in this situation even when the regime makes great efforts to make the profession of the short service or career non-commissioned officers more attractive. The main features of the non-commissioned officers' corps are dissatisfaction with their social status, insufficient education and training.

Among the ranks of the NPA is the general unwilligness of the youth of East Germany to military service at least latently in existence. Yet the desired results are achieved.

Hard training inevitably increases efficiency. When the young Germans of the GDR are forced to serve as conscripts in the NPA and thus all share the same fate, they are mostly, in the end, intent not to lag behind in training and fulfilment of their duties. The soldier who has first to reconcile himself with political pressure and constant demands for efficiency develops a kind of professional pride – even though he does not, perhaps, always think that being a "bad soldier" will prove to be a disadvantage for him in civil life. Despite all unfavourable circumstances – that is, even despite the existence of informers – the community of young men creates a feeling of togetherness which helps in maintaining the order in the unit.

The new disciplinary regulations and the lately stressed unity of military and political leadership, that is the unconditional command of military superiors, have also contributed to a better outward image of the NPA.

That blind, unconditional discipline is necessary is explained by the fact that even the 20 years of education to hatred against the West and especially against the Federal Republic could not make the Germans of the GDR see their enemy in either the West or West Germany. This is proved not only by the firing order on the Berlin Wall and the demarcation line but also by worried statements made by the NPA leadership that particularly among the "young members of the army who did not personally experience the hardships of class struggle the educational work must become very intensive".[4]

4 "Zeitschrift für Militärgeschichte" (Journal for Military History), published by the Institute of German Military History, Potsdam, No. 6/1965, p. 739.

Only an iron discipline can attempt to compensate for the weaknesses of the armed forces composed of such heterogeneous elements as there are in the officers' corps, the non-commissioned officers' cadre and among the conscripts of the NPA.

The type of discipline needed in the NPA was indicated by the Minister of National Defence, Army General Hoffmann:

> ... such a discipline which makes it impossible not to carry out any order without objections, exactly and in the ordered time.[5]

Political work

The communist regime tries to compensate for the weaknesses and shortages of its training and education by intensifying political work. But the threshold of personal endurance is overstepped to such an extent that it results in obtuseness or scepticism according to the disposition of the individual soldier. Since there is no opportunity for genuine discussion the soldiers do not accept as their own the slogans hammered into their heads. Prevention of the flow of free information, realization that one is so often deceived, and certain possibilities of comparison make the soldiers doubt the thesis of the alleged superiority of the communist system.

Weapons and equipment

The production of major military equipment in East Germany is negligible; but East Germany has efficient industries to supply the armaments production of the Soviet bloc. The norms and standards of NPA's weapons and equipment are the same as in the Soviet Union. The NPA is well provided with purposeful, modern weapons and some signs suggest that in recent years it has even had priority in receiving Soviet arms. Thus the NPA was issued with potential nuclear weapon carriers such as the guided or unguided surface-to-surface rockets (NATO designation Scud and FROG) and Osa guided missile patrol boats, and with other latest Soviet weapons, armoured vehicles and anti-aircraft guns.

5 "Volksarmee", No. 20/1963, p. 7.

Levels of training and efficiency

As for the level of training and equipment the combat value of the NPA is growing and has now, no doubt, reached a high degree.

The introduction of compulsory service has done away with the situation when the NPA was receiving only such "volunteers" who were not wanted by the factories. The NPA can now choose though, of course, it cannot take away from the factories skilled workers without any limitation when the economy of East Germany is suffering from a shortage of skilled labour.

Universal conscription has raised the general educational level of soldiers. Thus the quality of the NPA personnel is today in general better though not as far as "class consciousness" – that is the unconditional acceptance of the ideology and authority of the SED – is concerned. On the contrary, the influx of conscripts strengthens the elements which are more difficult to handle by the political officer but easier by the military trainer and leader when he understands his men.

Thus in general the NPA leadership can be satisfied with the level of equipment as well as with the level of weapon and tactical training. There are, however, no grounds for satisfaction with "civic education", that is subjugation of the conscripts to communist ideology. Here the norms have not been fulfilled. The party has not succeeded either in making the NPA a submissive politically *gleichgeschaltete* mass or in producing a worthwile number of ideal, hatred-filled, fanatical, "class conscious" fighters. The educational problem of the NPA still remains the same – political apathy in soldiers who have mastered the military craft.

The NPA in the Warsaw Pact

Good qualities for military service which the young soldiers bring with them from their homes, hard basic training and the relatively good weapons and equipment make the NPA an important military factor to be reckoned with.

Other preconditions for making the NPA a modern, efficient army were its strong dependence on the Soviet Army, its integration into the structure of the Warsaw Pact and its subordination to the United Supreme Command.

There are no parallels to the position of the Bundeswehr in NATO; appearance is deceiving. While the Bundeswehr was *integrated* with the contingents of other NATO states into a uniform armed force, that is was amalgamated in staffs and command structure, the Warsaw Pact consists of national elements which are linked in a Soviet command chain. The largest non-Soviet formation of the Pact's armed forces is an army formation corresponding to the western army corps. The NPA has, by now, been able to establish, together with the most efficient armies of the satellites, such a formation. Armies, possibly with attached Soviet and other formations, are subordinated to Soviet Fronts (corresponding to the western Army Groups) and a Soviet Supreme Command; in the latter there are, however, no NPA officers. This is the difference between NATO and the Warsaw Pact and these are the limitations of equality in the Pact.

The trend of the last years indicates that the satellites, including East Germany, will in the future press for more rights and more say into the day-to-day affairs of the Pact. However, there are no signs that the Soviets are willing to share with the East German government or supranational bodies the right to make final decisions on when and how the NPA and other armies subordinated to their command should be employed.

Concluding evaluation

In the concluding evaluation an important place must be reserved for the reliability of the NPA in the sense of the SED political expectations and its development in the coming years.

The moral fighting value of the NPA, based on communist ideology, depends on the attitude of the Germans in the GDR to the regime.

As long as the West is able to contain the expansion of communism, to neutralize the military forces of the Soviet bloc, to present credibly its own growing material and moral strength and to maintain, at least, the minimum of its share in informing the population of the GDR and thus forming its public opinion, a considerable "credibility gap" between communist indoctrination or propaganda in general and reality will remain and their effects will be limited.

A characteristic feature of the NPA is that – being fully dependent on the SED – it was not able to develop any independence. Its political dependence does not in any way bear comparison to the status of western armies and democratic control. The NPA is on all its levels and in all its activities supervised and led by the party. While, for example, the Soviet Army has among its leaders several independent, self-opinionated men, the holders of the highest commands and ranks in the NPA are either willing tools of the SED Politburo or political functionaries rather than military leaders.

The results of such a system are therefore opportunism in the higher ranks, hypocrisy and pretension among the lower ranks to avoid denunciation by informers.

Mistrust and insincerity lie heavily upon the lives of the young men in the army; the atmosphere is made even worse by the privileges given to those belonging to the party and by the great strain of constant "socialist emulation" for the title of the "best soldier" or self-commitments forced on the men on various political occasions.

Dishonesty and despondency bred by such circumstances will also remain in the future since the party is not willing to change the system.

Yet it would be a fatal mistake to regard, because of all this, the NPA as unreliable and without any fighting value. In a total dictatorship like that of the SED the masses of soldiers will be, even in the future, decisively influenced by force, habit and political reality. In addition, the majority of officers and part of the NCOs are reliable supporters of the SED regime and they are exercising a firm control over the soldiers.

Efficiency and reliability of an army in the war depend on many imponderabilities. They are therefore always questionable. The Soviets would apparently expect greatest efficiency if they would, in the event of war, employ the formations of the NPA, interspersed among its own troops, in the first wave.

As part of the first Soviet striking forces, the NPA would suffer particularly great strain and losses since it would have to open breaches for the advancing Soviet troops and would have no time to evaluate properly the situation.

That is theory and planning.

When, however, the spirit and morale are regarded as decisive factors, the situation is different because the masses of soldiers will remain, at least for some time, unreliable in the sense of the SED demands. The present spirit and morale of the NPA soldiers could become decisive when the soldiers could be sure that in a showdown with the totalitarian East the West would take into its hands the initiative. This is particularly true of the members of the "Combat Groups of the Working Class" who represent a good average of the East German working population when their functionaries are not taken into account. To a lesser extent it is also valid for the members of the paramilitary police units in which the SED is carrying out an even stricter selection of cadres.

The extent of hypocrisy required by the life in the SED totalitarian state is often well illustrated when the fleeing soldiers of the NPA report on other members of their units as faithful followers of the party line and shortly afterwards in talking to the suspects who, meanwhile, had also fled to the West, find out how they mutually deceived those around themselves on ther true views.

Only those who had to live, or still live, under the communist dictatorship can grasp and understand that under the spiritual, moral and material pressures of dictatorship, men must show two faces. One of them is the outward, everyday face which is accepted by many as their true face. The genuine face is, however, the other one which can be recognized only by those who know the essence of dictatorship, are not deceived by its propaganda and do not pass, from their safe place in freedom, hasty judgments on people behind the Iron Curtain.

INDEX